J. Dyer Ball

Readings in Cantonese Colloquial

Salzwasser

J. Dyer Ball

Readings in Cantonese Colloquial

1. Auflage | ISBN: 978-3-84604-726-2

Erscheinungsort: Frankfurt, Deutschland

Erscheinungsjahr: 2020

Salzwasser Verlag GmbH

Reprint of the original, first published in 1894.

READINGS IN CANTONESE COLLOQUIAL.

·

READINGS

IN

CANTONESE COLLOQUIAL:

BEING SELECTIONS FROM BOOKS IN THE CANTONESE VERNACULAR

WITH FREE AND LITERAL TRANSLATIONS OF THE CHINESE

CHARACTER AND ROMANIZED SPELLING

BY

J. DYER BALL, M.R.A.S., &c.

Author of

'THINGS CHINESE,'
'CANTONESE MADE EASY,'
'HOW TO SPEAK CANTONESE,'
'THE CANTONESE MADE EASY VOCABULARY,'
'EASY SENTENCES IN THE HAKKA DIALECT WITH A VOCABULARY,'
&C.,   &C.

HONGKONG :

KELLY & WALSH, LIMITED,

AND AT

SHANGHAI, YOKOHAMA AND SINGAPORE.

1894

OTHER WORKS BY THE SAME AUTHOR:

	Price.
'CANTONESE MADE EASY,' 2nd Edition	$3.00
'HOW TO SPEAK CANTONESE'	3.00
'THE CANTONESE MADE EASY Vocabulary,' 2nd Edition	1.00
'AN ENGLISH-CANTONESE Pocket Vocabulary,' 2nd Edition	.75
'EASY SENTENCES IN THE CANTONESE DIALECT with a Vocabulary:' being the first part of 'Cantonese Made Easy' and 'The Cantonese Made Easy Vocabulary,' bound in one volume	2.00
'EASY SENTENCES IN THE HAKKA DIALECT with a Vocabulary'	1.00
'HOW TO WRITE THE RADICALS'	.75
'HOW TO WRITE CHINESE,' Part I.	2.00
'THE SAN WÚI DIALECT'	.50
'THE TUNG KWÚN DIALECT'	.50
'THE ANGLO-CHINESE COOKERY BOOK'	2.00
'THINGS CHINESE,' 2nd Edition	3.50

In Course of Preparation. '*Tonic Exercises in Cantonese.*'

PREFACE.

HERALDED some five years ago as in course of preparation, the pressure of other duties has prevented the appearance of this book at an earlier date. The inquiries that have been made for it, since it has been known that the work was in contemplation, may be taken as a sign that such a collection of colloquial extracts will prove useful to the student of Cantonese.

It would have been an easier task to extract these passages from only one or two books; but the Author has considered it better to make selections from nearly every work which was suitable. From some books, a number of selections were made and even prepared for printing, but, though admirable for the learner, many of these had to be laid aside, as otherwise the book would have become too large. It is hoped that the taste here given will incite the learner to excursions by himself into the paths of colloquial literature where, unaided by literal translations and an English orthography, he may cull the flowers of the purest colloquial at his own sweet will.

An attempt has been made to graduate this course of lessons: the simplest colloquial will be found at the beginning of the book, and the mixed style, in which book-language words are more or less employed, towards the end.

Where the English original could be obtained, the compiler has given it; but in a few cases it has been necessary for the Author to translate back again from the Chinese into English. This explanation will prevent those who may chance to have the original English works from being at a loss to understand the difference between their own versions and some of those in this book. The cases where such a course has been necessary are in the extracts from 'Bible History for the Least and Lowest,' 'That Sweet Story of Old,' 'The King's Highway,' and 'the Four Character Book,' the last having been written originally in Chinese.

The English version of the extract from 'The Sacred Edict' is, with a few slight alterations, taken from Milne's translation.

The Author is responsible for the English translation of the portion of the native story of 'Old Cross Sticks.'

This last selection is given as a sample of one of the nearest approaches that the Chinese seem able unaided to make towards the use of colloquial in books; and the learner is hereby warned to be very careful in his study of it not to be led into the idea that all he sees therein may be used as colloquial. When reading it, constant reference to his teacher, as to whether the words or sentences in that Chinese work are pure colloquial or not, will therefore be necessary.

About a fifth of the book is from native sources, the 'Sacred Edict' and 'Old Cross Sticks' being Chinese works. The former originally appearing in the book-language, had a few pages of it rendered into colloquial under foreign supervision, and it is nearly the whole of this portion that appears in this book; the latter, as will be gathered from what has been said above, is not in pure colloquial, nor is it in the book-language, but consists of a mixture of the two. This mixed style of product will therefore be seen to be a sufficient reason for no further extracts from it or similar works being given, and the necessity therefore of selecting the majority of the passages from books which are translations from the English. The translators, it must be remembered, have had the assistance of good native speakers, consequently the Chinese teacher has left his imprint on the work that has passed through his hands.

The orthography employed is that used in the other books of the 'Cantonese Made Easy' series, with these two exceptions: the *k* of the final *chek* is dropped; and the Author has also adopted, in this book, Mr. E. H. Parker's *öü* instead of the *ui* previously used.

The advantages accruing from the use of the present book, the Author believes, will be many. First it supplements the other phrase and sentence books in use; gives the learner a larger vocabulary; extends his knowledge of colloquial, carrying it up into the mixed style, without which his knowledge of Cantonese colloquial will be incomplete. It has further this advantage that the various books from which the extracts in Chinese are taken are the work of different men. By its use he therefore gets familiar with the style of speech of different Chinese speakers—a most desirable consummation to be attained, as all who know anything of Chinese are aware. The extracts given, with the exceptions noticed above, are in good idiomatic colloquial. The learner need therefore feel no fear of assimilating them to his own use. In conclusion, the Author may say that he himself, though speaking Chinese from infancy, has derived great assistance from a systematic use of books in colloquial, and he doubts not that many more will do so in the future. This book, he believes, will assist them in their efforts and with this belief he has prepared it.

It only remains to acknowledge the assistance rendered to the Author by Mr. Mok Man-cheung in looking over the Chinese proofs, &c.

J. DYER BALL.

1st June, 1894.

CONTENTS.

			page	
Preface	...	... ...		
Introduction	... ...		page	iv
Lesson I.	'Peep of Day,'	... ...	,,	2
,, II.	,,	... ...	,,	2
,, III.	,,	... ...	,,	4
,, IV.	,,	... ...	,,	6
,, V.	,,	... ...	,,	6
,, VI.	,,	... ...	,,	8
,, VII.	,,	... ...	,,	8
,, VIII.	,,	... ...	,,	10
,, IX.	,,	... ...	,,	12
,, X.	,,	... ...	,,	14
,, XI.	'Four Character Book,'	... ...	,,	18
,, XII.	'The Ten Commandments,'	... ...	,,	20
,, XIII.	'The Creed,'	... ...	,,	24
,, XIV.	'Bible History for the Least and Lowest.'		,,	26
,, XV.	'Line upon Line,'	... ...	,,	34
,, XVI.	'The Sweet Story of the Cross,'	...	,,	48
,, XVII.	'Come to Jesus,'	... ...	,,	54
,, XVIII.	'The King's Highway,'	... ...	,,	58
,, XIX.	'The Gospel of Luke,'	... ...	,,	64
,, XX.	'The Twenty-third Psalm,'	... ...	,,	70
,, XXI.	'The Forty-sixth Psalm,'	... ...	,,	72
,, XXII.	'The Epistle of the Apostle Paul to the Romans,'	,,	74
,, XXIII.	'The Te Deum,'	,,	76
,, XXIV.	'The Gospel of John,'	,,	82
,, XXV.	'The Book of Ruth,'	,,	84
,, XXVI.	'The Pilgrim's Progress,'	,,	90
,, XXVII.	,, ...	,,	96
,, XXVIII.	'The Holy War,'	,,	112
,, XXIX.	'The Sacred Edict,'	,,	138
,, XXX.	'Conversations in Colloquial,'	,,	162

ABBREVIATIONS USED IN THIS BOOK:

―――〰〰〰〰〰―――

Class. = Classifier.

Lit. = Literally.

* Indicates that the tone the word is marked in is different from the tone in the book language—the tone is a colloquial one.

† Indicates that the pronunciation of the word as given in this book is different from that given to it in the book language.—the word is pronounced differently in colloquial.

INTRODUCTION.

I.—Hints for the Use of this Book.

A few hints as to the method to be adopted in the use of this book may not be amiss :—

Nothing is better in learning to read Chinese than to copy the Chinese. Let your teacher read over the passage to you, you following him clause by clause, imitating his every tone and inflexion of voice.

Do not be content with reading a passage over once or twice or even a dozen times, but keep on at it till you know it by heart, especially if it is a subject in which you are to be examined. Then make a point, if you can possibly get the time to do so, to memorise it *à la Chinoise*, so that if a sentence of it were given you without the book you could keep on with several sentences without looking at the book. The Author feels convinced from experience that this is one of the best ways to learn Chinese. It is splendid practice for the tones if rightly carried out. If you are to be examined in it, it gives you a confidence which is worth possessing.

This method is of course mechanical to a certain extent and that alone will not suffice to get up one's subject. It must not be allowed to descend into a mere mechanical, unreasoning process, but must be supplemented by thought, a learning of the meaning, analysis of the composition of the sentences, &c., &c., which go to make up a right comprehension of what one is reading.

But, as a firm basis for one's after work, the Author feels convinced that there is nothing like this memorising at first as much as possible. If pursued with a book of colloquial sentences or to a certain extent with a colloquial book, it has the additional advantage of furnishing ready-made speech for the beginner to use in conversation.

The student of Chinese requires constant, unremitting use of the language. He must make use of the living tongue—his own, his teacher's, and that belonging to the multitude of Chinese by whom he is surrounded. He finds, however, that at first and for some considerable time he seems surrounded by a confusion of tongues. His own, though awkwardly moving to the rhythm of this new and strange language, is understood by himself, of course, and to a less extent by his teacher, who has grown accustomed to its mistakes and makes allowances for them. His teacher's tongue, he likewise understands to a considerable extent, as he is familiar with it, and his teacher adapts his language to the capacity of his pupil.

But when he turns his attention to the speech of those he hears around him, it is humiliating to him to find that it is but a small percentage of what is said that is plain. It is advisable for him, notwithstanding the difficulties in his path, to persist in his attempts at conversation with the natives outside of the small circle formed by his teacher and servants, &c., whose talk, continual intercourse has rendered more intelligible to him than that of others. These attempts should be made as soon as he can put together a few Chinese words into a sentence. He thus increases his knowledge, adds to his limited vocabulary, trains his ear to take in the sounds, and his brain to interpret them, and also gives himself confidence.

At the same time there is another method which at the start and for some considerable time he must use even more than the preceding one, as by it he prepares himself for the preceding one—the preceding one being the aim and goal of his study. This other method is the use of the phrase and reading book. By memorising at first many of the sentences and making himself quite familiar with the others, he stores up many words, phrases, and sentences ready for use. The student of Cantonese, if he has gone through the fifteen lessons in 'Cantonese Made Easy,' and the fifty conversations in 'How to speak Cantonese' has, or ought to have, a fairly elementary knowledge of Cantonese colloquial. But, even before accomplishing this task, he will find it pleasant if he has a love for his work, and a relief if he is weary of it, as well as useful, to vary his labour by a careful perusal of some of the colloquial books of which there are not a few in Cantonese. These vary from the simplicity required by the child to the mixed style, as it is termed, in which not a few words primarily belonging to the book language are used. The first style is well adapted for the beginner when he is just commencing to talk in Cantonese; the latter should be well studied by him after he is familiar with ordinary common conversation. The present book commences with this simple style and proceeds gradually to the more difficult. If the student is not restricted in the time which he can give to the style of the language, and if he desires to be proficient in it, it would be well for him to supplement the present work by procuring some, if not all, of the books from which these extracts are made and read them as well.

II.—CANTONESE COLLOQUIAL LITERATURE.

A tribute of praise is due to those who have created a colloquial literature for Cantonese speakers. Infinite pains have evidently been taken in the production of the different books: some of them are beautiful specimens of the language—rich in their purity of form and in idiomatic phrase. By a perusal of them we have Cantonese as it is spoken; for they have all been prepared with the assistance of natives who, to a large extent, are responsible for the Chinese dress of the ideas presented to them by the foreigner.

One turns to the purely native literature, prepared entirely by natives, with the hope of finding something similar; but it is disappointing, after numerous enquiries, to find so little to reward one. With the exception of two or three books, there scarcely appears to be anything worthy of the name of a pure colloquial literature produced by the natives themselves—that is to say there appear to be scarcely any books entirely in colloquial.

It is only within about the last thirty-five years or so that any systematically continuous attempt, on a large scale, has been made to provide a colloquial literature for the Cantonese.

The efforts made previous to this were few in number; but they are interesting to the student of Cantonese from the fact of their being the precursors of the present mass of literature in the vernacular: first attempts made at introducing the Cantonese to their own spoken language—a language which will in time doubtless take the place of the present book-language, as the living English of our own day has long ere this superseded the dead language in use in books in Wickliff's time.

It is unfortunate that no specimens of these first attempts in Cantonese colloquial are procurable at the present day: they have been long out of print; nor are we able to fix with certainty the date of their production. As far as we are able to gather, Rev. James Legge, D.D., LL.D., for many years missionary of the London Missionary Society at Hongkong, and now Professor of Chinese at

Oxford, seems to have led the van in the production of Cantonese Colloquial Literature.* Unable to discover any copy of these colloquial books of Dr. Legge's, and equally unable to discover much definite information about them, we wrote to Dr. Legge with regard to them, having in view the production of the present monograph. The following extract from Dr. Legge's reply will doubtless prove of interest to our readers :—

'I published long ago the two leaflets, for they were hardly more, about which you ask me, though I do not think that either of them is now in my possession. They were produced early in my mission life in Hongkong, and before I was familiar with the speaking of Cantonese in any connected narrative or discourse. I used to go from house to house, and shop to shop; and where I had the opportunity, to tell off or read these two stories, which often led to interesting conversation.

'I wrote out in the same way Æsop's fables in Thom's Edition, and committed them to memory, and would often recite one or two; but I did not print any of them. In this way I laboured to help me in acquiring an easy and intelligible style in preaching which was for years the chief object of my ambition.'

From 'Memorials of Protestant Missionaries to the Chinese: giving a list of their Publications and Obituary Notices of the Deceased with Copious Indexes, Shanghai, American Mission Press, 1867,' page 121, we gather that the names of these two leaflets Dr. Legge mentions were as follows :—

' "Unscathed in the Furnace," six leaves, Hongkong. This tract, which is written in the Canton dialect, gives the story of Shadrach, Meshach, and Abednego, followed by a discourse on the subject.'

---

* No mention has been made here of a small tract by the Rev. I. J. Roberts, a missionary at one time of the Southern Baptist Convention of the United States, as this little book was in the Macao dialect. It may not be amiss to quote what 'Memorials of Protestant Missionaries' has to say concerning it. p. 96 :—

' "Catechism in the Macao Dialect :" Seven leaves, Macao 1840. This is divided into three parts; the first is a catechism of Christian truths, prefaced by a map of Jerusalem; the second is geographical, with a map of Asia; and the third is a collection of Scripture quotations. The author's signature is Heaóu.'

Several works by Rev. W. Lobscheid, a German missionary in Hongkong and sometime in charge of the Government Schools in the Colony, have not been noted in the text, as they are described as being in a half-colloquial style. To those who may be interested in knowing more about them, the descriptions of them in the book already quoted are given herewith :—

' "Thousand Character Classic, Hongkong," 1857. This is the popular little Chinese work of that name, with short notes explanatory of the Characters and the text, given in a simple half-colloquial style. It was prepared for the use of the Government Schools of Hongkong.'

' "Medhurst's Trimetrical Classic," 16 leaves, Hongkong, 1857. This is Medhurst's Tract * * annotated in the same manner as the preceding. It was reprinted at Hongkong in 1863.'

' "Odes for Children with notes," 17 leaves, Hongkong. This is another popular little book in Chinese Schools, to which Mr. Lobscheid has added simple explanations, clause by clause, uniform with the preceding.'

' "The Four Books with Explanations in the Local Dialect," 31 leaves, Hongkong, 1860. This is the Tái Hok, or first of the Four Books, annotated in the same style as the preceding, by one of Mr. Lobscheid's teachers, and published with his revision and imprimatur. There is a preface, followed by four questions and answers regarding the contents of the book, and a note regarding Confucius and his works.'

' "The Prodigal Repenting," six leaves, Hongkong. This is also in the Canton dialect, and gives the parable of the prodigal son, followed by a discourse on the subject.'

No date is however given of the publication of either of these small tracts. Dr. Legge came up to Hongkong from the Straits in the year 1843; consequently these little brochures must have been prepared some thirty years ago or so.

Rev. A. P. Happer, M.D., D.D., a missionary of the American Presbyterian Board, has the credit of the following two publications in the Cantonese colloquial in 'Memorials of Missionaries,' which states :—

' "Dialogues between Chöng and Yün," 16 leaves, Canton, 1862. This contains the first five chapters of Dr. Milne's tract with the same title ⁰ ⁰ adapted to the Canton dialect.'

' "Brown's Catechism," 22 leaves, Canton, 1862. This is a version in the Canton dialect.'

Dr. Happer writes to us in answer to enquiries concerning the colloquial books he prepared, that he translated several chapters of 'The Two Friends' into Cantonese colloquial and he continues :—

'But I cannot say in what year. It was continued in distribution till the blocks were burned in the printing shop in the city. I also translated "Brown's Shorter Catechism," into Cantonese, commencing "Who made you?" The blocks for it were burnt also. I also translated some others. I cannot locate them. You will find them mentioned in Wylie's "Notice of Chinese Missionaries and Publications" as published at the Mission Press, Shanghai. I took part in the translation of the gospels into Cantonese but I have no memo. of them.'

The dates as given above of two of these books are probably correct, as they would be supplied by Dr. Happer, thirty years ago, a few years after their publication, when his memory was clearer on the subject than it is now after the lapse of so many years, and when probably he had the books themselves to refer to.

A trio of missionaries were famous in Canton in the sixties for the production of Colloquial literature : there names were Mrs. French, later known as Mrs. Collins, and Messrs. Charles F. Preston and George Piercy.

Mr. Preston, who was a missionary of the American Presbyterian Board, was one of the few who spoke the language most remarkably well—a position which but few have the happy gift of attaining to. He drew crowds every day to hear him preach in a chapel in one of the most busy streets of the city of Canton. He was therefore well fitted for the task of putting some of the gospels and the Acts of the Apostles into colloquial. The following issued from Mr. Preston's study, according to the work ('Memorials of Missionaries') already quoted :—

' "Matthew's Gospel," 40 pages, Canton. A translation into the Canton Dialect.'

' "John's Gospel," 38 leaves, Canton. A translation into the Canton Dialect.'

' "Important selections from the life of Christ," in the Canton dialect, 108 leaves, Canton 1863. This consists of a hundred passages selected from the gospels, giving in a consecutive form the various events in the history of our Lord.'

' "Hymn book," 47 leaves, Canton. This is a collection of 81 hymns and two doxologies, translated into the Canton dialect. A later edition was published at Canton, in 51 leaves, with six additional hymns. The prefatory notice was published in a modified form as a separate tract, with the title : " A Child's Attachment to Jesus " in four leaves.'

For further reference to Mr. Preston's work see under heading ' New Testament.'

The Rev. George Piercy, a veteran missionary, now resident in England, in which country he is well known as the pioneer of Wesleyan missions in China, was also one of the pioneers in this glorious work of giving the Cantonese their language as it is spoken. His first effort was the rendering of the ' Peep of Day ' in 1862 into colloquial, with a preface printed in red and a table of contents, for the benefit of women and children. With this object in view the language was naturally of the simplest. The several extracts from it are therefore placed first of all in the present work.

Another lasting monument of Mr. Piercy's labours in China is ' The Pilgrim's Progress,' in Cantonese colloquial. This book being intended to reach a higher class of readers, as well as ignorant women and uneducated children, is in a higher style of colloquial ; and after the foreign learner has made himself familiar with the simplest style, as represented by the ' Peep of Day ' and other books, the ' Pilgrim's Progress ' will be found an excellent book to read, containing as it does idiomatic sentences, words, and phrases in the mixed style of Cantonese, as it is called. It will introduce one to the language in use by the teacher and educated man, a speech which it is necessary to acquire, but one which should not be attempted at the very first, else one will never learn in its purity the simple language of the people which forms the ground work of the whole spoken language, and without a correct knowledge of which one cannot be said to know the language. Two extracts are given in this book from the 'Pilgrim's Progress.'

'The Pilgrim's Progress,' in Cantonese colloquial, was illustrated by a native artist, and Pilgrim appears literally in Chinese dress: now as a literary student; now as a valiant warrior, clad in all the panoply of Celestial armour. Christiana and her children also appear in the dress of the Cantonese women and children—everything is in accord with Chinese ideas on the subject. There is nothing incongruous to the Chinese reader, and thus presented to the native it must appeal more readily to his sympathy than it would otherwise have done.

Mr. Piercy also translated portions of the New Testament, such as the Epistles, &c. To convey the logical and close reasoning of the apostle Paul, a high style of colloquial was necessary; and the difficulty in such a work was to keep the words colloquial enough— not, in fact, to be led too much into the book-language mode of writing. The study of such portions of the Cantonese colloquial should be left till the student is well grounded in the simple pure colloquial.

We may here remark that the student who desires to proceed to a knowledge of the book-language will find a graduated course of colloquial one of the best preparations possible: commencing with the easiest colloquial, he should proceed gradually after well mastering one style to the higher styles, and then take the simplest book-style such as that of the story-book after which he can gradually advance to more recondite works.

Mr. Piercy prepared a collection of 116 hymns in the Canton dialect in 1863.

A small pamphlet of only a few leaves was prepared by Mr. Piercy for the use of beginners. It consists of a collection of the simplest words and phrases with only the Chinese characters in it.

A portion of the 'Sacred Edict,' to which reference has been made in the Preface, was also put into been colloquial under the superintendence of Mr. Piercy.

For further reference to Mr. Piercy's work see under headings of New Testament and Old Testament, and Romanized colloquial.

NEW TESTAMENT.

We have seen that Messrs. Preston and Piercy both largely assisted in the translation of the New Testament, as well as Dr. Happer, and others have had a share in the work.

Dr. Henry has kindly given us the following information with regard to the New Testament, and, as it will probably prove of interest to our readers, we reproduce it :—

'Our Colloquial New Testament is in two parts—often bound together. Part First: Matt.—Acts is the work of a union committee, composed at the time the first translation was made by Rev. Charles Preston representing the Presbyterian Mission, Rev. George Piercy representing the Wesleyan Mission, and the Rev. Adam Krolczyk representing the Rhenish Mission. The London Mission took no part. I do not know exactly how the work was divided; but believe that Mark is chiefly Mr. Piercy's work, and John, Mr. Preston's; and Luke, Mr. Krolczyk's; Matthew and Acts being shared. The whole passed through the hands of the committee before being adopted; but many traces of the first translation and the style of each are preserved in the three books mentioned. This is a *bona fide* union version and is adopted by the American Bible Society and the British and Foreign Bible Society. It has been revised once or twice. ⚬ ⚬ ⚬.'

'Part II—Romans to Revelations is solely the work of our (American Presbyterian) Mission. ⚬ ⚬ ⚬ We took up the work ourselves. Our version has been adopted by the American Bible Society and, in the issue of that society, is bound with the union version of Matthew—Acts, forming the complete New Testament. The British and Foreign Bible Society has asked and received our consent to print it. ⚬ ⚬ ⚬ The work on this part was done by Dr. Happer, Mr. Noyes, and myself. Dr. Happer had the doing of Romans, First and Second Corinthians, First and Second Timothy, Titus, and Philemon. Mr. Noyes had Hebrew to Revelations inclusive. I had Galatians, Ephesians, Philippians, Colossians, First and Second Thessalonians. The translations of each member of the committee were submitted to the others, and all changes and suggestions receiving a majority vote were adopted. Mr. Piercy on his own account made and published a version of the New Testament, Part II, Romans—Revelation.'

OLD TESTAMENT.

A Commencement was made with the Old Testament some number of years ago, and the Book of Genesis was first put into Colloquial, Dr. Henry informs us, by Mr. Piercy and Dr. Graves. Exodus to Esther inclusive was the work of Rev. Mr. Noyes.

The Book of Psalms was translated into the vernacular in 1884 by Dr. Graves. From its diction and scope it scarcely needs to be said that the style of colloquial used is that of a high standard ; and to anyone who enjoys the reading of Chinese, it will be found a pleasure to read this version of the Psalms.

Another version of the Psalms had also been put into Cantonese colloquial by the Rev. A. B. Hutchinson of the Church Missionary Society in Hongkong, in the year 1875 or 1876. The Chinese title page bears the date A.D. 1875, while the English Preface is dated December, 1876. In the course of this preface Mr. Hutchinson says :—

'Appointed some four years since, to the management of the Church Mission here, I felt much the loss to the congregation at S. Stephen's Church resulting from the Psalms being in a form (Wan-li) unsuitable for use in Divine Service. Determined to do what I could towards giving my people this most precious aid to devotion, in their own tongue, I ventured to make this translation. * * * * * My thanks are due * * * to the Corresponding Committee of the British and Foreign Bible Society for accepting and publishing this translation.'

Mr. Hutchinson is now labouring in Japan.

The books of the Old Testament from Job and Proverbs to Malachi inclusive are in the hands of Rev. A. B. Henry, D.D., of the American Presbyterian Mission for translation.

At present the Pentateuch, Joshua, Judges, Ruth, Psalms, and Isaiah are published, and the whole of the Old Testament is expected to be ready within a year or so.

Extracts are given from the Book of Ruth and the Book of Psalms in the present work.

OTHER BOOKS.

At about the same time that Messrs. Preston and Piercy were engaged in their Colloquial translations, Mrs. French (née Ball) of the American Presbyterian Mission put the Rev. Mr. Hall's (of England) tract · Come to Jesus ' into Cantonese. This was produced or published in 1864. The next work undertaken by this lady was of a more ambitious character. It consisted of the translation from the English of a book in five volumes entitled · Bible History for the Least and Lowest,' being a compendium of the whole Biblical narrative in a simple style. The rendering of this work into Cantonese took a number of years. Mrs. French finished it while living in Hongkong, having left the Mission, and married Dr. Collins. The Colloquial in these two books is simple. though not puerile, good, and idiomatic—Mrs. Collins having spoken the language from her youth up like a native. Extracts are given from these two books in the present work. Mrs. Collins is now resident in the United States.

The late Mrs. Cunningham (née Happer) of Canton, in her quiet and diligent use of her leisure hours, made considerable additions to the Cantonese colloquial literature. Well qualified for the task, having spent her life in China and, as a consequence, speaking the language like a native, she devoted herself to this and other labours, when the weakness incident for many years to the insidious advances of a mortal malady would have been a sufficient excuse for rest and complete cessation from all toil.

'The Sweet Story of the Cross' was translated by her before her marriage, while yet Miss Happer, in 1874, and while labouring under the auspices of the American Presbyterian Mission. Mrs. Cunningham's great work in Cantonese, however, consists of three volumes of the 'Peep of Day Series.' The first of these three was the 'Peep of Day' itself, it appears to have been published in 1879. Not servilely following the original English work in its entirety, it better adapts itself for the Chinese women and children for whom it was intended. Its diction, though simple, is not childish in any way. The second volume is the Chinese rendering of 'Line upon Line' Part I, and bears the date of 1888. The third volume is Part II of 'Line upon Line,' and the date appearing on the title page is 1889.

Extracts from 'The Sweet Story of the Cross' and 'Line upon Line' are given in the present work.'

Another work of nearly equal size is a series of four volumes, consisting of the translation, by Mrs. Cunningham, of Sunday School Lessons on the gospels—a volume being devoted to each gospel. The passage from the gospel forming the subject of the Sunday School Lesson is first given in Cantonese; this is followed by the explanations. They are translations of the Westminster Sunday School Lessons, and were published in 1888. 'The Story of the Bible Women' by Mrs. Cunningham is also said to be another Colloquial book by the same lady, but no particulars seem to be procurable about it.

Miss Hattie Noyes of the American Presbyterian Mission has also contributed her quota towards the Cantonese colloquial publications. 'A Catechism of the Old Testament' and 'A Catechism of the New Testament' are from her study: we are unable to say whether they are original works or translations. They were published in 1888. Dr. Happer had originally prepared a Three Character and a Four Character Classic, in imitation of the Chinese native text books, for use in the Mission Schools, and intended to convey in rhythmical form a knowledge of the fundamental truths of religion and the facts contained in Scripture. Miss Hattie Noyes translated these two books into Colloquial. There is no date on their title-pages. An extract from the second of the two is given in this work.

'The King's Highway : Illustrations of the Ten Commandments by Rev. R. Newton, D.D.' was translated into Cantonese and published in 1886 by Mrs. Noyes, also of the American Presbyterian Mission. An extract from it appears in the present work. The same lady, we are informed, has also prepared, in Cantonese Colloquial, a book entitled, 'Little Pillows.'

Nor must we forget the work done by Miss Young of the American Southern Baptist Convention in the translation of Bunyan's 'Holy War' into the Cantonese Colloquial in 1887. A lengthy extract from it appears in this volume. It is well done, and in a high style of colloquial.

Miss Lewis of the American Presbyterian Mission prepared and printed at her own expense a small catechism of 18 pages in 1889.

The Rev. A. B. Hutchinson as we have already mentioned translated the book of Psalms in 1876. This translation has, however, not come into general use. The book of Common Prayer was also translated by the same Author in 1877.

Rev. J. S. Burdon, D.D., English Church Missionary Society's Bishop of South China, also translated a Prayer Book into Cantonese. 'The Memorials of Protestant Missionaries' gives the following account of it:—

' "Prayer Book," 69 leaves, Hongkong, 1866. This is a version of the preceding* in the Canton dialect, without the preface and introductory notes.'

We refer the reader to our paragraphs on the New and Old Testaments for mention of the Reverends A. Krolczyk, A. B. Henry, D.D., and H. V. Noyes.

HYMN BOOKS.

A hymn-book containing one hundred and sixteen hymns was prepared by Mr. Piercy in 1863.

'Gospel Hymns' was translated and issued by the Baptist Mission in two parts: the first part is dated 1884; the second, 1887. The first part contains sixty-four hymns; the second thirty-nine, and some doxologies. Amongst them are such favourites as 'Tell me the Old Old Story,' 'Wonderful Words of Love,' 'Hold the Fort,' and 'I am so Glad.'

A small hymn-book for children was prepared by Mrs. Happer, containing twenty-five hymns. No date is given on the title page.

---

* Of the preceding the same book says :—'This is a translation of a portion of the Anglican liturgy, containing the Morning and Evening Prayers. Litany, Baptismal and Communion Services. preceded by a preface and notes for the reader. It is in the Mandarin dialect, and was drawn up with the assistance of Mr. Schereschewsky.'

Bishop Burdon also published for the use of foreigners learning Cantonese, Sir Thos. Wade's ' Forty Exercises,' in the 'Tzu Erh Chi,' done into Cantonese with the following title :—

' The Forty Exercises of the Tzu Erh Chi adapted (by permission) to Cantonese. By J. S. Burdon, Bishop of Victoria, with a key. St. Paul's College, Hongkong, 1877.' It only contains the Chinese Characters.

A large hymn-book containing two hundred and ten hymns besides doxologies, anthems, and chants; has no name of compiler on its title page. The date is 1883. It was printed at the Presbyterian Mission premises.

A version of the Te Deum is given in the present work.

ROMANIZED CANTONESE COLLOQUIAL.

The latest development of the colloquial literature is in the use of the Romanized. Here more especially than in the character colloquial a spasmodic effort was made between twenty and thirty years ago.

At that time Mr. Piercy, whose name is so identified with the introduction of the colloquial, was the prime mover. Some of the scholars, in the boys' and girls' school in the Wesleyan Mission under his and Mrs. Piercy's oversight, were taught the Romanizing of Cantonese colloquial according to Dr. Williams's system of orthography, as exemplified in his Tonic Dictionary and other works; and such fluency did these scholars attain that they were able to write letters in it to Mrs. Piercy and Miss Gunson, their teachers, during their absence in England. The writer, being then a lad with a considerable amount of leisure time on his hands, had the pleasure of giving a little instruction to a small class of four boys who were then learning the Romanizing as an experiment. Mr. Piercy besides having fly sheets prepared for the elementary steps of learning the power of the vowels and consonants, singly and in combination, had the Gospel of Matthew (if the Author's memory is not at fault)* printed in this Romanized system. On Mr. Piercy's departure from China (if not possibly even before) the matter was dropped and no further efforts were made to continue this laudable attempt to introduce Romanizing of Cantonese—a system which is largely made use of in other parts of China, notably in Amoy and Swatow. It has been of the greatest usefulness, though a few foreign scholars in the extreme South of China, (who, mostly having had no practical proof of its utility) oppose it with all the force due to prejudging a system. It is looked at askance by the native literati (in common with their dislike to most foreign innovations) who, unacquainted with its benefits and wed to their own antiquated and cumbrous system, are too proud to concede that any good can result from its use. *En passant* it may be remarked that there is use for all the different styles of presenting the Chinese language in a written or printed form. To the literati whose whole time is taken up in

---

* The Author wrote to Mr. Piercy for further information as to his works in the colloquial, but has not received it.

delving amidst all the stores of the ancient classics, the highest classical style is welcome.

A simple style is of more general utility. not being beneath the notice of the Classical student, while, at the same time, it is more intelligible to the mass of the more or less (often less) educated body of Chinese, who, having been long enough at school, are able to understand books. But for a large mass of the population, the exigencies of whose existence have necessitated an abridgment of the years spent at school. the very simplest book language even is often unintelligible to a great extent. In many instances, the man who has spent a few years at school, as a boy, has gained little else than an ability to name a larger or smaller proportion of the different words. or rather characters, he comes across in the pages of a book accompanied by a very elementary knowledge of their meaning. It is very much as if a man. whose education was so restricted in its scope as not to embrace a knowledge of Algebra. should be asked to read the pages of a treatise on that branch of mathematics. His knowledge of the alphabet would enable him to read the equations, &c.. set forth in its pages ; but without any idea of the meaning, or with but a confused notion of it. To such persons, who have not the time to gain a thorough knowledge of the book language, the colloquial comes as a boon; and still more of a blessing will the Romanized be to those who have had next to nothing of a schooling course. For. in the course of a few weeks or months. a very fair knowledge of the Romanized can be acquired, whereas years are necessary for an adequate knowledge to be acquired of the character. With women, the case of Romanized *versus* character means the possibility of learning to read intelligibly *versus* the insuperable (in many if not most cases) difficulties of want of time, ability. &c., to acquire an adequate knowledge of the character. There are therefore distinct uses for all the different styles of books. And there can be no doubt that before very long the Chinese nation will, as the English did in Wickliff's time. awake to a use of their vernacular for books.

A committee formed of members representing different missions in Canton met in that City and, after taking in review the different systems of Romanizing used in different parts of China, evolved a new system from them. The chief idea in this system of Romanizing. as applied to Cantonese. has been to free the words from all diacritical marks appertaining to the pronunciation of the word as distinct from the tones : by this means, the diacritical marks are free to be used to represent the tones. The diacritical marks employed are the grave, the acute, the Latin circumflex, and the circumflex.

These marks are placed over the vowels, and, where two vowels occur together, they are placed over the second of the two.

The 上平 shöng p'ing, or upper even, tone and the 上入 shöng yap, or upper entering, tone have no mark placed over them at all, the fact of no mark shewing the word to be in one or other of those tones. The final k attached to all words in the 入 yap, or entering, tones being a sufficient sign, and showing alone that the word in question must be a word in the 入 yap, or entering, tone. No mark being over the vowel shows it to be a 上入 shöng yap, or upper entering, tone, while on the other hand all words without a mark over the vowel and also without a final k are in the 上平 shöng p'ing, or upper even, tone. The 上上 shöng shöng, or upper rising, tone is represented by the acute accent. The 上去 shöng höii, or upper retiring, tone by the grave (ˋ) accent. The 下平 há p'ing, or lower even, tone is represented by a dash (-) over the vowel of the word. The 下上 há shöng, or lower rising, tone is represented by the circumflex (˜) accent. The 下去 há höii, or lower retiring, tone is shown by the Latin circumflex (ˆ) accent over the vowel of the word. The 下入 há yap, or lower entering, tone is shown by a dash (-) over the vowel of the word; but the 下平 há p'ing, or lower even, tone it will be remembered is represented by the same mark, it may then be asked what serves to differentiate these two tones, both represented by the same mark? It will be remembered that all 入 yap, or entering, tone words end in k. consequently it will readily be seen that when any word which has a dash over its vowel ends in k, it must be a 下入 há yap, or lower entering, tone word, and all words with a dash over the vowel but not ending in k are in the 下平 há p'ing, or lower even, tone. The presence or absence therefore of a k in words with a dash over the vowel show which of the two tones the word belongs to.

The aspirate is represented by the inverted comma ('), the single quotation mark. which obviates the barbarism of two h's occurring together, as in some of the other Romanized systems in vogue in China, especially in the Lepsius system in use for the Romanized Hakka, as well as in those employed in Swatow and Amoy.

Compound words are united by a hyphen.

These then are all the signs employed; but they are not sufficient, as the 中入 chung yap, or middle entering tone, goes undesignated (though at the same time it must be remembered that most of the 中入 chung yap, or middle entering tone, words have long vowels); nor is that most important tone, the colloquial rising tone, represented at all; to say nothing of the what for want of a better term we shall call the 上 上 平 shöng shöng p'ing, or higher upper even, tone. It is a misnomer to call it a 中 平 chung p'ing, or medial even, tone as it is higher in pitch than the ordinary 上 平 shong p'ing, or upper even. tone. No system of Romanizing for Cantonese can be perfect till these important tones are fully recognised in it.

Barring these important omissions, the tonic marks used in this new Romanized system, once granted that such a method of using them is well, seem good and well chosen. Praise is also due for the improved spelling adopted in some of the words, such as ei instead of the erroneous and provincial i which has so disfigured the orthography employed for so many years in Cantonese. U also takes the place of the ü so inadequate to represent the proper sound of this class of words in Cantonese. What looks awkward in this new system is the use of double a to represent the Italian a; but as it was impossible to employ the acute accent (as in the old orthography) to represent this sound—the accents being required. as we have already said, to represent the tones—it is difficult to suggest any other method for representing this sound of the a, the single a being employed for the sound of u in much, except when it occurs alone and at the end of a word, when it has the same sound as the double a stands for in the middle of a word.

The o of the old orthography has an h placed after it when it occurs at the end of a word; but not when it is in the middle of a word—the learner has to remember that in the middle of a word the o has always this sound. The long o, i.e. the sound of o in the alphabet is unmarked in any way. The double o (oo) sound of the u, represented in the old orthography by an acute accent over it (ú), is shown by the use of double o (oo); and the French u (as pronounced in the French word une, and represented in the old orthography by a diæresis over the u (ü), is spelled ue, in the same manner as in Dr. Chalmers's Pocket English-Cantonese Dictionary. Otherwise, that is to say with the exceptions noted above. the system of spelling used to represent Chinese sounds is the same as Williams's. Thus, to free the words of all diacritical marks, spellings have been adopted from two or three other orthographies hitherto employed in Cantonese. The colloquial sounds are generally. if not always, given, when these differ from the book sounds, though unfortunately colloquial tones are not.

The whole system looks very simple and is an admirable attempt at dressing Cantonese in nineteenth century attire—an attempt that deserves to succeed; and we trust that no pains will be spared to improve away the few and little faults in it, and make it a success.

The Gospel of Mark has been printed in this style (prepared by a committee of missionaries in Canton) and published by the British and Foreign Bible Society in 1892. This unfortunately has typographical and other errors in it, and a second revised edition will shortly appear. The following Notice of it is in 'The Bible Society's Monthly Reporter' for March, 1894 :—

'Chinese. In the Canton Vernacular.—*The Gospel of St. Mark 1,000 Copies. Printed in London.* This is a reprint of an edition published in Canton. The proofs are being read in this country by Mr. Kenmure.'

A primer, to teach the use of this new Romanizing system either has, or will be, issued from the press.

The Gospel of Luke will also be published shortly in the same system; and we trust these are but the precursors of the whole New Testament and, eventually, of the whole Bible in Romanized Cantonese, for it is high time that Canton took her place with other less important centres of influence in China in having a Romanized literature for the use of women, children, and illiterate men.

These systems will doubtless, in the course of time, make the way clear for the disuse of the cumbrous, though interesting, Chinese characters which must, sooner or later, be relegated to the study of the scholar, the library of the philologist and the atelier of the art decorator, while for all purposes of every day use some alphabetical system will permit knowledge to be the common property of all.

As a specimen of this romanizing we give an extract, being Mark 13 : 46—52, as follows :—

Tò hiu Yŭ-leî-koh, Yĕ-So kúng moŏn-shang, k'áp taaî chùng ch'ut Yŭ-leî-koh shî, yaŭ kòh maäng ngaän hat-ī, tsĭk-haî Taî-maaî kè tsaí, Pa-taî-maaî, tsöh tó lô pin. Maŭ tak hâi Nä-saat-lăk Yĕ-So, tsaû taaî sheng kiù wâ, Taaî p'ĭk kè tsź-suen Yĕ-So, hóh-līn ngöh à. Chùng yän chaak shīng k'uï kiù maî ch'ut sheng, k'uï uĕt-faat taaî sheng kiù wâ, Taaî-p'ĭk kè tsź-suen, hóh-līn ngöh à. Yĕ-So hit-chuê keuk, wâ, Kiù k'uï laî. Kòh-ti yän tsaû kiù kòh maäng-ngaän kè wâ, Neï on sam, hei shan la, Yĕ-So kiù neî à. K'uï tsaû tiu-heî i-fûk, kap-ti heî shan, laî-tò Yĕ-So shuê. Yĕ-So tui k'uï wâ, Nei seúng ngöh kûng neï tsô mat yĕ ni. Maäng ngaän kè taap wâ, Chné à, ngöh seúng t'aî tak kin à. Yĕ-So tui k'uï wâ, Neï hnî la, neï kè sùn-tak i-hó neï lok, k'uï tsik shī t'aî tak kìn, tsaû hai lô sheúng kan ts'ùng Yĕ-So ī hnî.

---

* In one case, Mark 13 : 3, we find the há shŏng tonic mark used to represent it, but this would probably be considered to be a mistake.

Native Colloquial Literature.

It is a great pity that the Chinese have not used their beautiful colloquial in the production of books. Had they done so, the very words and thoughts of the natives fresh from their lips and tongues would have been open to our use instead of being, as at present, frozen into the dead book-language from which we have to thaw them out into our Western channels of thought and expression. The liveliness of expression, the sparkle of the spoken language, the vigour of the vernacular idioms, all are lost by the stiffening process; and the sentences are condensed into the rhythmic periods that the rules of composition make obligatory in literary composition.

A few attempts have been made by the natives in Canton to produce what they call colloquial books. One of the best of these is the Tsuk Wá K'ing T'ám, which might be put into English as 'Colloquial Chats,' or 'Conversations in Colloquial,' collected and commented on by Mr. Kéi T'ong of Pok Ling. The blocks from which it is printed are deposited at the Ng Kwai T'ong in Canton. It is a small book in four volumes, bound in two and paged as if in two volumes, but without any date. It has, however, evidently been written within the last century or two, as the events narrated are mostly stated to have taken place in the reigns of the earlier sovereigns of the present dynasty.

As the preface gives the key-note for the production of the book, we herewith give a free rendering of it :—

'The Proverb says, It enlarges the sphere of knowledge to know much about the affairs of the world ; and discernment is extended [lit. The two words to know and to understand] by understanding thoroughly about human matters, i.e. knowledge is acquired by one's own conception and reasoning, and it is also obtained by listening to the conversation of others. Whole crowds are often to be seen in the streets and lanes leisurely sitting under the moonlight and before the lanterns. It is not that there is nothing said ; but what is said is generally of no importance, and not sufficient to benefit either the body or the mind. Some talk about the recompenses that result from good or evil deeds ; then to this some listen, and some do not, while some, adjusting their dresses, leave. It is not because the words are not understood, but it is really that the subject matter is not interesting to them. But, if the narration is interesting, it will then find an entrance into the ear of men, move their hearts, and detain their footsteps longer. A good drummer generally strikes the side of the drum : a good story-teller always tells interesting and extraordinary tales. If the language used is too learned and obscure, women and children will find it difficult to understand. If the matters talked about are common matters of everyday occurrence and told in common speech, then all will easily understand, and furthermore they will feel entertained thereby.

I have gathered together several stories in the course of my reading during leisure hours. When I have told these stories, the hearers have sometimes forgotten to be wearied ; and, on this account, I have sent them to a fellow villager to meet the requirements of those in this world who are fond of narrating interesting matters.

The first and second volumes contain the stories of 'Old Cross Sticks,' from which a selection has been given in the present book, and 'The Seven Acres of Fertile Fields'; the third and fourth contain Yau K'ing Shán, and 'Sowing Happiness for One's Children,' 'A Sudden Mountain Gust,' 'The Advent of Nine Devils,' 'The Famine Song,' 'Meeting a Ghost in a Melon Watch-shed,' 'The Devils Fear Filial-hearted People,' and 'Chöng Acting for King Yama.'

In 'Conversations in Colloquial,' the diction employed for several sentences is a simple book language style, when a colloquial phrase will occur, or a conversation or description will ensue in which, if not entirely colloquial, the vernacular nearly entirely predominates. The continual employment of a number of book-language words in the midst of the colloquial also spoils the naturalness. Some, if not all, of the words are occasionally used by educated men in conversation; but the continual use of them and the use of a number of them in juxtaposition with too small a medium of Colloquial to unite them, is what is here complained of—such as, e.g. 不 pat, for *not*, and 是 shí for the verb *to be*. It is not that the native author entirely eschews the use of the colloquial forms, for 唔 m and 係 haí appear in the book as well, though sparingly. The third personal pronoun 其 k'éi and 他 t'á, the demonstrative 此 t'sz, the verb 曰 yüt, *to say*, the verb 來 loí, *to come*, the particle 而 yí— all of these either entirely exclude the use of the equivalent colloquial forms, or minimise their use.

It will thus be seen that the book is not in the book-language, nor is it in the colloquial entirely, though on the whole nearer the latter; it is a mixture of the two. Occasionally a mandarin word or phrase occurs. This may, of course, sometimes be allowable, as a French word may appear in an English book now and then; but when the mandarin form ná appears for the common demonstrative, it is really carrying the matter a little too far, and it sounds unpleasant to the ear accustomed to the pure sounds of Cantonese. If the student of Cantonese colloquial is sufficiently advanced to know what is colloquial and what is not, this book will prove of use to him, as he will find many good idiomatic phrases in it; and it might be useful as a stepping stone from the colloquial to the simple book-language style.

A second series of the same work is in two volumes. The blocks for printing the 'Second Collection of Conversations in Colloquial' were cut in the 12th year of T'ung Chi, A.D. 1873. The tales in them were collected and selected by Mr. Kéi T'ong of Pok Ling. It has no Preface. It is stated on the title page that the blocks are kept at the Ng Kwaí T'ong in Canton, but at the commencement of the first tale we are informed that the blocks are kept at the Fú King T'ong in front of the Examination Hall at Canton; probably the book is printed at the latter place. The first volume contains the following tales:—'True affection is a Test of Flesh and Blood,' 'A Shrew,' 'A Visit to Hades in a Trance,' 'Please Give Me a Light for My Pipe.' The Second Volume contains the following:—'A Good B.A.,' 'Instructions Given to Children in a Mat-shed. It is much more bookish than the first series.

Besides these, there is the Tsuk Wá Song Sam, which may be Englished as 'Entertaining Tales in the Colloquial: Collected and Selected by Mr. Kéí T'ong of Pok Ling.' It has no Preface. The blocks from which it is printed are deposited at the Ng Kwaí T'ong in Canton, the Fú King T'ong being the printing establishment from which it is issued. When the time of the incidents in the stories are laid in any particular reign, as they are in six of the tales, they are in Shun Chí's, K'ín Lung's, Ká Hing's, and Tò Kwong's reigns; consequently the book must have been compiled either during, or after, the reign of Tò-Kwong (A.D. 1820—1851). This book is also in four volumes bound in two. There are from two to four short tales in each volume. In the first volume are 'The Old Tea-seller,' 'Taming tho Shrew,' and 'Acting the Swell;' in the second volume, 'Stealing the Door-Key,' 'Renouncing the Property for the Sake of Her Fatherless Son,' 'The Venerable God of the Locality,' and 'Stealing a Bride;' in the third volume, 'An Encounter with a Tiger when gathering Firewood' 'Suing a Sister-in-law,' and 'Slumming;' in the fourth volume, 'A Spendthrift,' and 'Taking Refuge from Chü K'éí Lane.' The name of the person who selected them is put at the beginning of some of the tales. It is far more bookish in its style than the first series of the Tsuk Wá K'ing T'ám. These books all contain moral tales.

There is also the Yüt Au, 'Canton Lyrics,' the title of which was selected by 'A Wanderer through Skies and Seas,' in which much colloquial appears mixed up with more book language, the exigences of the poetic language used requiring the employment of a more exalted style than the common colloquial words could always supply; but the exigences of the rhyme are of more importance probably with the author than the sense. Love Songs, as some of these are, are lewd in the eyes of the Chinese. Doubtless some of these are not of the purest, but were the relations of the sexes what they are in the West, and were these songs not the property of the Chinese hetæræ, many of them, if not the great majority, would have nothing objectionable in them at all. Association and the unnatural relationship of the sexes giving rise to a whole system of false modesty and prudery, renders them almost all impure in the eyes of the Chinese. 'The Canton Lyrics' has a frontispiece representing a man accompanying himself on the p'éi p'á, or guitar, in the open air under the shade of a tree while his servant is preparing some refreshment for the inner man. On the other side of the page is a picture of the p'éi p'á, or guitar, with the notes marked on it and explanations at the side. After this, half of the next page is taken up with a voluntary for the guitar, followed on the other half of the page with the musical notation for a tune, probably for the first song. This is followed by two pages containing a glossary of Colloquial words, given their pronunciation and meaning. The book contains all but a hundred songs.

There is also the Tsoi Yüt Au, 'Further Cantonese Lyrics.' The songs in it are collected by someone under the pseudonym of Höng Mai Tsz, 'The Fragrance Bewitched One'—fragrance meaning the fragrance of flowers, and flowers standing for woman-kind. It is revised by The Taouist Priest Chöng, Who is Lifted Above The World. This book contains fewer songs than the preceding one, having only forty-six.

Besides these, some of the ballad books contain a good many colloquial words mixed up with the book-style words. This mixture of the two styles renders these song and ballad books of little use to the learner of Cantonese colloquial. Were extracts given of them in this book, it would be necessary to put constant notes of warning as to many words and sentences being in the book language.

From what has been said it will be seen, as things are, that in a work entirely devoted and limited to 'Readings in Cantonese Colloquial,' it would be a misnomer to call, without any qualifying explanations, such books pure colloquial books, or to include extracts to any large extent from them in it.

III.—A Bibliography of Books in the Cantonese Colloquial.*

(1).—**落爐不燒** 'Unscathed in the Furnace.' Written by Rev. J. Legge, D.D., L.L.D., L.M.S., Hongkong. Leaves 6. 'It gives the story of Shadrach, Meshach, and Abednego, followed by a discourse on the subject.' Published in Hongkong, probably in the early part of the decade, 1840-50. Out of print.

(2).—**浪子悔改** 'The Prodigal Repenting.' Written by Rev. J. Legge, D.D., L.L.D., L.M.S., Hongkong. Leaves 6. 'Gives the Parable of the Prodigal Son, followed by a discourse on the subject.' Published in Hongkong, probably in the early part of the decade 1840-50. Out of print.

(3).—**張遠兩友相論** 'Dialogues between Chang and Yuen.' Translated from the book language, by Rev. A. P. Happer, M.D., D.D., A.P.M., Canton: being 'the first five chapters of Dr. Milne's tract with the same title, adapted to the Canton Dialect.' Leaves 16. Published in Canton, 1862. Out of print.

(4).—**耶穌正教問答** 'Brown's Catechism.' Translated by Rev. A. P. Happer, M.D., D.D., A.P.M., Canton. Leaves 22. Published in Canton, 1862. 'Dr. Happer translated the same catechism' from the English 'into the book language previously and published it in 1852 at Canton.'

(5).—**曉初訓道** 'Peep of Day.' Translated from the English by Rev. G. Piercy, E.W.M., Canton. Leaves I., and 91. Size 6 inches by 4 inches. Printed from type. Illustrated. Preface printed in red. Published in Canton, at the E.W.M., 1862.

(6).—**啟蒙詩歌** 'Simple Hymns.' Translated by Rev. G. Piercy, E.W.M., Canton. Leaves 53. 'Contained 116 hymns.' Published in Canton, 1863.

---

* 'Written' means that the person whose name follows was the author, and that he wrote the work in question in the Cantonese Colloquial. When 'Translated' is used, it means that the book in question was originally written in English or in the Chinese book language and that it was translated into Cantonese Colloquial by the person whose name follows. The abbreviations used are as follows:—

L.M.S.=The London Missionary Society.
A.P.M.=The American Presbyterian Mission.
E.W.M.=The English Wesleyan Mission.
S.B.C.=The Southern Baptist Convention of America.
C.M.S.=The Church Missionary Society of England.
A.B.S.=The American Bible Society.
B. & F.B.S.=The British and Foreign Bible Society.

(7).—馬太傳福音書 'MATTHEW'S GOSPEL.' Translated by Rev. C. F. Preston, A.P.M., Canton. Leaves 40. Printed from wooden blocks. Published in Canton, probably in 1862 or 1863.

(8).—約翰傳福音書 'JOHN'S GOSPEL.' Translated by Rev. C. F. Preston, A.P.M., Canton. Leaves 38. Printed from wooden blocks. Published in Canton, probably in 1862 or 1863.

(9).—耶穌言行撮要俗話 'IMPORTANT SELECTIONS FROM THE LIFE OF CHRIST IN THE CANTON DIALECT.' Prepared by Rev. C. F. Preston. A.P.M., Canton. Leaves 108. 'This consists of a hundred passages selected from the Gospels, giving in a consecutive form the various events in the history of our Lord.' Probably printed from wooden blocks. Published in Canton, 1863.

(10).—讚美神詩 'HYMN BOOK.' Translated by Rev. C. F. Preston, A.P.M., Canton. Leaves 47. Printed from wooden blocks. Published in Canton, probably in 1862, 1863 or 1864. 'A collection of eighty-one hymns and two doxologies, containing a prefatory notice of the compiler's daughter who was fond of hymns and died in her youth. The preface was also printed as a separate tract of four leaves and entitled 孩童蹄耶穌.'

(11).—讚美神詩 'HYMN BOOK WITH SIX ADDITIONAL HYMNS.' Translated by Rev. C. F. Preston, A.P.M., Canton. Leaves 51. Printed from wooden blocks. Published in Canton.

(12).—親就耶穌 'COME TO JESUS BY REV. Mr. HALL.' Translated from the English by Mrs. French, A.P.M., Canton. Leaves 12. Size 6¾ inches by 4 inches. Printed from wooden blocks. Published in Canton, 1865.

(13).—述史淺譯 'BIBLE HISTORY FOR THE LEAST AND LOWEST.' Translated from the English by Mrs. French (Mrs. Collins), Canton and Hongkong. In five volumes. Vol. 1, leaves 1 and 172 : 2, 169 : 3, 124 : 4, 129 : 5, 128. Size 8¾ inches by 4¾ inches. Printed from wooden blocks. Published in 1866 and subsequent years at the A.P.M., Canton.

(14).—天路歷程 'THE PILGRIM'S PROGRESS.' Translated from the English by Rev. G. Piercy, E.W.M., Canton. In two volumes consisting of Part I and II. Vol. I., leaves II., 25, 24, 26, 29, 28. Vol. II., leaves 17, 20, 21, 21, 17, 18, at E.W.M. Size 9⅝ inches by 5¾ inches and 9⅝ by 5⅝. Illustrated with Chinese full-page wood-cuts. Printed from wooden blocks. Published in Canton, 1870. An edition of the first part was issued in 1871, but there was a prior edition of the first part.

(15).—使 徒 行 傳 'ACTS.' Translated from the Original Greek. Leaves 33. Union version, 1872. Size 7¾ inches by 5¼ inches. Printed from type. No place of printing or publication on title page. *See* New Testament No. 58.

(16).—馬 可 福 音 書 'MARK.' Translated from the Original Greek. Leaves 21. Union version, 1872. Size 7⅛ inches by 5¼ inches. Printed from type. No place of printing or publication on title page. *See* New Testament No. 58.

(17).—馬 可 傳 福 音 書 'MARK.' Leaves 38. Printed at the A.P.M. Press, in Shanghai, 1872. Size 9¼ inches by 5½ inches. Printed from type. *See* New Testament No. 58.

(18).—保 羅 達 曾 小 書 'PAUL'S LESSER EPISTLES.' Translated by Rev. G. Piercy, E.W.M., Canton. Leaves: Gal., 9. Eph., 8. Phil., 6. Col., 6, I. Thess., 6, II. Thess., 3, I. Tim., 7, II. Tim., 5. Titus, 3. Phil., 2. Bound in one volume. Size 9 inches by 5¼ inches. Printed from wooden blocks, probably in Canton, and published at the E.W.M. there, 1872.

(19).—使 徒 行 傳 'ACTS.' Leaves 61. Size 9¼ inches by 5¾ inches. Printed from type. Printed in Shanghai, A.P.M. Press, 1873. *See* New Testament No. 58.

(20).—馬 太 傳 福 音 書 'MATTHEW.' Leaves 60. Size 9¼ inches by 5¾ inches. Printed from type, probably in Shanghai at the A.P.M. Press, 1873. No place of publication on title page. *See* New Testament No. 58.

(21).—路 加 傳 福 音 書 'LUKE.' Leaves 65. Size 9¼ inches by 5¾ inches. Printed from type, in Shanghai at A.P.M. Press, 1873. *See* New Testament No. 58.

(22).—約 翰 傳 福 音 書 'JOHN.' Leaves 50. Size 9¼ inches by 5¾ inches. Printed from type, in Shanghai at A.P.M. Press, 1873. *See* New Testament No. 58.

(23).—舊 約 創 世 記 'GENESIS.' Translated by Rev. G. Piercy, E.W.M., Canton. and Rev. R. H. Graves, M.D., D.D., Canton. Leaves 48. Size 7¾ inches by 5¼ inches. Printed from type. Printed in Hongkong. Published by the A.B.S., 1873.

(24).—悅 耳 眞 言 'THAT SWEET STORY OF OLD.' Translated from the English by Miss Littie Happer, A.P.M., Canton. Leaves 7. Size 8¾ inches by 5⅛ inches. Printed from wooden blocks. Published in Canton, 1874.

(25).—聖諭廣訓 'THE SACRED EDICT.' Translated from the native work in the book language by Rev. G. Piercy, E.W.M., Canton. Leaves 2 and 4. Size 8⅞ inches by 5¼ inches. Printed from type. Published in Canton, 1875.

(26).—使徒雅各書彼得 'THE EPISTLES OF JAMES AND PETER.' Translated by Rev. G. Piercy, E.W.M., Canton. Leaves 7, 7, and 4. Size 9½ inches by 5¼ inches. No title page. Printed from wooden blocks, 1875 and 1876.

(27).—使徒雅各書 'EPISTLE OF JAMES.' Translated by Rev. G. Piercy, E.W.M., Canton. Leaves 7. Size 9¾ inches by 5¼ inches. No title page. Printed from wooden blocks. Bound separately, but the same as that contained in No. 26. Printed from wooden blocks.

(28).—舊約詩篇 'THE BOOK OF PSALMS.' Translated by Rev. A. B. Hutchinson, C.M.S., Hongkong. Leaves 149. Size 9⅝ inches by 5⅜ inches. Printed from wooden blocks. No local place of publication on title page. Published by the B. & F.B.S., 1876.

(29).—幼學問答 'EASY QUESTIONS FOR BEGINNERS, CANTON DIALECT.' Prepared by Rev. G. Piercy, E.W.M., Canton. Two vols. bound in one. First Vol. Leaves 3 and 35: Second Vol. 9. Size 7¼ inches by 5¼ inches. Printed from wooden blocks. Published in Canton, 1876.

(30).—聖日禱文 'COMMON PRAYER.' Translated from the English by Rev. A. B. Hutchinson, C.M.S., Hongkong. Leaves 96. Size 9⅝ inches by 5⅜ inches. Printed from wooden blocks. Published in Hongkong, 1877.

(31).—使徒保羅達希伯來人書 'HEBREWS.' Translated by Rev. G. Piercy, E.W.M., Canton. Leaves 18. Size 9½ inches by 5¾ inches. No title page. Printed from wooden blocks, 1877.*

(32).—訓蒙土音. Prepared by Rev. G. Piercy, E.W.M., Canton. Leaves 2. No date or title page. Size 7¼ inches by 4¾ inches. A book of words, phrases, and simple sentences, for beginners.

(33).—散語四十章 'THE FORTY EXERCISES FROM WADE'S TZU ERH CHI.' Translated from the Mandarin by Rev. J. S. Burdon, D.D., C. M. Society's Bishop of South China, Hongkong. Leaves 42. Size 10 inches by 5¼ inches. Printed in type. Published at St. Paul's College, Hongkong, 1877.

---

* We are informed that Rev. G. Piercy translated Rom. to Rev. inclusive.

(34).—曉 初 訓 道 ʻPEEP OF DAY.' Translated from the English by Mrs. Cunningham, (née Miss Lillie Happer), Canton. Leaves 114. Size 9¾ inches by 5¼ inches. Printed from wooden blocks. Published at the A.P.M., Canton, 1879.

(35).—ʻSTORY OF THE BIBLE-WOMEN,' by Mrs. Cunningham, Canton. (We have not seen this book nor or do we know anything about it but its title).

(36).—頌 讚 神 詩 ʻHYMN BOOK.' Translated by Miss Hattie Noyes, A.P.M., Canton, from the Hymn Book in the Mandarin language, adopted by the American Presbyterian Synod of China. Leaves 279 and 7. Size 9¹⁄₁₆ inches by 5¾ inches. Printed from wooden blocks. Published at A.P.M., Canton, 1883. The wooden blocks have been destroyed and it is not likely to be reprinted. It is now entirely out of print.

(37).—福 音 聖 詩 ʻGOSPEL HYMNS.' Issued by S.B.C., Canton. Leaves 25. Size 8⅛ inches by 5⅛ inches. Printed from wooden blocks. Published by the Baptist Tract Society, Canton, 1884.

(38).—讚 美 神 詩 ʻCHILDREN'S HYMN BOOK.' Translated by Mrs. Happer, A.P.M., Canton. Leaves 16. Size 8⅛ inches by 5¾ inches. Printed from wooden blocks, probably in Canton. No date.

(39).—舊 約 詩 篇 ʻBOOK OF PSALMS.' Translated by Rev. R. H. Graves, M.D., D.D., S.B.C., Canton. Leaves 114. Size 9½ inches by 5¾ inches. Printed from type, in Shanghai, at the A.P.M. Press. 1884. Published by the A.B.S.

(40).—神 道 指 正 ʻTHE KING'S HIGHWAY BY REV. JOHN NEWTON.' Translated from the English by Mrs. Noyes, A.P.M., Canton. Leaves 26, 14, 14, 16, 15, 11, 1, 11, 14 and 12. Illustrated with foreign pictures, 1886. Size 9¾ inches by 5¾ inches. Printed from wooden blocks, probably in Canton. No place of publication on title page.

(41).—ʻLITTLE PILLOWS.' Translated by Mrs. Noyes, A.P.M., Canton.

(42).—三 字 經 ʻTHREE CHARACTER BOOK.' Translated into Cantonese Colloquial by Miss Hattie Noyes, A.P.M., Canton, from the original in the book-language, which was written (in the book-language) by Rev. A. P. Happer, M.D., D.D., A.P.M., Canton. Leaves 24 and 5. Size 6¾ inches by 4¾ inches. No date. Printed from wooden blocks, probably at Canton. No place of publication on the title page.

(43).—幼 學 四 字 經 'Four Character Book.' Translated by Miss. Hattie Noyes, A.P.M., Canton, from the original in the book-language which was written (in the book-language) by Rev. A. P. Happer, M.D., D.D., A.P.M., Canton. Leaves 20. Size 8¾ inches by 5⅛ inches. Printed from wooden blocks, probably at Canton. No date or place of publication on title page. The Ten Commandments, Creed, Lord's Prayer, 'Now I lay me down to rest' and the Morning Hymn are at the end of the book.

(44).—人 靈 戰 紀 土 話 'The Holy War.' Translated from the English by Miss Young, S.B.C., Canton. Two vols. bound in one. Leaves I., 83 and 81. 1887. Size 9¼ inches by 5⅝ inches. Printed from wooden blocks. Published at Canton, S.B. Mission.

(45).—出 埃 及 記 'Exodus.' Translated by Rev. H. V. Noyes, A.P.M., Canton. Pages 85. Size 7¾ inches by 4⅝ inches. Printed in Shanghai, from type, at the A.P.M. Press. 1888. Published under the auspices of the A.B.S.

(46).—利 未 記 'Leviticus.' Translated by Rev. H. V. Noyes, A.P.M., Canton. Pages 62. Size 7¾ inches by 4⅝ inches. Printed from type, in Shanghai, at the A.P.M. Press. 1888. Published under the auspices of the A.B.S.

(47).—復 傳 律 例 書 'Deuteronomy.' Translated by Rev. H. V. Noyes, A.P.M., Canton. Pages 80. Size 7¾ inches by 5 inches. Printed from type, in Shanghai, at the A.P.M. Press. 1888. Published under the auspices of the A.B.S.

(48).—耶 穌 道 理 問 答. 'A small Catechism of Christian Doctrine.' Prepared by Miss Lewis, A.P.M., Canton, and printed at her own expense. Leaves 18. Size 6⅛ inches by 4⅛ inches. Printed from wooden blocks. No date, or place of publication on title page.

(49).—馬 太 傳 問 答 'Westminister Sunday School Lessons.' 4 vols. Translated from the English by Mrs. Cunningham, Canton. Matthew. Leaves 69. Size 9¾ inches by 5½ inches or 5¾ inches. Printed and Published in Canton, at the A.P.M.. 1888.

(50).—馬 可 傳 問 答. Do. Mark. Leaves 118. ⎤
                                                     ⎬ All uniform with the above. Published in the same year in Canton, as above.

(51).—路 加 傳 問 答. Do. Luke. Leaves 69. ⎥

(52).—約 翰 傳 問 答. Do. John. Leaves 86. ⎦

(53).—聖書問答舊約 ' OLD TESTAMENT CATECHISM.' Prepared by Miss Hattie Noyes, A.P.M., Canton.* Leaves 73. Size 9¾ inches by 5½ inches. Printed from wooden blocks, 1888. Published at A.P.M., Canton.

(54).—聖書問答新約 ' NEW TESTAMENT CATECHISM.' Prepared by Miss Hattie Noyes, A.P.M., Canton.* Leaves 44. Size 9¾ inches by 5¼ inches. Printed from wooden blocks, 1888. Published at A.P.M., Canton.

(55).—曉初再訓 ' LINE UPON LINE, Part I.' Translated from the English by Mrs. Cunningham, Canton. Leaves 124. Printed from wooden blocks, 1888. Published at A.P.M., Canton.

(56).—曉初三訓 ' LINE UPON LINE, Part II.' Translated from the English by Mrs. Cunningham, Canton. Leaves 117. Printed from wooden blocks, 1889. Published at A.P.M., Canton.

(57).—民數紀畧 ' NUMBERS.' Translated by Rev. H. V. Noyes, A.P.M., Canton. Pages 92. Size 7½ inches by 4⅝ inches. Printed from type, in Shanghai, at A.P.M., Press. 1889. Published under the auspices of the A.B.S.

(58).—新約聖書 ' NEW TESTAMENT.' In two vols. Leaves Vol. I., 58, 36, 63, 48, 59 and Vol. II., 196. Size 9¼ inches by 5¾ inches. Vol. I., Matt.—Acts, translated by a Union Committee representing several Missions. As far as we can learn now, Mark was chiefly the work of Rev. G. Piercy, E.W.M., Canton ; John, of Rev. C. F. Preston, A.P.M., Canton ; Luke, of the Rev. A. Krolczyk, Rhenish Mission ; while Matthew and Acts were either shared, or possibly the work of Rev. C. F. Preston. The whole passed through the hands of the Committee before being adopted, It has since been revised once or twice, the Union Version Committee being still in existence, Rev. H. V. Noyes now representing the A.P.M., on it. Vol. II., Rom.—Rev. is solely the work of the A.P.M., Canton : Rev. A. P. Happer, M.D., D.D., translating Rom., 1st. & 2nd. Cor., 1st. & 2nd. Tim., and Titus. ; Rev. B. C. Henry, D.D., Gal., Eph., Phil., Col., and 1st & 2nd. Thess. ; while Rev. H. V. Noyes did Heb.—to Rev. inclusive. Printed from type at A.P.M., Press, Shanghai, 1889. Vol. I., published under the auspices of the A.B.S., & B. & F.B.S. Vol. II., published under the auspices of the A.B.S., and will probably be also adopted by the B. & F.B.S.

---

* We are uncertain whether these are translations or original works.

(59).—約書亞記 ' JOSHUA.' Translated by Rev. H. V. Noyes, A.P.M., Canton. Pages 57. Size 7⅜ inches by 5 inches. Printed from type, in Shanghai, at A.P.M., Press. 1892. Published nnder the auspices of the A.B.S.

(60).—士師並路得記 ' JUDGES AND RUTH.' Translated by Rev. H. V. Noyes, A.P.M., Canton. Pages 56 and 8. Size 7⅜ inches by 5 inches. Printed from type, at A.P.M., Press, Shanghai. 1892. Published nnder the auspices of the A.B.S.

(61).—以賽亞書 ' ISAIAH.' Translated by Rev. B. C. Henry, D.D., A.P.M., Canton. Uniform with the above. Printed from type, at A.P.M., Press, Shanghai, 1893. Published under the auspices of the A.B.S.

(62).—Ma-Hoh Ch'uen Fuk Yam Shue. ' GOSPEL OF MARK.' Union Version, Pages 75. Royal 8vo. This is in Romanized Colloquial. Printed from type, 1892. Published by the B. & F.B.S.*

(63).—撒母耳書 ' SAMUEL.' Translated by Rev. H. V. Noyes, A.P.M., Canton. Uniform with Isaiah. Printed from type, at A.P.M. Press, Shanghai. Published nnder the auspices of the A.B.S. In the press.

(64).—列王紀畧 ' KINGS.' Translated by Rev. H. V. Noyes, A.P.M., Canton. Uniform with Isaiah. Printed from type, at A.P.M. Press, Shanghai. Published under the auspices of the A.B.S. In the press.†

---

* A revised edition of this is being printed. The Gospel of Luke and a Primer will also shortly be issued in the Romanized Colloquial.

† The rest of the books of the Old Testament have been translated by Rev. H. V. Noyes and Rev. B. C. Henry and are undergoing review and examination by the A.P.M., Canton, preparatory to being sent to the press. They will be issued shortly.

READINGS IN CANTONESE COLLOQUIAL.

LESSON, I.

You have seen the sun in the sky.

Who put the sun in the sky?

God.

Can you reach up so high?　No.

God lives in heaven; heaven is much higher than the sun.

Can you see God?

No.

Yet he can see you, for God sees every thing.

God made every thing at first, and God takes care of every thing.

God made you * * and takes care of you always.—'*Peep of Day,*' *pp. 1. & 2.*

你 睇 見 天 上 個 熱 頭。

係 乜 誰 擠 佢 喺 個 處 嘅 呢。

係 上 帝 略。

你 噲 舉 個 隻 手 到 熱 頭 咁 高 唔 呢，唔 噲 呀。

上 帝 喺 天 堂 處 住，天 堂 高 過 熱 頭 多。

你 睇 得 見 上 帝 唔 呢。

唔 睇 得 見。

上 帝 睇 見 你 嚛，因 上 帝 樣 樣 都 見 嘅。

上 帝 始 初 造 化 各 樣 物 件，到 而 家 都 保 佑 佢。

上 帝 造 化 你 亦 時 常 保 佑 你。

LESSON, II.

Who is it that dresses you and feeds you?　Your dear mother.

But how does your mother get money to buy the clothes, and the food? Father gives it her.

How does your father get money?

乜 誰 俾 飯 你 食，俾 衫 你 着 呢，係 老 母 略。

你 老 母 點 樣 有 錢 買 過 你 食，買 過 你 着 呢，係 父 親 揾 翻 嚟 嘅。

你 父 親 點 樣 揾 翻 嚟 呢。

LESSON, I.

⁵Néí ᶜt'ai-kín⁾ ᵤt'ín shöng² ko⁾ yit₂-ᶜt'áu*.	You look see sky up that sun.
Haí² mat₂-ᶜshuí* ᵤchai ⁵k'öü ⁵haí ko⁾ shü⁾ ke⁾ ₒni ?	Is what person place him at that place, eh ? 53.
Haí² Shöng²-taí⁾ lok₀.	Is God, 32.
⁵Néí-⁵wúí-⁵köü ko⁾ chek₀ ᶜshau tò⁾ yit₂ ᶜt'áu* kòm⁾ ₕkò ₑm ₒni ? ₑM ⁵wúí á⁾.	You can raise that [C.] hand to sun so high not, eh ? 53. Not can, 2.
Shöng²-taí⁾ ᶜhaí ₑt'ín-ₑt'ong shü⁾ chü² ; ₑt'ín-ₑt'ong ₕkò kwo⁾ yit₂-ᶜt'áu* ₑto.	God in heaven's place lives; heaven higher than sun much.
⁵Néí ᶜt'aí* tak₂ kín⁾ Shöng-²taí⁾ ₑm ₒni ? ₑM ᶜt'ai tak₂ kín⁾.	You see can perceive God not, eh ? 53. Not see can perceive.
Shöng²-taí⁾ ᶜt'aí*-kín⁾ ⁵néí po⁾, ₑyan Shöng²-taí⁾ yöng²-yöng² ₑtò kín⁾ ke⁾.	God look see you, 60, because God every kind also see, 15.
Shöng²-taí⁾ ᶜch'í-ₑch'o tsò²-fá⁾ kok₀ yöng² mat₂-ᶜkín*, tò⁾ ₑyí-ₑká ₑtò ᶜpò-yau² ⁵k'öü.	God at first created each kind thing, till now also protects them.
Shöng²-taí⁾ tsò²-fá⁾ ⁵néí yik₂ ₑshi-ₑshöng ᶜpò-yau² ⁵néí.	God created you also constantly protects you.

LESSON, II.

Mat₂-ᶜshuí* ᶜpéí fán² ⁵néí shik₂ ᶜpéí ₑshám ⁵néí chök₀ ₒni ? Haí² ⁵lò-⁵mò lok₀.	What person gives rice you eat, gives clothes you put-on, eh ? 53. Is mother. 39.
⁵Néí ⁵lò-⁵mò ᶜtím ᶜyöng* ᶜyau ᶜts'ín⁾ ⁵máí kwo⁾ ⁵néí shik₂, kwo⁾ ⁵néí ₑchök₀ ₒni ? Haí² fú²-ₑts'an ᶜwan ₑfán ₑlaí ke⁾.	Your mother how fashion have money buy for you to-eat for you to-wear, eh ? 53. Is father find back come, 15.
⁵Néí fú²-ₑts'an ᶜtím ᶜyöng* ᶜwan ₑfán ₑlaí ₒni ?	Your father how fashion find back come, eh ? 53.

He works in the fields.

佢 日 日 打 工 賺 翻 嚟 嘅。

Your father works all day long, and he gets money and brings it home to mother. He says to your mother, 'Buy some bread with this money, and give some of it to the children.'— *Peep of Day,' p. 11.*

你 爻 親 成 日 打 工, 賺 倒 錢 掅 翻 歸, 俾 過 你 老 母, 佢 對 你 老 母 話, 掅 呢 啲 錢 買 食 物 養 仔 女 啦。

LESSON, III.

In the spring he takes his scythe to mow the grass, and as he mows he bends his back till it aches. In harvest time he takes his sickle and reaps, while the hot sun beats upon his poor head.

In the cold weather he follows the plough, while the cold rain and sleet beat upon his face.

年 頭 之 時, 要 出 力 爬 田 掘 地, 有 時 去 撒 穀, 有 時 去 揷 禾, 喺 田 處, 個 啲 熱 頭 晒 得 好 關 係, 晒 到 個 頭 殼 都 痄 呀。

到 割 禾 個 時, 又 要 出 好 到 手 力 呀。佢 做 嘅 工 夫, 唔 論 冷 熱, 唔 論 好 天 落 雨, 都 要 去 做。

Why does he bear all this?

你 估 佢 爲 乜 做 咁 多 工 夫, 都 唔 怕 辛 苦 呢。

That you may have plenty of food and be fat and rosy.—*'Peep of Day,' p. 12.*

佢 都 係 想 你 唔 抵 肚 餓, 又 想 養 得 你 肥 肥 壯 壯 嗻。

ᶜK'öü yat₂-yat₂ ᶜtá-ₑkung chán² ₑfán
ₑlai ke⁾.

ᶜNéi fú²-ₑts'an ₑsheng† yat₂ ᶜtá-ₑkung
ₑchán²-ᶜtò ᶜts'ín* ₑním ₑfán ₑkwai,
ᶜpéi kwo⁾' ᶜnéi ᶜlò-ᶜmó, ᶜk'öü tui⁾
ᶜnéi ᶜlò-ᶜmò wä², ' ₑNím ₑni-ₑti
ᶜts'ín* ᶜmái shik₂-mat₂ ᶜyöng ᶜtsai
ᶜnui ₑlá.'

He day (by) day work earn back
come, 15.
Your father whole day work earn money
take back home give to your mother.
He to you mother says, ' Take this
money buy eatables to-rear sons and
daughters, 21.'

LESSON, III.

ₑNín-ₑt'au ₑchí ₑshí, yiú⁾ ch'ut₂ lik₂ ₑp'á
ₑt'ín kwat₂ ᶜtéi², ᶜyau ₑshí hui⁾ sät₀
kuk₂, ᶜyau ₑshi hui⁾ ch'áp₀ ₑwo, ᶜhai
ₑt'ín shü⁾, ₑkò-ₑti ỵit₂-ᶜt'au* shäi⁾ tak₂
ᶜhò ₑkwän-haí², shäi⁾ tò⁾ ko⁾ ₑt'au hok₀
ₑtò ts'ek₂† ä⁾.
Tò⁾ kot₀-ₑwo ko⁾ ₑshí, yau² yiú⁾ ch'ut₂
ᶜhò ₑto ᶜshau-lik₂ ä⁾, ᶜk'öü tsò² ke⁾
ₑkung-ₑfú, ₑm lun² ᶜláng yít₂, ₑm luu²
ᶜhò ₑt'ín lok₂ ᶜỵü, ₑtò ỵiú⁾ hui⁾ tsò².

Year head's time must put-out strength
to-rake fields dig ground. Have
times go scatter paddy, have times
go stick in rice-plant in field's place.
That sun shine very dreadfully,
shiuing till the head even aches ? 2.
Until cutting rice-plant that time also
need exert very much hand-strength.
2. He does that work (i.e. that work
that he does) not consider (whether)
cold (or) hot, not consider (whether)
good weather (or) descending rain,
also must go (and) do (it).

ᶜNéi ᶜkwú ᶜk'öü wai² mat₂ tsò² kùm⁾ ₑto
ₑkung-ₑfú, ₑtò ₑm p'á⁾ ₑsan-ᶜfú ₀ni ?

You think he on-account of-what do so
much work also not fear trouble,
eh ? 53.

ᶜK'öü ₑtò hai² ᶜsöng ᶜnéi ₑm ᶜtai ᶜt'ò
ngo⁾, yau² ᶜsöng ᶜyöng tak₂ ᶜnéi ₑféi
ₑféi chong⁾ chong⁾ ₑche.

He also is wishing you not sustain
hunger also wish rear to-be-able you
fat fat healthy healthy only, 7.

LESSON, IV.

This large place we live in is called the world. It is very beautiful. If we look up we see the blue sky, if we look down we see the green grass.

The sky is like a curtain spread over our heads, the grass like a carpet under our feet, and the bright sun is like a candle to give us light.—*'Peep of Day,' p. 37.*

我哋而家所住嘅地方，好見見帳，一似光嘅。地係你又布似吶，真頭頭大，好頭我野。住嘅抵青草，所世界垂青，似一張草個。家做略，擔天嘅青蓆，個大燈等得見野。而叫嘅個上好似，係上大盞睇。我哋就睇有地，天係地上張一猛。

LESSON, V.

When God made the dry land, there was nothing on it: it was bare. So God spake, and things grew out of the ground. Trees came out of it; they were covered with green leaves of different shapes. Some were called oak-trees, and some were called elm-trees, and some beech-trees. And some trees bore nice fruit, such as plum-trees, apple-trees, orange-trees, and fig-trees.—*'Peep of Day,' p. 41.*

個曾話，上木各做樹類，出啲梨，有沙類。地未又地有樹葉，叫做松之生，有沙類之生。旱件帝喺有樹嘅，做樹檜桃，生之類。起物上要，就嘅有叫竹樹檜，生嘅橙。造各樣出物，喇個嘅，有叫做多啲，有柑橙。經各生嘅嚟，同有叫做好，有枝生柑。已時得樣，出出唔樹啲，有啲荔啲生。上帝陣有各生，生有榕啲，有又菓生有啲。

LESSON. IV.

ᶜNgo-téi² ᵧvi-ₐká ᶜsho chü⁾ ke⁾ téi²-
ᵧfong tsau² kiú⁾-tsò² shai⁾-ᶜkái⁾, ₐchan
hai² ᶜhò ᶜt'ái ke⁾ lok₀, ᵧTám ₐkò ₐt'au,
ᶜnéi kín⁾ ᶜyau ko⁾ ₐt'in, ᵧshui ₐtái ₐt'au
yan⁾ kín⁾ téi² shöng² ke⁾ ₐts'ing ᶜts'ò.
ᵧT'ín hai² ᶜhò ᶜts'z yat, ᵧchöng tái² pò⁾
chöng⁾, téi² shöng² ke⁾ ₐts'ing ᶜts'ò ᶜhò
ᶜts'z yat, ᵧchöng tái² tsek₂†, ko⁾ yit₂-
ᶜtau*. ᶜhò ᶜts'z yat, ᶜchán tái² ₐtang,
ᶜtang ᶜngo-téi² ₐkwong-ᶜmáng ᶜt'ái
tak₂ kín⁾ ᶜye.

We now what live place just called
world. Truly is good to-see, 15, 32.
Lift high head you see have that
sky, drop low head also see earth on
green grass.
Heaven is very like one [C.] large cloth
curtain. Earth on green grass very
like a [C.] large mat. That sun
very like a [C.] large lamp, wait
(i.e. so that) we bright clear look
able see things.

LESSON, V.

Shöng²-tái⁾ ᶜyi-ₐking tsò²-ᶜhéi ᶜhon téi²,
ko⁾ chan² ₐshí, kok₀ yöng² mat₂-ᶜkín*
méi²-ₐts'ang ᶜyau tak₂ ᵧsháng ch'ut₂.
Shöng²-tái⁾ yau² wá², kok₀ yöng² ke⁾
mat₂ yíu⁾ ᶜhai téi² shöng² ᵧshángt
ch'ut₂ ₐlái, ᶜkòm tsau² ᶜyau shü²-muk₂
ᵧsháng ch'ut₂ lok₀, ko⁾-ₐti shü² yíp₂
kok₀ ᶜyau ₐm ₐt'ung ke⁾, ᶜyau ₐti kiú⁾-
tsò² ᵧyung-shü², ᶜyau ₐti kiú⁾-tsò²
ₐts'ung-shü², ᶜyau ₐti kín⁾-tsò² chuk₂
shü² ₐchí ᶜlui*. Yau² ᶜyau ᶜhò ₐto shü²
ᶜwúi ᵧshángt ch'ut₂, ᶜkwo ke⁾, ᶜyau ₐti
ᵧshángt ᶜt'ò*, ᶜyau ₐti ᵧshángt lái²-
ₐchí, ᶜyau ₐti ᵧshángt ᵧshá-ₐléi, ᶜyau
ₐti ᵧshángt ₐkòm, ᶜch'áng* ₐchí lui².

God already done finished dry land that
period of-time, every kind of-thing
not yet have able grown out. God
again said every kind of thing must on
earth surface produce out come. So
just have trees grow out, 32. Those
tree leaves each have not same, 15.
Have some called banian-trees: have
some called fir-trees; have some called
bamboo tree's species. Again have
very many trees able to-produce out
fruit, 15. Have some produce peaches,
have some produce lychis, have some
produce pears, have some produce
oranges' species.

LESSON, VI.

Vegetables grew out of the earth; potatoes and beans, cabbages and lettuces, they are called vegetables.

蔬芥多菜好白菜出豆又生薯地又有之類。個啲菜菜

Corn came of it. Some corn is called wheat, and some is called barley, and some is called oats. The ears of corn bend down when they are ripe, and look yellow like gold.

有啲做個啲低頭、有啲叫做粘米之類。唔會垂五穀嘅、有啲叫做大麥糯米時、又唔會生出五穀嘅顏色好似黃金一樣、實首好睇。熟嘅

God made the soft green grass to spring up, and flowers to grow among the grass; flowers of all colours and of the sweetest smell. The yellow buttercup, the blue violet, and white lily and the rose, the most beautiful of all flowers.—'Peep of Day,' pp. 41,42.

後來上帝又叫個啲青處、草生出嚟、生草個花、又有各樣色水嘅、如百合有聞見好香花、玫瑰花之花莱莉花、類。

LESSON, VII.

When Jesus was a man, he began to teach people about his Father. Jesus used to preach.

耶穌三十歲個時、起首講書、教人明白天父嘅道理。

Where did he preach?

佢喺邊處講書教人呢。

LESSON, VI.

Ko²-ₜti téi², yau² ₛsháng ch'ut, ʰhò ₜtó ₛsho-ts'oí², ˢyau ˢshü* ˢyau ˢtau*, pák₀ ts'oí², kái² ts'oí² ₛchí luí².

That earth also grow out very many vegetables, have potatoes 1, have beans 2, native cabbage, the mustard vegetable's kinds.

Yau² ˢwúi ₛsháng ch'ut, ˢng kuk, ₛlaí, ˢyau ₜti kiú²-tsò² táí²-ₜmak, ˢyau ₜtí kiú²-tsò² ₛchím-ˢmai no²-ˢmai ₛchí ˥luí.* Ko²-ₜtí kuk, shuk, ke² ₛshí, ˢwúi ₛshuí ₜtaí* ₜt'au, ₛngán-shik, ʰhò ˥ts'z ₛwong ₛkam yat, yöng², shat₂-ˢshau ʰhò ˢt'aí.

Also can grow out five grains come. Have some called wheat, have some called white rice, glutinous rice kinds. That grain ripe time able bend down head, colour very like yellow gold one same really good see.

Hau²-ₛloí Shöng²-taí² yau² kiú² ko²-ₜti ₜts'ing ˢts'ò ₛsháng ch'ut, ₛlai, ₛsháng ˢts'ò ko² shü², ˢyau kok₀ yöng² shik,-ˢshuí ke² ₛfá, yau² ₛman-kín² ʰhò ₛhöng ke², ₛyü pák₀-hòp₂ ₛfá, mút₂-léí² ₛfá, ₛmúi-kwaí² ₛfá ₛchí luí².

Afterward God again called that green grass grow out come, grow grass that place, have every kind coloured flowers, also smell very sweet 15, as lilies, jasmine, roses kinds.

LESSON, VII.

ₛYe-ₛò ₛsám-shap₂ suí² ko² ₛshí ˢhéí-ˢshau ˢkong-ₛshü kán² ₛyan ₛming-pák₂ ₜt'ín fú² ke² tò²-ˢléí.

Jesus thirty years that time began speak books (*i.e.* to preach) teach men understand Heavenly Father's doctrine.

ˢK'öü ˢhai ₛpín shü² ˢkong-ₛshü kán² ₛyan ₙni?

He at what place preach, teach men, eh? 53.

Sometimes he preached to people in a place like a church; sometimes he preached in the fields; sometimes he sat on the top of a hill and preached; and sometimes he sat in a ship, and the people stood by the edge of the water to hear him.

有時喺禮拜堂、有時喺山頂、又有時喺田間、有時喺船上、個啲聽嘅就企嗰岸邊嚟。

Jesus did not always live in the same place: he used to walk about from one place to another. Did Jesus walk about alone?—No; he had twelve friends always with him. He called them his twelve disciples.—
'Peep of Day,' pp. 83,84.

耶穌傳道教人、周圍都喺噉地道去、佢去、去唔係喺實一笡講、佢自己一個、係獨自呢、唔係、同佢係稱爲十嘅唔係個朋友同佢、係稱爲十十二個十二人、係稱爲十二門徒。

LESSON, VIII.

Jesus often went into a ship with his disciples. Peter had a ship of his own, and John had another ship, and they liked to lend their ships to Jesus.

耶穌常有同門徒坐船隻、有兩隻船、佢個隻船過海、彼得自己有隻、佢個隻船人、約翰都有借個隻、人好中意借耶穌嘅。過耶穌嘅。

Once they were all in a ship, when the wind blew very hard and the water moved up and down, and came over the ship. The disciples were afraid that they should be drowned.

有一日、大衆喺船上、到大入船海中間、忽然翻水打、個隻門徒死、風大浪、個啲土下滿、個係浸、船裏土下沉咁關怕嘓浸、各人好慌、

ᶜYau ˏshí ꜀hai ᶜlái-pái²-ˏt'ong; ᶜyau ˏshí ꜀hai ˏt'ín ˏkán; ᶜyau ˏshí ꜀hai ˏshán-ᶜtengt; yan² ᶜyau ˏshí ꜀hai ˏshün shöng², ko²-ˏti ˏt'engt ke² tsau² ᶜk'éi sái² ngon²-ˏpín ˏlai.

Have times at church; have times in fields; sometimes at hill top also; sometimes on ship-board, those listening just stand all shore side come.

ˏYe-ˏsò ˏch'ün-tò² káu² ˏyan ˏchau-ˏwai ˏtò hui², ˏm hai² ꜀hai sbat₂ yat₂ tát₀ téi²-ˏfong ke². ᶜK'öü ˏchau-ˏwai hui² ᶜkong tò²-ᶜléi hai² tuk₂ tsz²-ᶜkéi yat₂ ko² hui² ke² ˏm hai² ₀ni? ˏM hai²; ᶜk'öü ᶜyau shap₂-yí² ko² ˏp'ang-ᶜyau ˏt'ung ᶜk'öü hui². Ko² shap₂-yí² ˏyan hai² ˏch'ing wai² shap₂-yí² ˏmún-ˏt'ò.

Jesus disseminate doctrine teach men all round also go, not is at fixed one spot place, 15. He all round go speak doctrine is only himself one [C.] go not is eh? 53. Not is; he had twelve [C.] friends with him go. Those twelve men were styled twelve disciples.

LESSON, VIII.

ˏYe-ˏsò ˏshöng ᶜyau ˏt'ung ˏmún-ˏt'ò ᶜts'o*t ˏshün kwo² ꜀hoi. ᶜPéi-tak₂ tsz²-ᶜkéi ᶜyau chek₀ ˏshün, Yök₂-꜀hon ˏtò ᶜyau chek₀, ᶜk'öü ᶜlöng ˏyan ꜀hò ˏchung-yí² tse² ko² chek₀ ˏshün kwo² ˏYe-ˏsò ke²?

ᶜYau yat, yat₂ tái²-chung² ꜀hai ˏshün shöng², tò² ꜀hoi ˏchung-ˏkán fat₂-ˏyín ˏfán ꜀héi tái²-ˏfung tái²-long², ko²-ˏti ᶜshui ᶜtá yap₂ ˏshün ᶜlui shöng²-ᶜhá ᶜmún, ko² chek₀ ˏshün shöng²-ᶜhá ˏch'am kòm² ˏkwán-hai². ˏMún-ˏt'ò kok₀ ˏyan ꜀hò ˏfong, p'á² ᶜwúi tsam²-ᶜsz.

Jesus constantly have with disciples sit ship cross sea. Peter himself have [C.] ship, John also have [C.], they two men very pleased lend that [C.] ship to Jesus, 15.

Have one day all in ship on, arrive sea centre suddenly back rise gale (*lit.* great wind) great waves, that water beat into ship inside almost full, that [C.] ship almost sink so serious. Disciples each man very frightened, fear would drown to death.

Jesus had fallen asleep, and was lying on a pillow. The noise of the wind and of the water had not awakened him.

個陣耶穌啱啱瞓着。

His disciples ran to him and cried, 'O Master! do you not care for us? will you let us die?'

門徒叫醒佢嗽話，先生，我哋怕噲浸死嘑。

Then Jesus got up and said to the wind, 'Wind, be still!' and he said to the water. 'Be still.' The wind left off blowing, and the water was smooth and quiet.

耶穌起身，對住個啲風浪話，你好靜嘞，個啲風即時就息，浪就平咯。

Then Jesus said to his disciples, 'Why were you afraid? Why did you not believe that I would take care of you?'

耶穌又對門徒話，你為乜咁慌呢，你唔信我保佑得你咩。

Jesus knew that they were tossed about, and he would have kept them safe, though he was asleep.

耶穌雖係瞓着，佢都知到風浪點樣，縱使唔醒，都保佑得門徒嘅。

The disciples said one to another, 'Jesus is the Son of God; even the wind and the water obey him.'—'*Peep of Day*,' *pp. 98,99.*

個啲門徒睇見嘅樣，大眾就話，耶穌確係上帝嘅仔咯，風浪都聽佢話。

LESSON, IX.

When Jesus was in the world, he loved to think of his Father in heaven. He liked to be alone, that he might pray to his Father : sometimes the tears run down his cheeks while he prayed.

耶穌在世之時，時常記意上淚念佢嘅天父，好祈中眼淚獨自己喺處祈禱，帝，有時佢祈禱流得好凄凉。

ᶜKo chan² ⸜Ye-⸜ȯ ⸜ngám-⸜ngám fan²- chök⸜.

That time Jesus just exactly sleep.

⸜Mún-⸜t'ȯ kíú²-ᶜsengt ᶜk'öü ᶜkòm wá², 'ᶜSín-⸜sháng, ᶜngo-téi² p'á² ᶜwúi tsam²-ᶜsz ⸜lá.'
⸜Ye-⸜ȯ ᶜhéi ⸜shan tuí²-chü² ᶜko-⸜ti ⸜fung long² wá², 'ᶜNéi ᶜhȯ tsing² ⸜lá.' Ko²-⸜ti ⸜fung tsik⸜-⸜shí tsau² sik⸜, long² tsau² ⸜p'ing lok₀.

Disciples called awake him so said, 'Teacher, we fear will drown to death.' Jesus got up to that wind waves said, 'You better be quiet,' 21. That wind immediately then ceased, waves then peace, 32.

⸜Ye-⸜ȯ yau²-tuí² ⸜mún-⸜t'ȯ wá², 'ᶜNéi waí²-mat⸜ kòm² ⸜fong ₀ni? ᶜNéi ⸜m sun² ᶜngo ᶜpȯ-yau² ⸜tak ᶜnéi ⸜me?'

Jesus again to disciples said 'You on account of-what so afraid,' eh? 53. You not believe I protect able you, eh? 39.

⸜Ye-⸜ȯ ⸜suí hai² fan²-chök⸜, ᶜk'öü ⸜tȯ ⸜chí-tȯ² ⸜fung long² ᶜtim ᶜyöng,* tsung²-ᶜsz ⸜m ᶜsengt ⸜tȯ ᶜpo-yau² tak⸜ ⸜mún-⸜t'ȯ ke².
Ko²-⸜ti ⸜mún-⸜t'ȯ ᶜt'ai-kin² ᶜkòm ᶜyöng* taí²-chung² tsau² wá², 'ᶜYe-⸜ȯ k'ok₀ hai² Shöng²-⸜taí-ke² ᶜtsai lok₀; ⸜fung long² ⸜tȯ ⸜t'engt ᶜk'öü wá².'

Jesus although asleep he also know wind waves how fashion, even although not awake also protect able disciples, 15.
Those disciples see so fashion all then say, 'Jesus really is God's son,' 32; Wind waves also obey him speaking.

LESSON, IX.

⸜Ye-⸜ȯ tsoí² shaí² ⸜chí ⸜shi, ⸜shí-⸜shöng kéí²-ním² ᶜk'öü ke² ⸜t'ín fú², ᶜhȯ ⸜chung- yí² túk⸜ tsz²-ᶜkéí ᶜhaí shü² ⸜k'éí-⸜t'ȯ Shöng²-taí², ᶜyau ⸜shí ᶜk'öü k'éí-⸜t'ȯ ᶜngán-luí², ⸜lau tak⸜ hȯ ⸜tsaí-⸜löng.

Jesus in world's time constantly re-membered thought of his Heavenly Father much liked alone (by) him-self at place prayed God, have times he prayed tears flowed very bitterly.

One night Jesus prayed all night alone upon the top of a high hill.

Sometimes Jesus prayed to his Father while his disciples stood near and listened.

Once when Jesus had been praying with them they said, 'Teach us to pray.' Then Jesus taught them a little prayer.

It was this: 'Our Father which art in heaven, hallowed be thy name. Thy kingdom come. Thy will he done in earth, as it is in heaven. Give us this day our daily bread. And forgive us our trespasses as we forgive them that trespass against us. And lead us not into temptation, but deliver us from evil: for thine is the kingdom, and the power, and the glory, for ever and ever. Amen.'— 'Peep of Day,' pp. 110,112.

耶穌喺山頂祈禱。有時成夜喺山頂祈禱。

門徒常有企側便嚟聽。佢拜天父時，

呀耶穌嚟，主叮，耶穌文嚟。有日門徒求佢話，

教我哋呢章祈禱文。就拈呢章祈禱文教佢。

尊降得所求之救與世人之惑權，至所願。吾父在天，願爾之名，

願爾之國，願爾之旨如在天，我人之惑，願爾旨如今日賜我免試，與至心所誠。

爲至聖於世，願猶今日糧頁，使我出皆代代，臨於地在之我，使出皆爾代代，

成用免頁我榮世世，不因所誠，入國與有至所願。

LESSON, X.

One morning very early, when Jesus had been dead only two days, the poor women came into the garden. It was not quite light yet; for the sun was just rising.

到哪帶去花園。兩個人日，

死曉天光嘅香料，想時，個女人想去

已經三朝愛香膏香料，

耶穌第三敬齊香膏園。

Yau² ᶜyau ₍shí ₍sheng† ye² ᶜhaí ₍shán ᶜteng† ₍k'éí-ᶜt'ò.	Again have times whole night in mountain top prayed.
ᶜK'öü paí ᶜt'ín fú² ₍shi, ₍mún-₍t'ò shöng² ᶜyau ᶜk'éí tsak₀ ₍pin ₍laí ₍teng†.	He worshipped ` heavenly Father time, disciples constantly have stand side in-order-to hear.
ᶜYau yat₂ ₍mún-₍t'ò ₍k'au ᶜk'öü wá², ' ᶜChü a⟩, káu⟩ ᶜngo-téí² ₍k'éí-ᶜt'ò ₍á.' ₍Ye-₍sò tsau² nim² ₍ni ₍chöng ₍k'éí-ᶜt'ò-₍man ₍laí káu⟩ ᶜk'öü.	There-was a-day disciples begged him saying Lord, 2, teach us to-pray, 1. Jesus then said this [C.] prayer in-order-to teach them.
₍Ng fú² tsoí² ₍t'ín, yün² ᶜyí ₍chí ₍meng†, ₍tsün waí² chí⟩ shing⟩. Yün² ᶜyí ₍chí kwok₀, kong⟩-₍lam ₍yü shaí.⟩ Yün² ᶜyí ₍chí yí⟩, tak₂ ₍shing, tsoí⟩ téí² ₍yau-₍yü̇ tsoí² ₍t'ín. ᶜSho yung² ₍chí ₍löng, ₍kam yat₂ ts'z⟩ ᶜngo. ₍K'au ᶜmin ᶜngo fú², ₍yü ᶜngo ᶜmin ₍yan ₍chi fú². ᶜSz ᶜngo pat₂ yap₂ shí²-wak₂, kau⟩ ᶜngo ch'ut₂ ok₀ : ₍yan kwok₀, ᶜyü ₍k'ün, ᶜyü ₍wing, ₍kái ᶜyí ᶜsho ᶜyau, ₍chi ₍tò shaí⟩ shaí⟩ toí² toí². ₍Shing ₍sam ᶜsho yün².	Our Father in heaven, desire thy name honoured as most holy. Desire Thy kingdom descend to the world. Desire thy royal will be accomplished, in earth same as in heaven. What need food, to day give us. Beg forgive our debts, as we forgive men's debts. Send us not enter temptation. Save us out of evil : because kingdom and power, and glory, all those what hast until genera- tion (after) generation, age (after) age. Sincere heart what wishes.

LESSON, X.

₍Ye-₍sò ᶜyí-₍king ᶜsz-₍híú ᶜlöng yat₂, tò⟩ taí⟩ ₍sám chíú ₍t'ín-₍kwong ₍shí, ko⟩-₍ti king⟩-oí⟩ ₍Ye-₍sò ke⟩ ᶜnuí-ᶜyan*, táí⟩ ts'aí ₍höng-₍kò ₍höng-ᶜliú* ᶜsöng huí⟩ ₍fá-ᶜyün*.	Jesus already dead two days, arrived No. three morning, dawn time, those reverently loved Jesus women brought complete ointments spices wishing go flower garden.

As the women walked along with their ointment they said to each other, 'How shall we get into the grave? The men put a large stone before it; the stone is so big, we cannot roll it away.'

話、因爲我哋講開、誰替我哋轆開個墳口嘅石呢。嚿石咁大、我哋轆佢唔開呀。喺路上行嘅時、彼此相講。

The women did not know what to do. At last they came to the grave, but the stone was rolled away. The women were quite surprised. Then they were afraid some wicked people had rolled it away, and stolen the body of Jesus. This made them very sad: they looked into the grave, and saw that Jesus was not there.

好、知咯、奇、曉裏喺、子誰開出、偷嚇穌、耶穌閉繫。咁及個各估取頭處、嗷就唔知山墳已心見、法時轆好開、望見好閉。就行到石嘅係確實嗷就、已經轆好、轆咯見唔好。乜墳經見屍人嘅唔。

Soon they saw two beautiful angels standing by them. Their faces were bright like the sun, their clothes whiter than snow.

個呢、好好、歇有耐企、忽然見乜野、有兩個人面、衣服好好、人係天熱雪。使頭嘅光、白。似似。

The women trembled when they saw the angels; but the angels spoke sweetly and kindly to them, saying. 'Do not be afraid; we know that you are looking for Jesus. He is not here now; he is alive. Do you not remember how he said he would come to life again, after he had been crucified?'

好、使耶經該過日盯。個啲慌慌穌生記罪翻、女天我屍唔得人生、人使知喺話、你話你係呢佢、一見你你哋話、人話十幾個、心哋係處、釘字句就唔嚟我架說、嚟應解三話字句十幾句說話。

Lò² shöng² ‚háng ‚shí, táí² chung⁾ ‚söng ᶜkong wá², ‘Mat‚ ᶜshuí* t‘aí⁾ ᶜngo-téí² luk‚ ‚hoí ‚shán ‚fan ᶜhau ko⁾ kau² shek‚ ₒni ? ‚Yan-waí² ko⁾ kau² shek‚ kòm⁾ taí², ᶜngo-téí² ‚m luk‚ tak‚ ‚hoí á⁾.’

ᶜKòm tsau² ‚m ‚chí ᶜshaí mat‚ fát‚-ᶜtsz ᶜhò, k‘ap‚ ‚háng tò⁾ ‚shán ‚fan ‚shí, ‚shuí ‚chí, ko⁾ kau² shek‚, ᶜyí-‚king luk‚ ‚hoí lok₀. Kok₀ ‚yan-ke⁾ ‚sam kín⁾ ᶜhò ch‘ut‚-‚k‘éí, ᶜkwú haí² ok₀ ‚yan luk‚ ‚hoí, ‚t‘au ‚hiú ‚Ye-‚sò ke⁾ ‚shí lok₀. Mong² ᶜhá ᶜluí-‚t‘au k‘ok₀-shat‚ ‚m kín⁾ ‚Ye-‚sò ᶜhaí shü⁾, ᶜkòm tsau² ᶜhò paí²-aí⁾.

Hít₀ ᶜmò ᶜnoí* fat‚-yín⁾ kín⁾ ᶜyau ᶜlöng ko⁾ ‚yan ᶜk‘éí shü⁾. Haí² mat‚-ᶜye ‚yan ₒni ? Haí² ‚t‘ín-sz⁾ á⁾. ᶜK‘öü-ke⁾ mín², ᶜhò ᶜt‘sz yít‚-ᶜt‘au* kòm⁾ ‚kwong, ᶜyí-fuk‚ ᶜhò-ᶜts‘z süt₀ kòm⁾ pák₀.

Ko⁾-‚ti ᶜnuí-ᶜyan* yat‚ kín⁾, ‚sam tsau² ᶜhò ‚fong. ‚T‘ín-sz⁾ wá², ‘ᶜNéí-téí² ‚m ᶜshaí ‚fong, ᶜngo ‚chí ᶜnéí haí² ‚laí ᶜwan ‚Ye-‚sò ‚shí ke⁾; tán² ᶜk‘öü ᶜyí-‚king ‚fán-‚sháng, ‚m ᶜhaí ‚ni shü⁾. ‚Néí ‚ying-‚koí kéí⁾-tak‚ ᶜk‘öü wá², “ᶜNgo pít‚ ᶜk‘áí kwo⁾ tsuí² ‚yan, ‚tengt shap‚ tsz²-ká⁾, ‚sám yat‚ ‚fán-‚sháng,” ko⁾ ᶜkéí kuí⁾ shüt₀-wá² ‚á⁾.

Road on walking time all together talk saying, 'Who for us roll away hill grave's mouth that lump stone, eh ? 53. Because that lump stone so large we not roll able away 2 ?'

So just not know use what means good, and walked to hill grave time, who would have know that lump stone already rolled off 32. Each person's heart perceived very extraordinary, thought was wicked men rolled off, stolen away Jesus's corpse, 32. Look a-bit inside really not see Jesus at place, so then very sad.

Stop not long suddenly see have two [C.] men standing place. Is what thing man, eh ? 53. Is angel, 2. His face very like sun so bright, clothing very like snow so white.

Those women one see, heart then very frightened. Angels say, 'You not need fear, we know you are come to-look for Jesus corpse, but he already returned to life, not at this place. You ought to remember he said, "I must be-handed over-to sinful men, nailed cross, three days return to-life" those several sentences words, 1.'

'Come,' said the angels, 'and look at the place where Jesus lay. Run quickly, and tell his disciples that Jesus is alive, and that they shall see him very soon.'

The women were very glad indeed they ran as quickly as they could to tell the disciples.—'*Peep of Day*,' *pp. 178,179.*

佢唔喺門生佢
見過翻必見佢
話去經耐嘅
實快已有
確你救主你呲
你哩主你呲
家知
而處
徒咯
嘅。

天使講完，個啲女人，心
好歡喜，即時走去話
過門徒知。

LESSON, XI.

Compare the feelings of others by your own.

將自己心，嚟比較人。

If you do not like any thing yourself, do not give it to others.

自己唔想，咪俾過人。

By acting in this way, your steps will tread the right road.

依住嗽樣，行翻正路。

Observe the rules do not rebel against the Lord.

遵守規條，咪背逆主。

I would not wish anyone to steal my things.

人偷我野我心唔想。

Other people have the same feelings.

別人嘅心，亦同一樣。

I would not like to be struck.

我俾人打，我心唔甘。

Other people feel the same.

別二個人，亦同嗽心。

If I am in trouble, I wish people to help me.

我有艱難，想人幫我。

If I see any one else in trouble, I ought to render my help.

見人艱難，我當幫助。

By acting in this way, you will be able to escape calamities.

不論在家，與及在外。

Whether at home or abroad.—'*The Four Character Book*.'

照依嗽做，可免災害。

'ͺYi-ͺká ᶜnéí k'okͺ-shat, kín'-ᶜk'öü ͺm ᶜhaí shü' ͺle, ᶜnéí fáí' huí' wá² kwo' ͺmún-ͺt'ò ͺchí Kau'-ᶜchü ᶜyí-ͺking ͺfán-ͺsháng† lokͺ, ᶜnéí-téí² ᶜmo ᶜnoí* pít, kín' ᶜk'öü ke'.'

ͺT'in-sz' ᶜkong ͺyün, ko'-ͺti ᶜnuí-ᶜyan*, ͺsam ᶜhò ͺfún-ᶜhéí, tsik,-ͺshí ᶜtsau huí' wá² kwo' ͺmún-ͺt'ò ͺchí.

'Now you really see he not at place, 24. You quickly go say to disciples to-know Saviour already return to-life, 32. You not long must see him.'

Angels talked finished those women's hearts very happy, immediately ran away tell to disciples to-know.

LESSON, XI.

ͺTsöng tsz²-ᶜkéí ke' ͺsam ͺlaí péí²-káu' ͺyan.

Tsz²-ᶜkéí ͺm ᶜsöng ᶜmaí ᶜp... kwo' ͺyan.

ͺYi-chü² ᶜkòm ᶜyöng* ͺháng ͺfán ching' lò².

ͺTsun-ᶜshau ͺkw'aí-ͺt'iú, ᶜmaí puí'-ͺyik, ᶜChü.

ͺYan ͺt'au' ͺngo ᶜye, ᶜngo ͺsam ͺm ᶜsöng.

Pít, ͺyan ke' ͺsam, yik, ͺt'ung yat, yöng².

ᶜNgo ᶜpéí ͺyan ᶜtá, ᶜngo ͺsam ͺm ͺkòm.

Pít,-yí² ko' ͺyan, yik, ͺt'ung ᶜkòm ͺsam.

ᶜNgo ᶜyau ͺkán-ͺnán, ᶜsöng ͺyau ͺpong ᶜngo.

Kín' ͺyan ͺkán-ͺnán, ᶜngo ͺtong ͺpong-cho².

Pat, lun² tsoí² ͺká, ᶜyü-k'ap, tsoí² ngoí².

Chíú'-ͺyí ᶜkòm tsò², ᶜho ᶜmíu ͺtsoí-hoí².

Take (or Use) your own heart to compare men.

Yourself not wish, don't give to men.

According to such manner walk back correct road.

Observe regulations, not rebel against Lord.

Man steal my things, my heart not wish.

Other men's hearts, also same one kind.

I by men beaten, my heart not like.

Another [C.] man, also same such heart.

I have troubles, wish men help me.

See men (in) troubles, I ought to assist.

Not matter in family or at outside.

According to such do, able to avoid calamities.

LESSON, XII.

The Ten Commandments.

十聖誡。

The First Commandment.—

第一誡。

God said, 'Thou shalt have no other God before me.'

神話、除曉我之外、你唔好有別個神。

The Second Commandment.—

第二誡。

'Thou shalt not make unto thee any graven image, or any likeness of anything that is in heaven above, or that is in the earth beneath, or that is in the water under the earth : thou shalt not bow down thyself to them, nor serve them : for I the Lord thy God am a jealous God, visiting the iniquity of the fathers upon the children unto the third and fourth generation of them that hate me ; and shewing mercy unto thousands of them that love me, and keep my commandments.

翻水唔好有別個神、你唔好雕刻偶像、學天上地下、共地下各物嘅樣子、你唔好拜佢、而且服事佢、因爲我耶和華係你嘅神、不容你拜別神、憎我嘅[我就]罰佢子孫嘅罪、自祖父到我到三四代、愛我嘅、就施恩過佢到誡嘅、千百代。

The Third Commandment.—

第三誡。

'Thou shalt not take the name of thy Lord in vain ; for the Lord will not hold him guiltless that taketh his name in vain.'

你唔好亂叫你神耶和華嘅名、亂叫嘅、耶和華是必定佢罪。

LESSON, XII.

Shap₂ ʿShingʾ Káiʾ.	The Ten Commandments.

Tai² yat, káiʾ.—

ʿShan wá², 'ʿChʻü-ʿhiú ʿngo ʿchí ngoi², ʿnéi ʿm ʻhò ʿyau pit, koʾ ʿShan.'

The First Commandment.—

God said, 'Excepting me beyond, you not good have another God.'

Tai² yí² káiʾ.—

'ʿNéi ʿm ʻhò ʿtʻiú-hak, ʿngau-tsöng², hok, ʿfán ʿtʻín shöng² téi² há², kung² téi² há² ʿshui ʿchung kok₀ mat,-keʾ yöng²-ʿtsz. ʿNéi ʿm ʻhò pái² ʿkʻöü, ʿyí-ʿchʻe fuk,-sz² ʿkʻöü : ʿyan-wai² ʿNgo, ʿYe-ʿwò-ʿwá, hai² ʿnéi-keʾ ʿShan, pat, ʿyung ʿnéi páiʾ pit, koʾ ʿShan, ʿtsang ʿNgo-keʾ [ʿngo tsauʾ] fat, ʿkʻöü-keʾ tsui², tsz² ʿtsò-fú² tòʾ ʿtsz-ʿsün ʿsám szʾ toi² ; oiʾ ʿNgo-keʾ, ʿshau ʿngo káiʾ keʾ, tsau² ʿshí-ʿyan kwoʾ ʿkʻöü tòʾ ʿtsʻin pák₀ toi².'

'You not good carve images, copying (or in imitation of) heaven above, earth below, and earth below water midst (i.e. that is in the water) any thing's fashion : you not good worship them, moreover serve them : because I, Jehovah, am your God, not allow (or permit) you to worship another [C.] God. Hate me those [I then] punish their guilt or sin, from ancestors to descendants third fourth generations ; love me those, observe my command ment those, then show mercy to them until thousand hundred generations.'

Tai² ʿsám káiʾ.

ʿNéi ʿm ʻhò ʿlün* kiúʾ ʿnéi ʿShan ʿYe-ʿwò-ʿwá-keʾ ʿmeng*†, ʿlün* kiúʾ keʾ, ʿYe-ʿwò-ʿwá shí²-pit, ting² ʿkʻöü tsui².

The Third Commandment.—

You must not disorderly call your God Jehovah's name, disorderly call those Jehovah certainly convict them of-guilt.

The Fourth Commandment.—

'Remember the Sabbath Day to keep it holy. Six days shalt thou labour and do all thy work : But the seventh day is the Sabbath of the Lord thy God : in it thou shalt not do any work, thou nor thy son, nor thy daughter, thy manservant, nor thy maidservant, nor thy cattle, nor thy stranger that is within thy gates : For in six days the Lord made heaven and earth, the sea, and all that in them is, and rested the seventh day : wherefore the Lord blessed the Sabbath Day and hallowed it.'

第四誡。

你要記念安息日，守佢做日。六日內，要做日。安你做各樣工夫，第七華嘅工夫婢嘅六係你神即和好做女，內爲天物，故息你個日唔嘅仔你屋因造萬息，你共牲與及要嘅華創嘅息，故畜人客，都耶和華中就安福安人日地間，海第七日，和華祝聖日。地到此即以個日爲聖日。

The Fifth Commandment.—

'Honour thy father and thy mother : that thy days may be long upon the land which the Lord thy God giveth thee.'

第五誡。

你要孝敬你父母，等你可以長久喺你神耶和華所賜過你嘅地。

The Sixth Commandment.—

'Thou shalt not kill.'

第六誡。

你唔好殺人。

The Seventh Commandment.—

'Thou shalt not commit adultery.'

第七誡。

你唔好行淫。

The Eight Commandment.—

'Thou shalt not steal.'

第八誡。

你唔好偷野。

The Ninth Commandment.—

'Thou shalt not bear false witness against thy neighbour.'

第九誡。

你唔好妄（或誓假願做）證人。

Taí² sz³ káí³.

ᶜNéí yíú³ kéí³-ním² ˏOn-sik, Yat² ᶜshau ᶜk'öü tsò² shing³ yat². Luk² yat² noí² yíú³ tsò² ᶜnéí kok. yöng² ˏkung-ˏfú : taí² ts'at, yat² haí² ᶜnéí ˏShan, ˏYe-ˏwò-ˏwá-ke³ ˏOn-sik. Ko³ yat² ˏm ᶜhò tsò² ˏkung-ˏfú, ᶜnéí kung³ ᶜnéí-ke³ ᶜtsaí ᶜnuí, puk² ᶜp'éí, ch'uk,-ˏshang, ᶜyü-k'ap, ᶜnéí uk, noí² ke³ ˏyan-bák. ˏtò yíú³ ᶜkóm. ˏYau-waí² luk² yat² ˏkán, ˏYe-ˏwí-ˏwá ch'öng³-tsò² ˏt'ín téí² ᶜhoi, kung² ˏk'éí ˏchung-ke³ mán² ˏmat² tò³ taí² ts'at, yat², tsan² ˏOn-sik, : Kwú³-ᶜts'z ˏYe-ˏwò-ˏwá ch'uk,-fuk, ˏOn-sik, Yat² ᶜyí ko³ yat² waí² shing³ yat².

Taí² ᶜng káí³.

ᶜNéí yíú³ hán³-king³ ᶜnéí fú²-ᶜmò, ᶜtang ᶜnéí ᶜho-ᶜyí ˏch'öng-ᶜkau ᶜhaí ᶜnéí ˏShan, ˏYe-ˏwò-ˏwá, ᶜsho ts'z³ kwo³ ᶜnéí-ke³ téí².

Taí² luk² káí³.

ᶜNéí ˏm ᶜhò shát. ˏyan.

Taí² ts'at, káí³.

ᶜNéí ˏm ᶜhò ˏháng-ˏyam.

Taí² pát. káí³.

ᶜNéí ˏm ᶜhò ˏt'au ᶜye.

Taí² ᶜkau káí³.

ᶜNéí ˏm ᶜhò mong² (or shaí² ᶜká yün² tsò²) ching³ ˏyan.

The Fourth Commandment.—

You must remember Sabbath Day keep it to be holy day. Six days within must do your each kind work. No. seventh day is your God, Jehovah's, Sabbath. That day must not do work, you with your son, daughter, man slave, maid-slave, animals and your house within's guest, also must so. Because six days time Jehovah created heaven, earth, sea with its midst's myriad things until No. seven day, then Sabbath; therefore Jehovah blessed Sabbath Day considered that day to be holy day.

No. 5 Commandment.—

You must reverence your parents : so-that you may long be-in your God, Jehovah, what give to you's land.

No. 6 Commandment.—

You must not kill man.

No. 7 Commandment.—

You must not commit adultery.

No. 8 Commandment.—

You must not steal things.

No. 9 Commandment.—

You don't false witness against man (or swear false oath being a witness).

The Tenth Commandment.—

'Thou shalt not covet thy neighbour's house, thou shalt not covet thy neighbour's wife, nor his manservant, nor his maidservant, nor his ox, nor his ass, nor anything that is thy neighbour's.'

第十誡。

你唔好貪人屋舍，唔好僕所
貪人妻，與及人嘅人有
婢牛驢，共佢凡嘅，
有嘅，(or 有嘅野)。

LESSON, XIII.

The Creed :—

I believe in God the Father Almighty, Maker of heaven and earth.

And in Jesus Christ his only Son our Lord, who was conceived by the Holy Ghost, Born of the Virgin Mary Suffered under Pontius Pilate, Was crucified, died, and buried, He descended into Hades : The third day he rose again from the dead, He ascended into heaven, and sitteth on the right hand of God the Father Almighty ; From thence he shall come to judge the quick and the dead.

信篇。

我信全能真神聖父造
成天地嘅。

我信佢獨子，耶穌基督，
我哋嘅主，我信佢因處本受上日落嘅由
聖靈感動，我信利亞當時架三坐者將來死
女丟彼拉多官做十字府
難，被釘落陰升天能
死，葬埋去生父全信佢
由死翻便，我信佢生
真神嘥，我信佢審判生
個嚱嘥，審

I believe in the Holy Ghost ; The Holy Church ; The Communion of Saints ; The Forgiveness of sins ; The Resurrection of the body and the life everlasting.

我信聖靈，我信聖公會，我信生，
又各聖徒相合，我信得翻
罪得赦，身肉，
至到永生。

Taí² shap₂ kái⁗.

ᶜNéi ₍m ᶜhò ₍t'ám ₍yan uk₂-she⁗, ₍m ᶜhò ₍t'ám ₍yan ₍ts'aí, ᶜyü k'ap₂ ₍yan ke⁗ puk₂ ᶜp'éi ₍ngau ₍luí, kung² tán²-₍fán ₍yan ᶜsho ᶜyau ke⁗ (or ᶜyau ke⁗ ᶜye).

No. 10 Commandment.—

You must not covet man's house, must not covet man's wife, and man's male servant female servant, cow donkey, and whatever man has.

LESSON, XIII.

Sun⁗ ₍P'ín :—

ᶜNgo sun⁗ ₍tsün-₍nang ₍Chan ₍Shan shing⁗ fú² tsò² ₍shengt ₍t'ín téi² ke⁗. ᶜNgo sun⁗ ᶜK'öü tuk₂ ᶜtsz ₍Ye-₍sò ₍Kéi-tuk, ᶜngo-téi² ke⁗ ᶜchü, ᶜngo sun⁗ ᶜk'öü ₍yan Shing⁗-₍ling ᶜkòm-tung², ᶜMá-léi²-à⁗ ᶜch'ü-ᶜnuí tsau² ₍sháng. ᶜNgo sun⁗ ᶜk'öü, ₍tong ᶜPún-₍tíú ᶜPéi-₍lá-₍to tsò² ₍kwún ₍shí, shau² ₍nán, péi² ₍tengt lok₂ shap₂-tsz²-ká⁗ (sometimes pronounced ᶜká, but more often as ká⁗) shöng² ᶜsz, tsong⁗-₍máí, húi⁗ ₍yam-₍fú, ₍sám yat₂ yau² ᶜsz ₍fán ₍sháng, ₍shing ₍t'ín ᶜts'o*t lok₂, ₍Chan ₍Shan shing⁗ fú² ₍tsün-₍nang-ᶜche ke⁗ yau² pín². ᶜNgo sun⁗ ᶜk'öü tsöng-₍loí ₍yau ko⁗ shü⁗ ₍laí, ᶜsham-p'ún⁗ ₍sháng ᶜsz ke⁗. ᶜNgo sun⁗ Shing⁗-₍ling, ᶜngo sun⁗ shing⁗ ₍kung-wúi², yau² kok₀ shing⁗-₍t'ò ₍söng-hòp₂. ᶜNgo sun⁗ tsuí⁗ tak₂ she⁗, yuk₂ ₍shan tak₂ ₍fán-₍sháng, chí⁗-tò⁗ ᶜwing ₍sháng.

The Creed :—

I believe-in Almighty True God, Holy Father, made complete heaven earth. I believe-in his only son Jesus Christ our Lord, I believe that he on account of Holy Spirit affected Mary virgin then was given-birth-to. I believe he, at the time Pontius (₍tong ₍shí— at the time) Pilate was official, suffer troubles, was nailed down the cross on and died, buried, went Hades. Three days from the-dead again lived, ascended heaven, sat down True God, Holy Father, Almighty's right side. I believe he in the future from that place come to-judge alive dead.

I believe-in the Holy Ghost, I believe holy church from all believers to-gether joined, I believe sin obtain forgiveness, fleshly body get again life until eternal life.

LESSON, XIV.

Jacob had twelve sons. * * * Joseph was only seventeen years old and Benjamin was but a small child. All the others were grown up. The ten brothers were very bad: they had no fear of God in their hearts at all. Joseph was not like this: he really loved God. Jacob loved Joseph most of all his sons and made him a coat of many colours for him to wear. When his ten brothers saw that their Father loved Joseph, they hated him, and always oppressed him. God loved Joseph and always took care of him. One night Joseph dreamed he was in the field with his brother binding up sheaves of corn; and his brothers' sheaves all bowed down before his sheaf. God told Joseph what this meant.

雅各有十二個仔，＊＊＊約瑟十七歲，都有十神嘅，至着嘅，時約處禾兄地一特個神，佢愛個就佢時共把弟處把登。個陣時個十個兄弟敬畏係各佢親時約晚田的個仆束係，其餘十哋就神花爻時約一喺起個把瑟意瑟。有瑟愛件弟約好佢自弟個把瑟意瑟，有己束時都所思知。約首整兄弟約好佑自弟個把約哋約。雅個大大大惡心寶佢十好神保夢埋束嘅拜呢令。

It meant that Joseph's brothers at some future time would serve Joseph. His brothers were very angry with Joseph when they heard him say so. Before very long Joseph had another dream.

約瑟嘅過夢。必服約瑟嘅，是見約瑟發，弟聽見佢又嬲佢，兄弟好又試，後來約瑟兄子冇耐，佢兄弟樣有耐。

LESSON, XIV.

$_{c}$Ngá-kok$_{o}$ ^{c}yau shap$_{2}$-yí^{2} ko$^{)}$ ^{c}tsai.
* * * Ko$^{)}$ chan^{2} $_{c}$shí Yök$_{2}$-shat$_{2}$
shap$_{2}$-ts'at$_{2}$ suí$^{)}$ tái^{2} chek$_{o}$, Pín^{2}-^{c}ngá-
^{c}man tsan^{2} ^{c}mo ^{c}kéi tái^{2}ko$^{)}$. $_{c}$K'éi-
$_{c}$yü ko$^{)}$ ko$^{)}$ $_{c}$tò ^{c}t'höng-tái^{2} lok$_{o}$.
^{c}K'öü shap$_{2}$ $_{c}$hing-tai^{2} shap$_{2}$-$_{c}$fan
ok$_{o}$ ke$^{)}$: ^{c}mò $_{c}$ti king$^{)}$-wai$^{)}$ $_{c}$Shan
ke$^{)}$ $_{c}$sam. Yök$_{2}$-shat$_{2}$ tsan^{2} $_{c}$m hai^{2}
^{c}kòm: ^{c}k'öü shat$_{2}$-^{c}shan oi$^{)}$ $_{c}$Shan.
^{c}Ngá-kok$_{o}$ chí$^{)}$ oi$^{)}$ ^{c}k'öü, ^{c}ching kin^{2}
$_{c}$fá $_{c}$shám ^{c}k'öü chök$_{o}$. Ko$^{)}$ shap$_{2}$
$_{c}$hing-tai^{2} kin$^{)}$ fú^{2}-$_{c}$ts'an ^{c}kòm, tsan^{2}
^{c}hò $_{c}$tsang Yök$_{2}$-shat$_{2}$, $_{c}$shí-$_{c}$shí $_{c}$há
^{c}k'öü. $_{c}$Shan tsan^{2} ^{c}hò oi$^{)}$ Yök$_{2}$-shat$_{2}$,
$_{c}$shí-$_{c}$shí ^{c}pò-yan^{2} ^{c}k'öü. ^{c}Yau yat$_{2}$
^{c}mán Yök$_{2}$-shat$_{2}$ mung^{2} kin$^{)}$ tsz^{2}-^{c}kéi
^{c}hai $_{c}$t'in shü$^{)}$, kung^{2}-$_{c}$mái $_{c}$hing-tai^{2}
ch'uk$_{2}$ ^{c}héi $_{c}$ti $_{c}$wo ^{c}pá; ch'uk$_{2}$ ^{c}héi
ko$^{)}$ $_{c}$shí, ko$^{)}$-$_{c}$ti $_{c}$hing-tai^{2} ke$^{)}$, ^{c}pá-
^{c}pá $_{c}$to p'uk$_{2}$ ^{c}tò téi^{2} shü$^{)}$ pái$^{)}$
Yök$_{2}$-shat$_{2}$ ^{c}sho ch'uk$_{2}$ ko$^{)}$ yat$_{2}$ ^{c}pá.
$_{c}$Ni-$_{c}$ti yí$^{)}$-sz$^{)}$ hai^{2} $_{c}$Shan tak$_{2}$-$_{c}$tang
ling^{2} Yök$_{2}$-shat$_{2}$ $_{c}$chí.

Hau^{2}-$_{c}$loi ^{c}k'öü $_{c}$hing-tai^{2} shí^{2}-pít$_{2}$ fuk$_{2}$
Yök$_{2}$-shat$_{2}$. $_{c}$Hing-tai^{2} $_{c}$t'engt kin$^{)}$
Yök$_{2}$-shat$_{2}$ ^{c}kòm ^{c}yöng*-$_{c}$tsz ^{c}hò $_{c}$nau
Yök$_{2}$-shat$_{2}$. Kwo$^{)}$ $_{c}$híu ^{c}mò ^{c}noi*
^{c}k'öü yau^{2} shí$^{)}$ fát$_{o}$-mung^{2}.

Jacob had twelve [C.] sons. * * *
That period time Joseph seventeen
years big only 7, Benjamin, just not
much big [C.] Remainder each [C.]
also grown-up 32. They ten brothers
ten parts had: not (even a) little
reverence and fear God (kind of)
heart. Joseph just not was so, he
really loved God. Jacob most loved
him, made him flowery jacket (for)
him to wear. Those ten brothers
seeing (their) father so, then much
hated Joseph, constantly bullied him.
God just much loved Joseph, always
protected him. There-was one night
Joseph dreamt (he) saw himself in
field place together with (his) brothers
binding up the paddy sheaves;
binding up that time those brother's
(ones) sheaf sheaf even prostrated to
(the) ground place and did reverence
(to) Joseph what binded that one
sheaf. These meanings had God determinately caused Joseph to know.
Afterwards his brothers must be-sub-
ject-to Joseph. The brothers hearing Joseph so fashion very angry at
Joseph. Passed done not long he
again dreamed.

In his dream he saw the sun, moon, and eleven stars worshipping him. Joseph told this dream to his father and brothers. When Jacob heard these things, he did not know exactly what they meant, but he thought about them all the time. Joseph's brothers were still more angry with him.

Jacob's twelve sons were shepherds; they always helped their father by looking after sheep. The ten grown-up sons of Jacob took the sheep once to Shechem to feed; but Joseph and Benjamin did not go.

One day Israel, that is Jacob, called Joseph and said to him, 'I want you to go now and see how your brothers are getting on with the sheep at pasture, and then come back and give me an answer.'

Joseph went at once as soon as his father told him to go. Perhaps he was a bit afraid at first when his father told him to go, because his brothers were so angry with him. He knew that he ought to obey his father; and he knew that God could take care of him, so he went at once.

一粒講各分不越
又聽雅各就幾處弟
有約瑟弟事，就心處兄弟
共己兄嘅意思，係嘅兄弟
月自親呢意起，
日拜父見得想嬲
夢見星過聽曉歇發嬲咯。

羊羊大示雅
看看長去便
係親個十個
仔，父嘅羊同
個十個約瑟去。
二時排個唔
各時帶養，去。
雅嘅有仔處就
各十仔劍憫

各家嘅兄就我
雅而你嘅過
係我你黗我
即話睇嘅生氣
列嘅去得俾聲氣
色瑟你養嚟俾
以約你弟翻嚟
一日叫要弟翻

咐與時，為都親保
嘅者陣因俾俾父能刻去。
吩咛個定俾俾聽有刻去
父親或叫唔嘅該到神即
見去，親都嚟應知故此
聽就父呲兄弟應知俾
瑟時聽慌慌兄到又知俾
約即工慌俾知話佑俾

Mung² kín⁾ yat₂, yüt₂, kung² ⁵yau shap₂-yat, nap, ₍sing pái⁾ tsz²-⁵kéí. Yök₂-shat, yan² ⁵kong kwo⁾ fú²-₍ts'an ₍hing-taí² ₍te'ng†. ⁵Ngá-kok₀ ₍t'engt kín⁾ ₍ni-₍ti sz², tsan² ⁵kéí ₍fan ⁵híú tak₍ yí⁵-sz⁾, ⁵haí ₍sam shü⁾ pat₍ hít₀ ⁵söng ⁵héí. ⁵K'öü-ke⁾ ₍hing-taí² yüt₂-fát₀ ₍nau lok₀.

⁵Ngá-kok₀ shap₂-yí² ko⁾ ⁵tsaí haí² ₍hon ₍yöng ke⁾; ₍shí-₍shí ₍pong fú²-₍ts'an ₍hon ₍yöng. ⁵Yau yat, ⁵p'áí* ko⁾ shap₂ ko⁾ ⁵chöng-táí² ke⁾ ⁵tsaí táí⁾ ko⁾-₍tí ₍yöng huí⁾ Shí²-kím⁾ shü⁾ ⁵yöng. Yök₂-shat, ₍t'ung Pín²-⁵ngá-⁵man tsau² ₍m huí⁾.

Yat, yat₂ ⁵Yí-shik₍-lít₂, tsik₍ haí² ⁵Ngá-kok₀, kíú⁾ Yök₂-shat, ⁵kòm wá², ‘⁵Ngo ₍yí-₍ká yíú⁾ ⁵néí hüí⁾ ⁵t'aí ⁵há ⁵néí-₍ti ₍hing-taí² ⁵yöng tak, ₍ti ₍sháng-⁵hau ⁵tím, tsau² ₍fán ₍laí ⁵péí ₍shengt-héí⁾ kwo⁾ ⁵ngo.’

Yök₂-shat, ₍t'engt-kín⁾ fú²-₍ts'an ⁵kòm ₍fan-fú⁾, tsik₍-₍shí tsan² huí⁾. Wák₍-⁵che ⁵k'öü ₍hing-₍kung ₍t'engt fú²-₍ts'an kíú⁾ ko⁾ chan² ₍shí ₍fong-₍fong-⁵téí* ₍tò ₍m ting², ₍yan-waí² ⁵k'öü ₍hing-taí² kòm⁾ ₍nau ⁵k'öü. ⁵K'öü ₍tò ₍chí-tò⁾ ₍ying-₍koí yíú⁾ ₍t'engt fú²-₍ts'an wá²; yau² ₍chí-tò⁾ Shan ⁵yau ₍nang ⁵pò-yau² ⁵k'öü, kwú⁵-t'sz tsik₍-hak₍ huí⁾.

(In his) dream (he) saw sun, moon, together-with there-were eleven [C.] stars worshipping him. Joseph again spoke to (his) father brothers to-hear. Jacob hearing these matters then several tenths understand able meaning, in heart place without ceasing think. His brothers still more angry, 32.

Jacob's twelve sons were shepherds, always helped (their) father to-watch sheep. There was once the ten [C.] grown-up sons led the sheep away-to Shechem place to feed (them). Joseph with Benjamin then not go.

One day Israel, that is Jacob, called Joseph so said, ‘I now want you to-go see a bit your brothers rearing the live stock (lit. live mouths) how, then back come give answer to me.’

Joseph hearing (his) father so direct, immediately then went. Perhaps he at first hearing (his) father telling at that time frightened a bit, also not certain (i.e. he was very likely a bit frightened), because his brothers so angry-at him. He also knew by-rights ought to-obey (his) father's words; Further (he) knew God had power to-protect him, therefore (he) immediately went.

Joseph started from Hebron and when he got to Shechem he could not find his brothers. A man then told him, 'Your brothers have gone to Dothan; you will find them there.'

約瑟離開希伯倫個處，去搵佢兄弟，到倒示劍個處搵佢唔得，搵佢唔曉。個陣有個人話佢聽，你個兄弟去咗多丹個處，喺個處就搵得倒佢。

When some of Joseph's brothers saw him coming, they said, 'The dreamer is coming. Let us kill him, and throw his body into a pit; when we go home we can say to his father that a wild beast has eaten him up; and then we shall see whether his dreams will come to pass or not.'

But Reuben said, 'Do not kill him, but throw him into this pit.' Reuben was not so wicked as his brothers. He wanted to put him into the pit, then wait till all his brothers had gone away, when he would take him out again and give him back to his father.

有幾個兄弟見約瑟佢至一來，有後事，揪佢歸，就緊緊話，殺佢等親食佢，丟屍落坑處，過惡獸嚇佢，睇下佢嘅夢發應驗有冇。

流便話，唔好殺佢，丟落呢個坑處。流便冇佢哋咁惡。佢想丟佢落坑，等各個兄弟行翻，佢就攬佢翻，交返佢父親。

When Joseph got to his brothers, they seized him, took off his coat of many colours and threw him into a pit. It was a good thing there was no water in the pit; it was dry.

約瑟弟到倒佢，佢哋就捉佢，揪佢件花衫好彩係乾嘅，除佢落坑。個坑冇水喺個處，個坑冇水，係乾嘅。

Yŏk₂-shat, ₌léí-ₐhoí ₐHéí-pák₀-ₐlun huí⁾
tò⁾ Shí²-kím⁾ ko⁾ shü⁾, ₌m ⁽wan tak,
⁽tò ₐhing-taí². Ko⁾ chan² ⁽yan ko⁾
₌yan wá² ⁽k'öü ₐt'engɬ, '⁽Néí ₐhing-
taí² huí⁾ ₐbíú ₐTo-ₐtán shú⁾, ⁽haí ko⁾
shü⁾ ⁽wan tak, chök₀ ⁽k'öü.'

⁽Yau ⁽kéí ko⁾ ₐhing-taí² ⁽t'aí kín⁾ Yŏk₂-
shat, ₐlaí-⁽kan, tsau² ⁽kòm wá², 'Ko⁾
fat₀-mung²-ke⁾ ₐlaí-⁽kan lok₀; shát₀
⁽k'öü ₐlá; ₐwing ⁽k'öü ₐshí lok,
ₐháng shü⁾; ⁽tang huí⁾ ₐkwaí chí⁾ wá²
kwo⁾ fú²-ₐts'an ₐt'engɬ, wá², ⁽yau yat,
chek₀ ok₀ shau⁾ shik, ₐhíú ⁽k'öü;
hau²-ₐloí ⁽t'aí ⁽há ⁽k'öü fát₀ mung²
ₐti sz⁾ ⁽yau ying⁾-yím² ⁽mò.'

₌Lau-pín² wá², '₌M ⁽hò shát₀ ⁽k'öü,
ₐwing ⁽k'öü lok, ₌ni-ko⁾ ₐháng shü⁾.'
₌Lau-pín² ₌m ₐt'ung ko⁾-ₐti ₐhing-taí²
kòm⁾ hak, ₐsam. ⁽K'öü ⁽söng ₐchaí
⁽k'öü lok, ₐháng shü⁾, ⁽tang kok₀
ₐhing-taí² ₐháng ₐhoí ko⁾ chan² ₌shí,
tsau² ⁽lo ⁽k'öü ₐfán ch'ut, ₌laí, ₐkáu-
₌wúí fú²-ₐts'an.

Yŏk₂-shat, ₌laí tò⁾ ko⁾ ₐshí, ⁽k'öü ₐti
ₐhing-taí² chuk₀ (or chuk₂) ⁽tò ⁽k'öü,
ₐch'ü ⁽k'öü kín² ₐfá ₐshám, ₐwing
⁽k'öü lok₀ ₐháng shü⁾. ⁽Hò ⁽ts'oí
ko⁾ ₐháng ⁽mò ⁽shuí ⁽haí shü⁾, haí²
ₐkòn ke⁾.

Joseph separated-from Hebron went to
Shechem that place, not find able
arrive (*i.e.* the finding did not
arrive at the conclusion wished for)
brothers. That period have [*C.*] man
say to-him to-hear, 'Your brothers
gone have Dothan place; at that
place find able right them.'

There-were several brothers seeing
Joseph coming, then so said, 'The
dreamer is-coming, 32; kill him;
21, throw his corpse down pit place;
wait-till go home until say to father
to-hear, say, there-was one [*C.*] fierce
animal eat have him; afterwards
see a-bit his dreaming matters have
fulfilment (*or*) not.'

Reuben said, 'Do-not kill him, throw
him down-into this pit place.'
Reuben not with those brothers so
black heart. He wished to-place
him down-into the-pit place, (and)
wait-till èach brother had-walked off
that period-of time, then take him
back out come, hand back-again-to
(his) father.

Joseph come arrived that time, his
those brothers caught him, took-
off his [*C.*] flowered coat, threw
him down-into pit place. Very fortunate that pit no water at place,
was dry.

When his brothers had thrown him into the pit, they sat down and had their lunch. It was great pity they did this; it was because they hated their little brother Joseph that they did so. * * * .

While Joseph's brothers were eating, they looked up and saw a great many people coming. These people were the descendants of Ismael the son of Hagar. They came from Gilead, riding on camels, and brought many spices with them to take down into Egypt to sell.

When Judah saw these people coming, he said to his brothers, 'Let us sell Joseph to these men.' His brothers were pleased and took Joseph out of the pit at once, and sold him for twenty pieces of gold, which would now be worth about ten or eleven dollars.

The Ishmaelites took Joseph to Egypt and sold him to Potiphar. Reuben was not there when his brothers sold Joseph. When he came back he wanted to find Joseph; he was unable to find him; he was very sad, and tore his clothes.

兄弟揾佢落坑倒，坐低食晏，佢哋咁做個細佬呢，可惜，因爲憎約瑟呌。

* * *

約瑟啲兄弟食緊嘅時候，擡高個頭睇，見好多人嚟，呢啲人實係夏甲仔以實馬利嘅子孫，喺基列嚟，騎住駱駝，帶好多香料，想掉去埃及處賣。

猶大見呢啲人嚟處，約瑟就話，拉二十零個金，賣約瑟過呢啲人好，啲兄弟知嘵，就話好，即時上佢坑處，即賣佢，賣得二十零個金銀錢。

以實馬利人就帶約瑟去到埃及，賣過波提乏。約瑟啲兄弟賣約瑟嗰陣，流便唔喺嗰處，佢翻嚟個時，想搵約瑟，搵唔倒，好閉翳，傷心得自己撕爛件衫。

ᴄWing ꞓk'öü lok₂ ꞔháng ko⁾ ꞔshí, ko⁾-ꞔti ꞔhing-taí² ꞓts'ò*† ꞓtò téi² shü⁾ shik₂ án⁾. ꞓHo-sik₂ ꞓk'öü-téi² tsò² ꞔni-ꞔti sz² ; ꞔyan-wái² ꞔtsang ko⁾ saí-ꞓlò Yök₂-shat₂ che₂.

Yök₂-shat₂ ꞔhing-taí² shik₂ ꞓkan án⁾ ko⁾ ꞔshí, ꞔtám ꞔkò ꞔt'au, kin⁾ ꞓhò ꞔto ꞔyan ꞔlaí ꞓkan shü⁾. ꞔNi-ꞔti ꞔyan haí² ꞔHá-káp₀ ko⁾ ꞓtsaí ꞓYí-shat₂-ꞓmá-léi² ke⁾ ꞓtsaí ₀sün. ꞓHaí ꞔKéi-lít₂ shü⁾, ꞔk'éi lok₀-ꞔt'o ꞔlaí tò⁾ ke⁾, taí tiing² ꞓhò ꞔto ꞔhöng líú², ꞓsöng ꞔning huí⁾ ꞔOí-k'ap₂ shü⁾ máí².

ꞔYau-táí² kín⁾ ꞔni-ꞔti ꞔyan ꞔlaí-ꞓkan shü⁾, tsau² wá² kwo⁾ ꞔhing-taí² ꞔchí, 'Yök₂-shat₂ ꞓk'áí ꞔlaí máí² kwo⁾ ꞓk'öü ꞔti ꞔyan, tsau² chök₀ lok₀.' ꞓK'öü ꞔti ꞔhing-taí² wá², 'ꞓHò.' Tsau² tsik₂ ꞔshí ꞓhaí ꞔháng shü⁾ ꞔláí ko⁾ Yök₂-shat₂ ꞓshöng ꞔlaí, máí² ꞓhíú yí²-shap₂ ꞔkam, tsik₂ haí² ꞔkam-yat₂ shap₂ leng²† ko⁾ ꞔngan-ꞓts'in*.

ꞓYí-shat₂-ꞓmá-léi² ꞔyan tsau² táí⁾ Yök₂-shat₂ huí⁾ tò⁾ ꞔOí-k'ap₂, máí² ꞔhúí kwo⁾ ꞔPo-ꞔt'aí-fat₂. ꞓK'öü ꞔhing-ꞓtaí² máí² Yök₂-shat₂ ko⁾ chan² ꞔshí, ꞔLau-pín² tsau² ꞔm ꞓhaí shü⁾. ꞓK'öü ꞔfán-ꞔlaí ko⁾ ꞔshí, ꞓsöng ꞓwan Yök₂-shat₂, ꞓwan ꞔm tak₂ ꞓtò; ꞔsam tsau² ꞓhò paí²-aí⁾, mák₂ lán² tsz²-ꞓkéi ꞔshám.

Threw him down-into pit that time, those brothers sat on ground place eat lunch. To be pitied they did these things ; (it was) because (they) hated the younger brother, Joseph, only, 7.

Joseph's brothers eating in-progress lunch that time, lifted high (their) heads, saw very many men coming in-progress to-the-place. These men were Hagar that son Ismael's sons grand-sons. From Gilead place riding-on camels coming arrived bringing prepared very many spice materials, wishing to-take to-go-to Egypt place to-sell.

Judah saw these people coming in-progress-to the-place, then said to brothers to-know, 'Joseph take come sell to them these people just correct,' 32. His these brothers said, 'Good.' Then immediately from pit place pull that Joseph up come, sold done two tens gold, just is to-day ten odd [C.] dollars.

Ishmaelite men just led Joseph go to Egypt, sold done to Potiphar. His brothers sold Joseph that [C.] time, Reuben just not (is) at place. He back come that time wish find Joseph, find not able arrive-at (the finding) ; heart then very sad, rending tore own clothes.

He went quickly to his brothers and said, 'The child is not here. I do not know what to do.' The brothers paid no attention to him. They killed a kid at once, and taking Joseph's coat of many colours they dipped it into the blood of the kid, and took it home to show to their father. They said, 'Is this coat which we have found Joseph's?' As soon as Jacob saw it, he said, 'It is his. A wild beast has eaten him, my son Joseph is not.'

急啲去對兄弟話個細唔
蚊仔唔處話我總唔
知點筭個我弟一件揸
唔喋即弟劏件倒
隻仔將個個處掉話倒係
花衫落血瞇係
去浸過親認個
呢俾係我得野
嘅件約瑟嘅佢獸瑟
雅衫見就野約
件約一錯係仔約
喋話被隻瑟
食必定我個仔
必定佢唱咯

Jacob had deceived his father, and now his children were deceiving him. * * *.

本來雅各已經呃自己
父親而家仔又呃翻
佢。 * * *

Jacob thought that his son was really dead and he was very sad; he wept aloud, tore his clothes, and would not be comforted.—'Bible History for the Least and Lowest.'

雅各個時估個仔就真好正閉自慰
死喇佢大聲心喊攀人安
翳已衫又嗌唔受爛
已己又人嘅

LESSON, XV.

King Darius was a proud man, and he worshipped idols.

大利烏王係好驕傲嘅
人，又係拜偶像嘅。

Kap,-ᵪti huí̄ tuí̄ ᵪhing-taí̄² wá², 'Ko'
sai-ᵪman-'tsai ᵪm 'haí̄ shü' lok₀.
ᶜNgo ᵪm ᵪchí 'tím sün'.' Ko'-ᵪti
ᵪhing-taí̄² 'tsung ᵪm 'ts'oi ᶜk'öü; tsik,-
ᵪshí chung² ᵪt'ong yat, chek₀ ᵪyöng-
tsai, ᵪtsöng Yök₂-shat, ko'-kín ᵪfá
ᵪshám tsam' lok, ᵪyöng hüt₀ shü',
ᵪning huí̄ ᵪkwai 'péí kwo' fú²-ᵪts'an
't'ai, wá², 'Ni kín² ᵪshám haí̄² ᶜngo-
téí̄² 'wan-'tò ke'. Haí̄² Yök₂-shat, ke'
ᵪshám ᵪm haí̄² ?' ᶜNgá-kok₀ yat, kín'
tsan² ying²-tak, ko' kín² ᵪshám wá²,
' ᶜMò ts'o'; haí̄² ᶜk'öü-ke' lok₀. Pít₀-
ting² péí̄² yat, chek₀ ᶜye shaṅ' shik,
ᶜsz ᶜk'öü. ᶜNgo₀ ko' 'tsai Yök₂-shat,
pít₀-ting² ᶜmò ᵪhíú lok₀.'

ᶜPún-ᵪloí̄ ᶜNgá-kok₀ ᶜyí-ᵪking ngak,
tsz²-ᶜkéí̄ fú²-ᵪts'an, ᵪyí-ᵪká ᶜtsai yan²
ngak, ᵪfán ᶜk'öü. * * *.
ᶜNgá-kok₀ ko' ᵪshi ᶜkwú ko' ᶜtsaí̄
ᵪchan-ching' ᶜsz ᵪlá. ᶜK'öü ko' ᵪsam
tsau² ᶜhò pai²-ai' lok₀; taí̄² ᵪshengt
hám', mák, kán² tsz²-ᶜkéí̄ ᵪshám, yan²
ᵪm shau² ᵪyan ᵪon-waí̄'.

Quickly went answered brothers, saying,
'The child not at place, 32. I not
know how to-consider (what is best
to be done).' Those brothers entirely
not pay-attention-to him; just at-that-
time even slaughtered a [C.] kid, taking Joseph that [C.] flowered coat, im-
mersed down-into kid's blood place,
took (it) away home to-give to (their)
father to-see, saying, 'This [C.] coat
was (what) we found. Is (it) Joseph's
coat (or) not is ?' Jacob (at) one
sight (of it) then recognised able that
[C.] coat, saying, 'No mistake ; (it) is
his, 32. Certainly by one [C.] wild
animal eaten to-death him. My that
son Joseph certainly is not, 32.'
Originally Jacob already deceived his-
own father, now (his) son also cheat
back him. * * *.
Jacob that time thought that son
really was-dead, 21. His that heart
then very sad, 32 ; great sound cry,
tore-to pieces his-own clothing, also
not receive (from) man comfort.

LESSON, XV.

Taí̄²-léí̄²-ᵪwú ᵪwong haí̄² ᶜhò ᵪkiú-ngo² ke'
ᵪyan, yau² haí̄² páí̄' ᶜngau-tsöng² ke'.

Darius King was very proud man, also
did pray-to images.

Yet he liked Daniel very much; and he set him over all the other judges and lords, and told all the people to mind him. Daniel was a very wise old man, and he was fit to be a judge. There were a great many rich men, who hated Daniel, because the King told them to mind Daniel, and because the King liked him better than them. These men were envious of Daniel. * * *.

These wicked rich men wished to hurt Daniel, and to get him into disgrace with King Darius; but they did not know how to get him into disgrace; they never saw Daniel do anything wrong. I suppose they were afraid of telling the King lies of Daniel, lest they should be found out. But at last they thought of a way to get Daniel into disgrace. They knew that he prayed very often to his God.

So they went to the King and asked him to make a law, that no one should pray to any God or man, but to the King himself, for thirty days.

理，嘅佢時慧人，爲以王佢妒忌佢。以大聽陣智主，因但個過嘅。但至要個好財理，聽爲多個，以哋因理生。個中人理多嘅，以哋因理。又以佢心就歡喜，國眾以又個。做哋但大，多憎叫佢。又以好國眾以大，多憎叫咄以。但佢份訓老好好，王份喜嘅。心。但立官教係，有就個理歡哋忌。

呢啲爲利係，子得做出利理理要。啲惡烏佢正出錯一烏咯，一拜。嘅以王唔做但嘅，個王佢一日拜神。財理唔知得，以佢法唔嘅。主又歡揾，因理哋子，歡知間。人想喜也佢，有收喜到好。想令佢野，唔乜尾，令但多。難大但法查野想大，以以賬。

命日唔個，出十都拜，王三神係，個人嘅淨，求眾樣拜，個人嘅拜。就份耐，佢哋令咁准王。嚟吩咐，佢咋。佢哋就嚟求個王，命令三十日都唔拜個神三個，淨係拜個王咋。眾人樣樣拜，咁耐，唔准佢哋拜，淨係個王咋。

Tán² ⁵k‘öü ⁵hò ‚fún-⁵héï ko⁾ Tán²-⁵yí-
⁵léï; láp₂ ⁵k‘öü tsò² kwok₀ ‚chung chï⁾
táï² ke⁾ ‚kwún, ‚fan-fú⁾ chúng⁾ ‚yan
yíú⁾ ‚t‘eng† ⁵k‘öü káu⁾-fan⁾. Tán²-⁵yí-
⁵léï ko⁾ chan² ‚shí haï² ⁵lò-⁵táï*, yau²
⁵hò ‚to chï⁾-waï². ⁵Yau ⁵hò ‚to ko⁾-‚ti
‚ts‘oi-⁵chü ‚yan tsau² ⁵hò ‚tsang Tán²-
⁵yí-⁵léï, ‚yan-waï² ko⁾ ‚wong kíú⁾
⁵k‘öü-téï² ‚t‘eng† Tán²-⁵yí-⁵léï ‚fan-
fú⁾, yau² ‚yan-waï² ko⁾ ‚wong ‚fún-
⁵héï Tán²-⁵yí-⁵léï ‚to kwo⁾ ⁵k‘öü-téï².
⁵Kòm ⁵k‘öü tsau² ‚sháng ko⁾-‚ti tò⁾-
kéï² ke⁾ ‚sam. * * *.

‚Ni-‚ti ok₀ ke⁾ ‚ts‘oi-⁵chü ‚yan ⁵söng
‚nán-waï² Tán²-⁵yí-⁵léï, yau² ⁵söng
ling² Táï²-léï²-‚wú ‚wong ‚m ‚fún-⁵héï
⁵k‘öü; tán²-haï² ⁵k‘öü ‚m ‚chí ⁵wan
mat₂-⁵ye fát₀-⁵tsz ching⁾ tsò² tak₂;
‚yan ⁵k‘öü ‚m ‚ch‘á tak₂ ch‘ut₂ Tán²-
⁵yí-⁵léï ⁵yau mat₂ ⁵ye tsò² ts‘o⁾ ke⁾.
⁵K‘öü-téï² ‚shau-₀méï ⁵söng ch‘ut₂
yat₂ ko⁾ fát₀-⁵tsz, ⁵wui ling² Táï²-
léï²-‚wú ‚wong ‚m ‚fún-⁵héï Tán²-⁵yí-
⁵léï lok₀. ⁵K‘öü-téï² ‚chí tò⁾ Tán²-
⁵yí-⁵léï yat₂ yat₂ ‚chí ‚kán ⁵hò ‚to
chöng⁾ yíú⁾ páï⁾ ‚Shan ke⁾.

⁵K‘öü-téï² tsau² ‚laí ‚k‘au ko⁾ ‚wong
ch‘ut₂ ming²-ling², ‚fan-fú⁾ chúng⁾
‚yan ‚sám-shap₂ yat₂ kòm⁾ noï²,
yöng²-yöng² ke⁾ ‚Shan ‚tò ‚m ⁵chun
⁵k‘öü-téï² páï⁾, tsing² haï² páï⁾ ko⁾
‚wong che₂.

But he (was) very pleased-with that
Daniel; appointed him to be country's
midst greatest officials, directed all
men must obey his instructions.
Daniel at-that [C.] time was old, had
very much wisdom. There-were very
many-of those wealthy men just
much hated Daniel, because the King
told them to-obey Daniel, (giving)
directions further because the King
was-pleased-with Daniel more than
with-them. So they then grew those
envious hearts. * * *.

These wicked wealthy men wished to-
oppress Daniel, also they-wished to-
cause Darius King not to-be-pleased-
with him; but they (did) not know
to-find what means properly to-do
to-be-able; because they not find able
out Daniel had what thing doing
wrong. They finally thought out one
[C.] means, (which) could cause
Darius King not to-be-pleased-with
Daniel, 32. They knew Daniel one
day's course very many times would
pray-to God.

They then came (and) begged the
King to-issue a-decree, directing all
men thirty days so long within every
kind of God also not to-allow them
to-pray-to. Only to-pray-to the King
only.

And that if any one did pray to any one else, he should be cast into a den of lions. Now the King did not know why these men asked him to make this law: if the King had known that Daniel always prayed to his God, I do not think he would have made this law, for the King loved Daniel.

The King was so foolish as to say that he would do as these men wished, because, you know, the King was a heathen, and he did not love the true God. * * *.

Daniel heard of the law that the King had made.

Do you think that he went on praying?

Daniel would have thought it very dreadful not to pray to God for thirty days. He wanted to praise God very often, and ask Him to bless him.

He used always to pray before the open window in his room. Perhaps you wonder why he did so. The reason was, he liked to look towards the place where he knew Jerusalem was. He could not see Jerusalem from his window, because it was so very far off; but still he knew which way it was, and he knew that God loved Jerusalem. * * *.

揾個人拜第二個神，就要掟佢落個獅子窿。個王實唔知佢哋爲乜叫佢出呢條令，或者個王知到但以理成日拜佢個神，我估佢實唔會出呢條令，因爲個王愛但以理嘅。

個王唔係愛個真神，係拜個菩薩嘅。可惜個王真係咁嘅。 * * *

但以理聽聞個王出嘅命令。

佢都照舊一樣拜神嘅。

但以理點得三十日唔讚美神，唔多謝恩典呢。

佢時時都喺自己間房度，向個開嘅窓拜神。因爲佢好愛個城，就係耶路撒冷。佢做乜咁拜呢？因爲佢鍾意向住佢知到耶路撒冷城嘅嗰便睇。佢喺個窓睇唔到耶路撒冷城，因爲個城離到咁遠，但佢都知到個城喺邊，又知到神愛個城。 * * *

Wăk₂ ͻyau păi⁾ tai²-yi² ͻwai*, tsau² yiú⁾ ͻwing ⁵k'öü ɽap₂ ko⁾-ͻti ͻsz-tau⁾ shü⁾. Ko⁾ ͻwong ͻm ͻchí wai²-mat₂ ͻni-ͻti ͻɽan kiú⁾ ⁵k'öü ch'ut₂ ͻkòm-ke⁾ ming²-ling². ⁵Ngo ͻkwú wăk₂ ⁵k'öü ͻchí-tò⁾ Tán²-⁵yi-⁵léí ɽat₂-ɽat₂ kòm⁾ ͻtò chöng⁾ păi⁾ ͻShan, ⁵k'öü tsau² ͻm ⁵wui ch'ut₂ ͻkòm-ke⁾ ming²-ling⁾, ɽan-wai² ⁵k'öü 'hò oi⁾ Tán²-⁵yí-⁵léí ke⁾.

Tán⁾ 'ho-sik₂ ko⁾ ͻwong ͻm hai² oi⁾ ko⁾ ͻwai* ͻchan-ke⁾ Shan, ⁵k'öü hai² păi⁾ ͻp'ò-sàt₀ ke⁾. * * *.

Tán²-⁵yí-⁵léí ͻt'engᵗ-ͻman ko⁾ ͻwong ch'ut₂, ͻkòm ke⁾ ming²-ling².

⁵K'öü ͻtò chiú⁾ kau² ɽat₂ yöng² păi⁾ ͻShan ke⁾.

Tán²-⁵yi-⁵léí 'tim tak₂ ͻsàm-shap₂ ɽat₂ kòm⁾ noi² ͻm ͻto-tse² ͻm tsán-⁵méí ͻShan ke⁾ ͻyan-'tín ₀ni?

⁵K'öü ͻshi-ͻshí ͻtò hai² 'hai tsz²-⁵kéí ͻfong* 't'ă-hoi tò² ch'öng ⁵kòm ͻlai păi⁾ ke⁾. ⁵K'öü ͻkòm tsὸ⁾ ͻyan ⁵k'öü 'hò oi⁾ ͻYe-lò⁾-sàt₀-⁵láng ko⁾ ͻshengᵗ. ⁵K'öü tsau² ͻfún-'héi 'péi min² höng⁾-chü² ko⁾ ͻshengᵗ ͻlai păi⁾. ⁵K'öü ͻm 't'ăí-kin⁾ ko⁾ ͻYe-lò²-sàt₀-⁵láng ͻshengᵗ, ɽan-wai² kăk₀ tak₂ ⁵yün; tán² ⁵k'öü ͻchi-tò⁾ ko⁾ ͻshengᵗ 'hai ͻpín pín². ⁵K'öü ɽau² ͻchi-ͻtò ͻShan 'hò oi⁾ ko⁾ ͻshengᵗ. * * *.

If there-was praying-to another [C.], then must throw him into those lions' den place. The King not know why these men told him to-issue such decree. I think if he knew Daniel daily so many times prayed-to God, he then not would-have issued such a-decree, because he much loved Daniel.

But it-is-to-be-pitied-that the King not did love the [C.] true God. He did pray-to idols. * * *.

Daniel heard (that) the King had-issued such-a decree.

He also according-to old (manner or time) one same prayed to-God.

Daniel how could thirty days so long not thank (and) not praise God's mercy eh? 53.

He constantly also did in his own room throw open [C.] window in-that-way in-order-to pray. He so did because he very loved Jerusalem that city. He then pleased to-put (his) face facing that city in-order-to pray. He not see that Jerusalem city, because separated able far; but he knew the city at what side. He also knew God very loved the city. * * *.

So Daniel liked to look that way when he prayed. He knelt down three times every day, and prayed, and thanked God for all His kindness to him.

嘑，但以理歡喜面向嗰便嘅拜。佢日日跪倒三次拜神，多謝神咁大恩典待佢，而家都係照一樣嘅拜。

The men who hated Daniel heard that he went on praying: so they went one day to look at him praying, that they might tell the King that they had seen him.

個啲憎但以理嘅人，聽聞佢照舊嘅拜，知到係佢，一日時候就去賍佢，做得話個王知，佢哋親眼見佢拜。

Then they asked the King, 'Did you not make a law that if any one prayed to any god or man, excepting you, that he should be cast into a den of lions?'

佢哋就嚟對個王話，你命令，十日之內，或者一個人咁耐有拜神，唔係拜你，就要拣佢落獅竇。

And the King said, 'Yes, it is true, and I cannot change the law.'

個王話，係真嘅咯，我又唔改得呢個命令嘅。

Then the men said, 'That Daniel, who was brought from Jerusalem to be a slave, does not mind you, nor your law, but prays three times a day.'

個啲人就話，耶路撒冷帶嚟嗰個但以理，唔聽你嘅命令，一日三偏拜神。

ˊKòm ˹k‘öü ˌfún-ˊhéí mín² höng⌐ ko⌐ pín² ˌlaí paí⌐. ˊK‘öü yat₂-yat₂ ˌsám chöng⌐ ˌtò haí² ˊkòm kwaí²-˹tò ko⌐ shü⌐ ˌlaí paí⌐ ˌShan, ˌto-tse² ˌShan kòm⌐ táí² ˌyan-˹tín, toí² ˹k‘öü. ˌYí-ká ch‘ut₂ ˌhíú ko⌐ ming²-ling², ˹k‘öü ˌtò haí² chíú⌐ yat₂ yöng² ˊkòm paí⌐.

Ko⌐-ˌti ˌtsang Tán²-˹yí-˹léí ke⌐ ˌyan ˌt‘eng†-ˌman ˹k‘öü chíú⌐ kam² ˊkòm paí⌐ : ˹k‘öü-téí² yat₂ yat₂ ˌchí-tò⌐ haí² ˹k‘öü paí⌐-ke⌐ ˌshí-hau² tsau² huí⌐ ˌchong ˹k‘öü, ˹tang ˹k‘öü-téí² ˌtsò⌐-tak₂ wá² ko⌐ ˌwong ˌchí, haí² ˹k‘öü-téí² ˌts‘an ˹ngán kín⌐ ˹k‘öü paí⌐.

˹K‘öü-téí² tsan² ˌlaí tuí⌐ ko⌐ ˌwong wá², ‘ˊNéí ˌm haí² ch‘ut₂ ˌhíú yat₂ ko⌐ ming²-ling², wák₂-˹che yat₂ ko⌐ ˌyan ˌsám-shap₂ yat₂ kòm⌐ noí², ˹yau paí⌐ ˌShan, ˌm haí² tuk₂ paí⌐ ˹néí, tsan² yíu⌐ ˌwing ˹k‘öü lok₂ ˌsz-tau⌐.’

Ko⌐ ˌwong wá², ‘Haí² ˹chan ke⌐ lok₀, ˹ngo yau² ˌm ˹koí tak₂ ˌni-ko⌐ ming²-ling² ke⌐.’

Ko⌐-ˌti ˌyan tsau² wá², ‘Haí ˌYe-lò⌐-sát₀-˹láng táí⌐ ˌlaí ko⌐ Tán²-˹yí-˹léí ˌm t‘eng† ˹néí-ke⌐ ming²-ling², yat₂ yat₂ ˌchí kán⌐ ˌtò ˌsám p‘ín⌐ paí⌐ ˌShan.’

So he was-pleased (to have his) face towards that side in-order-to pray. He day (by) day three times also did so kneel-at that place in-order-to pray to-God to-thank God such great grace towards him. Now issued had the decree, he also did according-to one same so pray.

Those (who) hated Daniel people heard he according-to old (time) so prayed : they one day knew it-was his praying time then went to-spy-on him so-that they do could say-to the King to-know it was they with-their-own eyes saw him pray.

They then came (and) to the King said, ‘You not have (i.e. Have you not) issued done a [C.] decree (to the effect that), if a [C.] man (for the space of) thirty days so long did pray to-God, (and) not did only pray to-you, then must thrown down lions' den ?’

The King said, ‘It is true, 32, I also not change able this decree.’

The men then said, ‘From Jerusalem brought to-come (here) that Daniel not obey your decree, one day's course also three times pray-to God.’

Then the King was very sorry that he had made a law against praying, and tried to think of some way of not letting Daniel be killed.

But he could think of no way. In the evening the men came to him and said, 'You cannot alter the law that you have made, for in our country it is a law that laws may not be altered.'

Then the King desired Daniel to be brought, and he was cast into a den of lions; the lions lived in a deep place underground. Lions are always very hungry in the evening, and roar for their food. Would they not eat up Daniel as soon as he was thrown into the den?

But Darius knew that Daniel's God was a very great God, and he said to Daniel, 'Your God whom you serve always, is able to deliver you.'

I think Darius must have heard how God once saved three men from being burnt in the furnace.

A stone was brought, and laid upon the top of the den.

個王個時就好閉翳咯，就想揾法子，等佢唔使俾個啲獅咬死。

但冇法子嚟，到晚個啲人對個王話，你個命令出過，改唔得嘅，因為呢個國，係必唔改得嘅咯。

個王就吩咐人帶但以理嚟，揾佢落獅寶處，個獅寶係一個大都好深嘅困落地底，啲獅到晚時時好肚餓嘅。

所以大話，但以理你所事嘅神，係好大嘅神，佢就對但以理話，你時時所服事嘅神，有能救你嘅。

大概大利烏聽聞過人講，神先日救過三個人出火爐。

佢嚟揾落大石，之後就俾個大石塞住個獅寶大籠口。

Ko꞉ ꞇwong ko꞉ ꞇshi tsau² ꞇhò páí꞉-aí꞉ lok₀, tsau² ꞇsöng ꞇwan fát₀-ꞇtsz ꞇlaí kau꞉ ko꞉ Tán²-ꞇyí-ꞇléí, ꞇtang ꞇk'öü ꞇm ꞇshaí ꞇpéí ꞇti ꞇsz ꞇngáu ꞇsz.

The King at-that time then very sad, 32, then wished to-find means in-order-to save that Daniel, so-that he not need allow those lions to-bite (him) to-death.'

Tán² ꞇmò fát₀-ꞇtsz. Tò꞉ ꞇáí-ꞇmán ko꞉-ꞇti ꞇyan ꞇlaí tuí꞉ ko꞉ ꞇwong wá², 'ꞇNéí ꞇm tak, ꞇkoí-pín꞉ ꞇnéí ko꞉-ꞇti mìng²-ling², ꞇyan ꞇni-ko꞉ kwok₀ ch'ut, kwo꞉ mìng²-ling², shí²-pít, ꞇm ꞇkoí tak, ke꞉ lok₀.'

But (there-were) no means. At evening those men came to the King said, 'You not can change your those decrees, because this country issue have decrees, certainly not change able, 32.'

Ko꞉ ꞇwong tsau² ꞇfan-fú꞉ ꞇyan táí꞉ Tán²-ꞇyí-ꞇléí ꞇlaí ꞇwing lok, ꞇsz tau꞉ shü꞉; ko꞉-ꞇti ꞇsz haí² k'wan꞉ lok, yat, ko꞉ táí꞉ ꞇlung. Tò꞉ ꞇáí-ꞇmán ꞇk'öü ꞇshí-ꞇshí ꞇtò ꞇhò ꞇt'ò-ngo² ke꞉.

The King than directed men to-lead Daniel to-come, (and) throw down lion's den place; the lions were shut-up down-in a [C.] large hole. At evening they always also very hungry.

Táí꞉-léí²-ꞇwú ꞇchi-tò꞉ Tán²-ꞇyí-ꞇléí ꞇsho páí꞉ ko꞉ ꞇwaí* ꞇShan haí² ꞇhò ꞇtsün táí²-ke꞉, ꞇk'öü tsau² tuí꞉ Tán²-ꞇyí-ꞇléí wá², 'ꞇNéí ꞇshí-ꞇshí ꞇsho fuk, -sz² ke꞉ ꞇShan, ꞇyau ꞇnang kan꞉ ꞇnéí ke꞉.'

Darius knew Daniel what prayed-to that [C.] God was very exalted (and) great, he then to Daniel said, 'You constantly what serve (that) God (i.e. that God you constantly serve) has ability to-save you.'

Táí² ꞇk'oí* Táí꞉-léí²-ꞇwú ꞇt'engṭ-ꞇman ꞇyan ꞇkong kwo꞉ ꞇShan sín-yat, kau꞉ kwo꞉ ꞇsám ko꞉ ꞇyan ch'ut, ꞇhíú ꞇfo-ꞇlò.

Probably Darius heard people talk had (that) God former days saved had three [C.] men out-of the-furnace.

ꞇK'öü-téí² ꞇwiug-híú Tán²-ꞇyí-ꞇléí lok, ꞇsz tau꞉ ꞇchí hau², tsau² ꞇpéí kau² táí² shek, sak,-chü² ko꞉ ꞇlung ꞇhau.

They thrown had Daniel down-into the-lions' den, after (that) then put a-piece of-large stone to-stop-up the hole mouth.

And the King put his seal on it, that none might take away the stone, and he put on it also the seal of the men that hated Daniel.

Why did the King put his own seal on it? That he might find out if any one came and took Daniel away, for no one else had a seal like the King's: so if any one broke the seal, the King would find it out. Why did he put the wicked men's seal? That they might see that the King did not take Daniel out in the night.

The King went to his palace that evening, but he was so unhappy that he could not eat, * * * and when he went to bed he could not sleep.

He got up very early in the morning. Where did he go? To the den of lions. When he came to the den, he cried out in a very sad voice, 'O Daniel, is thy God, whom thou servest always, able to deliver thee from the lions?'

The King longed to hear Daniel's voice—and he heard it.

個王就俾自己嘅印封住個石，又俾個惡人嘅印封住添。

個王俾自己嘅印封住，為要知到或者有人攞但以理出去，因為佢嘅印，第二個人冇，同個王嘅印一樣，個王就知到。個王等，或者攞但以理嘅人，半夜嚟攞佢去，等佢哋知。又俾個啲惡人嘅印封住，等王有理知半夜冇攞但以理去。

個王夜就翻去屋企，但成夜都唔得安樂，*** 食又食唔得，瞓又瞓唔得。

第二朝天光佢就起身，佢去邊處呢？去個獅竇以理佢。佢到個獅竇處，就大聲好傷心話，但以理呀，你時時所服事嘅神，有能到救你出個啲獅係唔係呢。

佢就好留心聽吓有聲冇，佢答佢。

Ko⁾ ₎wong tsau² ⁾péí tsz²-⁽kéí-ke⁾ yan⁾
₍fung-chü² ko⁾ kau² shek₎†, yau² ⁾péí
ko⁾-₍ti ok。 yan-ke⁾ yan⁾ ₍fung-chü²
₍t'ím.

Ko⁾ ₎wung ⁾péí tsz²-⁽kéí ke⁾ yan⁾ ₍fung-
chü², ⁾tang wǎk₎-⁽che pún⁾ ye² ⁽yau
₍yan ₍laí ⁽söng ⁽lo Tán²-⁽yí-⁽léí ₍fán
ch'ut₎ huí⁾, ko⁾ ₎wong tsau² ₍chí-tó⁾;
₍yau-waí² ⁽mo taí² yí² ko⁾ yan⁾ ₍t'ung
⁽k'öü ke⁾. ⁽K'öü yau² ⁾péí ko⁾ ₍ti ok。
₍yan-ke⁾ yan⁾ ₍fung-chü², ⁾tang ⁽k'öü-
téí² ₍chí-tó⁾ ko⁾ ₎wong ⁽mò pún⁾ ye²
₍laí ⁽lo Tán²-⁽yí-⁽léí huí⁾.

Ko⁾ ₎wong tsau² ₍fán huí⁾ uk₎-⁽k'éí,
tǎn⁵ ₍sheng†ye²₎₍tò ₍m tak₎ ₍on-lok₎
shik₎ yau² ₍m shik₎ tak₎, * * *
fan⁾ yau² ₍m fan⁾ tak₎.

Taí² yí² ₍chïu ⁽k'öü ₍t'ïn ₍kwong tsau²
⁽héí ₍shan, ch'ut₎ ko⁾ sz tau⁾ shü⁾,
tsau² taí² ₍sheng† kíu⁾ Tán²-⁽yí-⁽léí,
⁽kòm wǎ², 'Tán²-⁽yí-⁽léí a⁾. ⁽Néí
₍shí-₍shí ⁽sho† fuk₎-sz² ko⁾ ʳwaí*
₍Shạn ⁽yau ₍nang ₍m ⁾péí ko⁾-₍ti
₍sz ₍shöng tò⁾ ⁽néí haí² ₍m haí²
。ni?'

⁽K'öü tsau² ⁽hò ₍lau ₍sam ₍t'eng† ⁽há
⁽yau ₍sheng† tǎp。 ⁽k'öü ⁽mò.

The King then gave his-own seal (and) sealed that piece of-stone, further (he) gave those wicked men's seal to-seal (it) as-well.

The King put his-own seal sealed, so-that if in-the-middle of-the-night there-were people came wishing to-take Daniel back out away the King then would-know; because no other [C.] seal the-same (as) his. He further put the wicked men's seal to-seal, so that they would-know (if) the King had-not in-the-middle of-the-night come (and) taken Daniel away.

The King then back went home, but the-whole night also (he was) not able (to-be-at) peace. (As to) eating (he was) also not to eat able; * * * (as to) sleeping (he) also (was) not to sleep able.

The next morning he at-dawn then got up, (and) out to-the lions' den place. Then (with a) loud noise called Daniel so saying 'Daniel, 2, You constantly (that God) that (you) serve that [C.] God has (had) power not allow those lions wound you, is (it so) (or) not is (it so) eh? 53.'

He then very carefully listened a-bit (whether there) were (any) sound answering him (or) not.

Daniel said, 'O King, live for ever. My God hath sent his angel, and hath shut the lions' mouths, that they have not hurt me : because I had done nothing wrong.'

Then the King was very glad indeed, and he desired that Daniel should be taken up, and he was not the least hurt.

Why did God take such care of Daniel ? Because Daniel loved Him, and feared Him, and God wanted to show the King that he was able to save Daniel, and that He was the true God.

The King was very angry with those who had asked him to put Daniel in the den, and he commanded them to be thrown down into the den, with their wives and their children. It was very cruel of the King to have the wives and children put into the den, but the wicked men deserved to be put there.

答打個傷做
理神住唔有
以嘅住唔係有
但問佢我有錯
見呀、我使等因我
聽王呀嘅天口、係錯事。
即話佢嘅獅我倒
佢佺發啲得錯事。

個王個時就好歡喜、叫
人土即刻共見到翻都
有傷到。

神嗽樣保全但以理因因
但以理俾個王愛佢、又到佢佺
佢有能救但以理、又佢
係個位真嘅神。

個王惡出但人埋都嗽子因就
個人、個命以理即佢揪樣落為就
時即刻令理、嘅捉妣獅揪去爲唔呢嘅
就係個嘅個令住妻子、處妣黑妣落去
好惱個嘅叫王住妻子、個嘅心事去
啲佢爲啲共個王妻嘅呀、叱。

ᶜK'öü tsik͵-hak͵ ͵t'engǂ-kiu² Tán²-ᶜyi-
ᶜléi táp₀ ᶜk'öü wá², 'ᵕWong á', ᶜngo-
ke² ᵕShan ᶜtá-fát₀ ᶜk'öü-ke² ͵t'ín-sz²
ᵕshán-chü² ko²-͵ti ͵sz-ke² ᶜhau, ᶜtáng
ᶜk'öü ͵m ᵕshöng tak͵ ͵tò ᶜngo: ͵yan
ᶜngo hai² ᶜmò tsò² ts'o² sz².'

Ko² ͵wong ko² ͵shi tsan² ᶜhò ͵fún-ᶜhéi,
kiú² ͵yan tsik͵-hak͵ kung² Tán²-ᶜyí-
ᶜléi ͵fán ᵕshöng ͵lai, ᶜt'ái-kín² ᶜk'öü
yat͵ ͵ti ͵to ᶜmò ͵shöng tò².

͵Shan ᶜkòm ᶜyöng⁕ ᶜpò ͵tsün Tán²-ᶜyí-
ᶜléi, ͵yan Tán²-ᶜyí-ᶜléi hai² oi³ ᶜk'öü;
yan² ͵yan ᶜk'öü ᵕsöng ᶜpéi ko² ͵wong
͵chí-tò² ᶜk'öü ᵕyau ͵nang kan² Tán²-
ᶜyí-ᶜléi; yan² ᶜk'öü hai² ko² ᶜwai⁕
͵chan-ke² ͵Shan.

Ko² ͵wong ko² ͵shi tsan² ᶜhò ͵nò ko²-
͵ti ok₀ ͵yan, tsik͵-hai² ko²-͵ti kiú²
ᶜk'öü ch'ut͵ ko² ming²-ling² ᶜkòm
͵lai ͵nán-wai² Tán²-ᶜyí-ᶜléi ke². Ko²
͵wong ͵fan-fú² ͵yan tsik͵-hak͵ chuk₀-
chü² ᶜk'öü-téi², kung²-͵mai ᶜk'öü-téi²
ke² ͵ts'ai ᶜtsz ko²-ko² ͵tò ͵wing lok͵
͵sz-tau² shü². Ko² ͵wong ᶜkòm ᶜyöng⁕
͵wing-͵mai ᶜk'öü-téi²-ke² ͵ts'ai ᶜtsz
lok͵ hui² hai² ᶜhò hak͵ ͵sam ke²,
͵yan-wai² ͵m ͵kwán ᶜk'öü-téi² sz² á²;
tsau² ͵wing ͵ni-͵ti ͵yan lok͵ hui²
che͵.

He immediately heard Daniel. He
said, 'King 2, my God has-sent his
heavenly messengers (and) shut the
lions' mouths, so-that they not hurt
able to-reach mé: because I have not
done wrong matters.'

The King at-that time then (was)
very pleased, (and) called men immediately with Daniel back up come,
(and) saw he one mite also not
hurt arrived.

God so fashion preserved intact Daniel,
because Daniel did love him; further
because he wished to-give the King
to-know he had power to-save Daniel;
further (that) he was the [C.] true
God.

The King that time then (was) very
angry-at-those wicked men, that-is
those (who) told him to-issue the
decree so that (they might) oppress
Daniel. The King directed people
immediately to catch them with their
wives (and) children every one also
to-throw down-into the-lions' den
place. The King so fashion threw
along-with (them) their wives (and)
children down away. It was (the
deed of a) very dark heart, because (it
did) not concern their doings (*i.e.* they
had nothing to do with it), 2; just
threw these men down away only, 7.

The lions eat them up in a moment, and broke all their bones before they came to the bottom of the den. So you see that the lions were very hungry—though they did not eat Daniel.

佢雖以餓，嚟出、但肚死咬得咬，好即刻就睇，有獅都即就嘅，獅嘅個時嗷個，佢啲嚿然理，嘅。

Then King Darius wrote a letter, and sent it to all countries, and said that he had made a law that every one should fear the God of Daniel, because He was the true God, who could do wonders, and who had saved Daniel from the lions.—'*Line Upon Line*' pp. 314-322.

信話個尊位神，救啲封國，一要個嘅，又啲寫嘅出一人拜嚿幹嘅，就有又各所個能俾王佢人所知個唔，即人吩以理係，烏去咐佢大，利各令以，大寄過命令敬神，佢得傷。

LESSON, XVI.

When the proper time arrived, Jesus came down to earth, and was born as a little baby in a village in Judaea. That village was called Bethlehem.

耶穌嗷係個，到合時候，就好似一間個穌仔出世，降生世太省佢係一條村，猶叫個條村做百利恒。

When he became a man, he went all about doing very many extraordinary things, thus revealing his power.

圍事顯，就去週嘅能，後來佢大好多嗷出奇嘅權，出佢嘅。

ᶜK'öü ₌ti ₌sz tsik₎-hak₎ ᶜngáu ᶜsz sái⁾ ᶜk'öü-téí² lok₀. ᶜKòm tsan² ᵗ'aí tak₎ ch'ut₎ ₌suí-₌yin ko⁾-₌ti ₌sz ᶜmò ᶜngáu Tán²-ᶜyí-ᶜléí, ko⁾ ₌shí ᶜk'öü ₌tò ᶜhò ᶜt'ò-ngo² ke⁾.

Táí²-léí²-₌wú ₌wong tsan² ᶜse yat₎ ₌fung sun⁾, keí⁾ huí⁾ ᶜk'öü ᶜsho ᶜyau ke⁾ kwok₀, wá² kwo⁾ kok₀ ₌yau ₌chí; ₌yan² ch'ut₎ yat₎ ko⁾ ming²-ling². ₌fan-fú⁾ kok₀ ₌yan yiú₎ ₌tsün-king⁾ Tán²-ᶜyı-ᶜléí ᶜsho paí⁾ ko⁾ ᶜwaí⁎ ₌Shan. ₌yan ᶜk'öü haí² ko⁾ ₌chan ke⁾ ₌Shan. ᶜK'öü ᶜyau kòm⁾ táí² ₌nang-kòn⁾. yan² kau⁾-tak₎ Tan²-ᶜyí-ᶜléí. ₌m ᶜpéi ₌ti ₌sz ₌shöng-tò⁾ ᶜk'öü.

They those lions immediately bit to-death all-of them, 32. So then (it is) see able out although those lions (did) not bite Daniel that time they also (were) very hungry.

Darius King then wrote a [C.] letter, (and) sent (it) away (to) his whatever he-had countries saying to every one to-know; further he-issued a [C.] decree directing every one (that they) must venerate Daniel what he-prayed-to that [C.] God because he was that true God. He had so great power, further save able Daniel not permit the lions injure him.

LESSON. XVI.

To⁾ hòp₂ ₌shí-han² ko⁾ chan² ₌shi, ₌Ye-₌sò tsan² ᶜhò ᶜts·z yat₎ ko⁾ ₌sò-tsaí ᶜkòm kòng⁾ ₌shàng shaí⁾-₌kán. ᶜK'öü ch'ut₎ shaí⁾ haí² ᶜhaí ₌Yan-t'áí⁾ ᶜSháng yat₎ ₌t'iú ₌ts'ün. ko⁾ ₌t'iú ₌ts'ün kiú⁾ tsò² Pák₎-léí²-₌hang.

Hau²-₌loí ᶜk'öü taí²-₌hiú, tsan² ₌hü ₌chau-₌waí tsò² ᶜhò ₌to ch'ut₎-₌k'éí ke⁾ sz⁾, ᶜhín ch'ut₎ ᶜk'öü-ke⁾ ₌k'ün-₌nang.

Arrived proper time that [C.] time, Jesus then very like one [C.] baby so descend-into life (in the) world's midst. His coming-out-into-the world was in Judæa Province one [C.] village, that [C.] village called to-be Bethlehem.

Afterwards he grown-up, then went all-round (every where) did very many wonderful things, to-reveal (display or make clear) out his power.

He once met a man who had been born blind. Jesus pitied him and cured him, so that he was able to see at once.

佢有一囘、遇着一個人、出世就盲曉眼嘅、耶穌可憐佢、就醫好佢、令佢即時睇得見。

He also made the lame, whom he met and who had been ill for many years, quite well again.

又遇着啲跛脚嘅、患病遠年嘅、都即時令佢哋好翻。

Jesus did not heal the sick, as the doctors do, by giving them medicine to cure them: he just said a few words, telling them to be well immediately, and they were well at once.

耶穌醫好人、唔係同啲醫嘅醫生俾藥材嚟醫嘅、係出一句說話、叫個啲人就好翻、即時好翻嘅咯。

The sick that came to Jesus are to be counted by the thousands, and not by the hundreds. It did not matter what the sickness was, Jesus made them well.

講嚟病人也好、論千論萬、唔止幾百咁多處、唔論乜野病、耶穌都醫翻好佢。

Besides this Jesus did a great many wonderful things: he caused the dead to rise again.

出個至多、耶穌又做過好多奇嘅事添、即係令個啲死曉嘅人翻生。

There was once a girl who was dead. Her father and mother were very sad, and very distressed about it; but, when Jesus came, he immediately told her to come to life again.

有一囘、有個女仔已經死曉嘅咯、佢嘅父母好凄涼、好閉翳、好愁到、耶穌一嚟到、就即時叫佢翻生。

Again there was a poor widow woman whose only son had died, and when they were carrying him away to bury him, Jesus met them on the street.

又有個貧窮嘅寡母婆、死曉一個孤獨仔、抬佢去葬之時、耶穌喺街遇着佢。

ᶜK'öü ᶜyan yat, ₍wúi, yü²-chök₂ yat, ko⁾ ₍yan, ch'ut, shai⁾ tsau² ₍máng-₍hiú ᶜngán ke⁾. ₍Ye-₍sò ᶜho-₍lín ᶜk'öü, tsau² ₍yí-ᶜhò ᶜk'öü, ling² ᶜk'öü tsik₍-₍shí ᶜt'ai tak, kín⁾.

Yau² yü²-chök₂ ₍ti ₍pai kök₀ ke⁾, ᶜyün ₍nín wán²-peng²† ke⁾, ₍tò tsik₍-₍shí ling² ᶜk'öü-têí² ᶜhò ₍fán.

₍Ye-₍sò ₍yi ᶜhò ₍yan, ₍m hai² ₍t'ung ₍ti ₍yi-₍shang ᶜpéí yök₍-₍ts'oí ₍lai ₍yí ke⁾: hai² ch'ut, yat⁾ köü² shüt₀-wá², kin² tsik₍-₍shí ᶜhò ₍fán. ko⁾-₍ti ₍yan, tsau² ᶜhò ₍fán ke⁾ lok₍.

ᶜKong ts'ín ₍m ᶜkong pák₀, kòm⁾ ₍to peng²† ₍yan ₍lai tò⁾ ₍Ye-₍sò shü⁾. ₍M lun² mat⁾ ᶜye peng²†, ₍Ye-₍sò ₍tò ₍yi ₍fán ᶜhò ᶜk'öü.

₍Ye-₍sò yau² tsò²-kwo⁾ ᶜhò ₍to chí⁾ ch'ut₍-₍k'éí ke⁾ sz² ₍t'ím: tsik₍-hai² ling² ko⁾-₍ti ᶜsz-₍hiú-ke⁾ ₍yau ₍fán ₍sháng.

ᶜYau yat⁾ ₍wúi, ᶜyau ko⁾ ᶜnüi ᶜtsai ₍yí-₍king ᶜsz-₍húi-ke⁾ lok₀. ᶜK'öü-ke⁾ fú²-ᶜmò ᶜhò pai²-aí⁾, ᶜhò ₍ts'ai-₍löng: ₍Ye-₍sò ₍lai tò⁾ tsau² tsik₍-₍shí kiú⁵ ᶜk'öü ₍fán ₍sháng.

Yau² ₍yau ko⁾ ₍p'an-₍k'ung-ke⁾ ᶜkwá-ᶜmò-p'o*, ᶜsz-₍hiú yat⁾, ko⁾ ₍kwú-tuk₂ ᶜtsai, ₍t'oi huí⁾ tsong ₍chí ₍shí, ₍Ye-₍sò ᶜhai ₍kái yü²-chök₂ ᶜk'öü.

He did one time meet one [C.] man born blind of-his-eyes Jesus pitied him, then healed-well him, caused him, immediately look able to-see.

Also met some lame feeted ones, far-away years got ill, also immediately caused them (to get) well again.

Jesus cured people not is same those doctors give medicine in-order-to heal: was issued one sentence (of) words, told immediately well again. those people then well again, &c.

Talk (of) thousands not talk (of) hundreds, so many sick people came to Jesus's place. Not matter what thing sickness, Jesus also heal back well him.

Jesus also did very many most wonderful things besides: just is cause those dead men back live.

Have one time have one female child already dead, &c. Her parents very sad, very distressed: Jesus came to (there), then immediately called him back to-live.

Also have a poor widow dead one [C.] only son, carried (by two or more) away to-be-buried time, Jesus in street met him.

He went up to the side of the corpse and told the dead man to rise, and the only son at once came to life again. When the widow woman saw her son come to life again, she was very happy.

There was another dead man whose name was Lazarus. He had been buried for four days; but Jesus went to the grave and called him back to life again; and he came out of the tomb at once. * * *.

There was still one thing that he did besides. That was the best; so I must tell you about it; it is healing very serious illness.

What illness is that? It is a disease of the heart: it is sin. That illness you, I, and every one have; but if we can have him say, 'Your sins are forgiven'—if every could hear those words, they would certainly be glad and would have no more sickness.

If anyone comes and asks him now to heal him, he will not say he is unwilling to do so; and when he heals people, he does not take their money, so the poor and the rich can come to him.—*The Sweet Story of the Cross.*

就埋去叫佢起身,個獨生仔即時就翻生咯。個孤寡婆見個仔翻生,就十分歡喜。

又有一個死人,名叫嘵拉撒路,已經葬咗四日,葬咗一路咁耐嘅處,耶穌即翻去墳墓時,叫佢翻生,佢即翻出嚟。 * * *

佢重有一樣事做出添,故知關你哋好嘅事,個樣係我至好嘅,要講過你哋知,即係醫好人嘅病症咯。

個啲係乜野病呢,係心嘅病,即係罪,呢啲病你,我,惡人,個個都有嘅話,你若赦免嘵人嘅罪,令人開心,人人聽見嘵個句說話,都係必有病嘅咯。

佢嘅人,窮佢都愛得嚟求醫,唔肯唔醫人嘅;而家有人嚟求佢醫人,佢話唔肯醫人,敢都嚟得嘅,而且醫人唔要人銀錢添,唔愛人錢財主嘅,或者貧窮富貴都嚟得嘅處咯。

Tsau² ͜maí-huí² kíú³ ᶜk'öü ᶜhéi ͜shan. Ko³ ͜kwú-tuk₂ ᶜtsaí tsik₃-͜shí tsau² ͜fán ͜sháng lok₀. ͜Tong ͜shí ko³ ᶜkwá-ᶜmò-ᶜp'o* kín³ ko³ ᶜtsaí ͜fán ͜sháng, tsau² shap₂ ͜fan ͜fún-ᶜhéi lok₀.

Yau² ᶜyau yat₂ ko³ ᶜsz ͜yau, ᶜmeng*† kíú³ ͜Lá-sát₀-lò². ᶜYi-͜king tsong³ ͜hiú sz² yat₂ kòm³ noí² ke³ lok₀; ͜Ye-͜sò huí³ ͜fan-mò² shü³, kín³ ᶜk'öü ͜fán ͜sháng; ᶜk'öü tsik₃-͜shí tsau² ᶜhaí ͜fan-mò² ͜fán ch'ut₂ ͜laí. * * *.

ᶜK'öü chung² ᶜyau yat₂ ͜yöng² sz² tsò² ch'ut₂ ͜t'ím. Ko³ ͜yöng² hai² chí³-ᶜhò ke³ sz²; kwú₃-ᶜt'sz ᶜngo yiú³ ͜kong kwo² ᶜnéi-téi² ͜chí; tsik₃ hai² ͜yi ᶜhò ͜yan-téi² ᶜhò ͜kwán-hai² ke³ peng²†-ching³ lok₀.

Ko³-͜ti hai² mat₂ ᶜye peng²† ͜ni? Hai² ͜sam-ke³ peng²† ; tsik₃ hai² tsuí² ok₀ ͜laí. Ko³-͜ti peng²†, ᶜnéi, ᶜngo, ͜yan-͜yan ͜tò ᶜyau ke³. ᵀ'ong-yök₂ tak₃ ᶜk'öü wá², ᶜNéi-ke³ tsuí³ she³-ᶜmín ͜hiú,' ko³ köü³ shüt₀-wá², ling² ͜yan-͜yan ͜t'eng† kín³, ͜to shí²-pit₃ hoí ͜sam, ᶜmò ͜hiú peng† ke³ lok₀.

Wak₂-ᶜche ͜yí-͜ká ᶜyau ͜yan ͜laí ͜k'au ᶜk'öü ͜yí, ᶜk'öü ᶜmò wá² ͜m ᶜhang ͜yí ke³; ͜yí-ᶜch'e ᶜk'öü ͜yi ͜yan, ͜m oí³ ͜yan-téi³ ͜ts'ín-ᶜngan* ͜t'ím, ͜kòm tsau² ͜p'an-͜k'ung ke³, ͜ts'oí-ᶜchü ke³, ͜tò ͜laí-tak₃ ᶜk'öü shü³ ke³ lok₀.

Then near-up-to-went called him to-get up. The only son immediately then again lived, 32. When the widow saw the son again lived, then ten parts happy, 32.

Also have one [*.] dead man, name called Lazarus. Already buried four days so long, 32. Jesus went grave place, called him back-to life; he immediately then from grave again out came. * * *.

He besides have one sort-of thing did out as well. That kind is best matter; therefore I want to-speak to you to-know; just is healed well people's very serious sickness diseases, 32.

Those are what thing illness, ch ? 53. Is heart's sickness: just is sins, wickednesses. Those illnesses you, I, every man also have. If get him to-say, 'Your sins forgiven,' that sentence words cause every one to-hear, also must open heart, got none illness, 32.

Perhaps now have man come beg him to-heal, he not say not willing to-heal; moreover he heal man, not want men's money too, so just poor, rich, also come can his place, 32.

LESSON, XVII.

How delightful is the description the Bible gives of heaven. We are told that sickness, sorrow, and death never enter there; that cares, fears, and anxieties are never felt there; that poverty, privation, unkindness, and disappointment are never. known there. The body that will rise from the grave will be 'incorruptible,' and will never experience pain, weariness, or decay. Old age will never enfeeble, for there will be perpetual youth; and death will never snatch away those we love, for death itself will be destroyed. What is still better, there will be no more sin, but all hearts will be full of holy love to God, and to one another. Every one will rejoice in the society and happiness of every one else, and God himself will dwell among them. All the good men of former ages will be there—the martyrs, and apostles, and prophets. There, too, we shall meet with angels and arch-angels; and more then all, we shall behold Jesus in his glorified human body—we shall see his face, and ever be with the Lord.

十翳、唔曉驚好、久中用愛一面、則三泉美

處閉窮、唔使你日其脫神喜、嘅二惡人讚

天堂、冇病痛、冇貧慮、唔待所欲老、其惡真歡穌住、有罪善齊

嚟病、冇掛人心生、係心長見埋己古處、

講冇難、使唔怕從長嘅、熱家喜同自喜嚟

所好、冇艱唔使事變好、好大歡喜時歡使神

書分有死慌事不至嘅人則時歡則天真

聖書分有死慌事不至嘅人、則時歡、則天真眞。

LESSON, XVII.

Shing²-ₛshü ᶜsho ᶜkong ᶜhaí ₛt'ín-ₛt'ong shü², shap₂-ₛfan ᶜhò: ᶜmò peng²†-t'ung²; ᶜmò paí²-aí²; ᶜmò ₛkán-ₛnán; ᶜmò ₛp'an-ₛk'ung; ₛm ᶜwúi ᶜsz, ₛm ᶜshaí kwá²-lúí²: ₛm ᶜshaí ₛking-ₛfong; ₛm p'á² ₛyan toí² ᶜneí ₛm ᶜhò, sz²-sz² ₛts'ung ₛsam ᶜsho yuk₂; yat₂ ᶜkau pat₂ pín²; ₛch'öng ₛsháng pat₂ ᶜlò; ₛK'éi ₛchung chí² ᶜhò ke², haí² tsuí²-ok₀ t'üt₀ lat₂ sáí², ᶜho yít₂ ₛsam oí² ₛchan ₛShan oí² ₛyan, táí²-ₛká ₛch'öng-ₛch'öng fún-ᶜhéi. Yat₂ tsak₂: ₛfún-ᶜhéi kin² ₛYe-ₛsò ke² mín², ₛshí-ₛshí ₛt'ung ₛmáí ᶜk'öü chü². Yi² tsak₂: ₛfún-ᶜhéi tsz²-ᶜkéi ᶜmò tsuí²-ok₀. ₛSám tsak₂: ₛfún-ᶜhéi ᶜkwú shí² shín² ₛyan, chung² ₛt'ín-sz² ᶜhaí shü²: yat₂ ₛts'aí tsán²-ᶜméi ₛchan ₛShan.

Holy book (according-to) what (it) says, (there is) at heaven's place ten parts good, no illness, no sorrow, no trouble, no poverty, not able to die, not need anxious-caring-for (matters), not need to-be-frightened, no fear peopleact-towards you not well. Thing thing (*i.e.* every thing) according-to. heart what like. Days long not change, long life not old. Their midst most good is sin evil take off altogether, very hot heart love true God, love man. All long long happy. First place: happy see Jesus's face, always together with him live. Secondly: happy self not have sin, evil. Thirdly: happy (because) ancient times good men, all angels at place: one altogether praise true God.

To show how glorious heaven is, it is compared to a city with streets of gold, gates of pearl, and walls of jasper and emerald; to a paradise with a river clear as crystal, and the tree of life with healing leaves; to a place of rest after labour: to a father's house, a happy home.

'They shall obtain joy and gladness, and sorrow and sighing shall flee away. Everlasting joy shall be upon their heads. In his presence is fulness of joy, and at his right hand are pleasures for evermore.' The best joys of earth are soon gone. Riches fly, health decays, friends depart, death is written on all things.

But the joys of heaven are for ever, and for ever, and for ever. Reader, this heaven may be thine. Jesus keeps the door, but he has opened it wide for all sinners to enter. If you will not come to Jesus, you cannot enter heaven; for he is the door, the only door.

聖書話天堂大城，地方都係珍玉石，似平天父好似珠嘅快安
一個金造砌樂嘅地方嘅屋蹤。天城門基城嘅天堂園又叫做地方都撼又好叫做又叫做

聖書又話，歡愁快活都飛在歡右來假處，都離都
嚟到，永上到快世上嘅錢嚟開，嚟憂遠嘅好樂各過嚟朋友吔多失世毀爛喜嗟快樂神滿到無嘅陣曉都物件喜嘆面真窮本係嚟神嚟都

單係天堂嘅永遠不變天堂耶穌你入，就有別係路福遠嘅都嘅蘇你嘅係路份就今做門打肯親路呀就唔千你耶人門就入呀
係噉樣萬想蘇信等耶得，你都嘅就唔路呀門

Shing²-ₛshü wá² ₛt'ín-ₛt'ong téí²-ₛfong,
ᶜhò-ᶜts'z yat, ko² táí² ₛsheng† : ₛt'íú-
ₛt'íú ₛtò haí² ₛkam ₛkáí ; ₛsheng†
ₛmún ₛtò haí² ₛchan-ₛchü tsò² ke² ;
ₛsheng† ₛkéí ᶜk'áí yúk₂-shek₂† ₛlai
ts'aí² ke². ₛT'ín-ₛt'ong yau² ᶜhò-ᶜts'z
fáí²-lok₂-kc² ₛyün ; yan² kíú² tsò²
ₛp'ing-ₛon-ke² téí²-ₛfong ; yau² kíú²
tso² ₛt'ín-fú² ke² nk₀ ᶜk'éí.

Shing²-ₛshü yau² wá², 'Fún-ᶜhéí fáí²-wút₂
ₛtò ₛlaí tò², ₛyau-ₛsbau ₛtse-t'án² ₛtò ₛféi
hui². ᶜWing-ᶜyün ke² fáí-lok₂ táí²
tsoí² ₛt'au shöng². 'Haí ₛchan ₛShan
mín²-ₛts'ín fún-ᶜhéí tò² ᶜhò ᶜmün, ᶜhaí
ₛchan ₛShan yau²-pín² fáí²-lok₂ tò²
ₛmò-ₛk'ung.' ᶜPún-ₛloí shaí² shöng²
kok₀-yöng²-ke² fuk₂ haí² ᶜká-ke², pat₂
kwo² yat, chan² ₛshí ᶜhaí shü². ₛTs'ín-
ₛts'oí ᶜwúí ᶜmò ₛhíú, ₛtsing-ₛshan ₛtò
ᶜwúí shat₂-höü², ₛp'ang-ᶜyau ₛtò ᶜwúí
ₛléi-ₛhoí, shaí ₛyan kòm² ₛto mat₂-
ᶜkin* ₛtò ᶜwúí ᶜwaí-lán² ke².

ₛTán-haí² ₛt'ín-ₛt'ong-ke² fuk₂-fan², tsau²
ₛm haí² ᶜkòm ᶜyöng*, ᶜwing-ᶜyün ᶜhaí-
shü², ₛts'ín-mán² ₛnín pat₂ pín²-ke².
ₛYí-ₛkam ᶜnéí ᶜsöng yap₂ ₛt'ín-ₛt'ong
ₛtò tsò² tak₂, ᶜYe-ₛsò haí² ₛt'ín-ₛt'ong-
ke² ₛmún. ᶜYau ₛyan sun² ᶜk'öü, ᶜYe-
ₛsò tsau² ᶜtá-ₛhoí ₛmún ᶜtang ᶜnéí
yap₂, ᶜNéí ₛm ᶜhang ₛts'au-tsau², ᶜYe-
ₛsò, tsau² ᶜmò pát₂ ₛt'íú lò² yap₂ tak₂,
ₛYe-ₛsò haí² lò² á², ₛmún á².

Holy book says, Heaven place very like
one [C.] large city : length length
(*i.e.* each) also is golden streets ; city
gates, also are pearls made ; city walls
take jade-stone to lay. Heaven also
very like a pleasure garden ; further
called to-be peaceful place ; further
called to-be heavenly father's house.

Holy book also says, ' Pleasure (and)
joy also come arrived, sadness (and)
sighing also fly away. Eternal joy
wear on head above. In true God's
presence pleasure even-to very full,
at true God's right side pleasure
even-to endlessness.' Originally earth
on all kinds-of happiness are false,
not over one [C.] time at place.
Wealth can-become none, health also
can be-lost away, friends also can
disperse-apart, world's men so many
articles also can spoil.

But heaven's happiness just not is so
fashion, eternally present, thousand
myriad year not change. Now you
wish to-enter heaven, also do can,
Jesus is heaven's door. Have man
believe-on him, Jesus just throw open
door wait (for) him to-enter. You
not willing come to Jesus, then not-
have another [C.] road enter can,
Jesus is road 2, door 2.

But he invites you to come. Yes, however guilty and vile you are, heaven may, and certainly *will* be yours, if you come to Jesus. 'To YOU is the word of this salvation sent.' O then for heavenly bless, come to Jesus.—'*Come to Jesus*, pp. 16 and 17.'

你唔惡後嘅個善改、總堂心拜中聖唔心嘅、你感心、者惡改然、一條係悔心、天你喜、唔見糟嘥靈新過。或罪、罪腸處、都曾你爲共歡佢道音、唔汚堂聖做世。嘥多悔心堂嘅、個未天、因都多愛善福禱、係天得叫出。你咁要副得潔個、你天樂嘅、你唔嘅講祈心、得就再。請己就轉入係嘅、此嘵安嘅、你又穌味、見個入改、就。而今自得轉入係住嘅、故入得事、同神、即冇聽樣、唔悔你叫。佢怕入換至都處人、雖唔嘅唔眞意書好嘵、就要化又

LESSON, XVIII.

Our God must always have power to help us. Little children always want their mothers to help them.

我哋嘅神當時時有嫩能幫助。細小嘅仔要老母幫助。

ᶜK'öü ₍yí-₍kam ᶜts'eng† ᶜnéi ₍lai. Wăk₎-
ᶜche ᶜnéi p'á⁾ tsz²-ᶜkéi kòm⁾ ₍tò tsuí²-
ok₀ ₍m yap₂ tak₎, tsan² yíú⁾ fuí-
tsuí² ᶜkoi ok₀, wún²-ehün⁾ ko⁾ fuk₎
₍sam ₍ch'öng ; ₍yín-han² chí⁾ yap₂-
tak₎. ₍T'ín-₍t'ong shü⁾, yat₎ ₍tí ₍tò
haí²·shing⁾-kít₂ ke⁾ sz² ; ᶜhaí ₍ko shü⁾
chü² ke⁾, ko⁾-ko⁾ ₍tò haí² shín² ₍yan ;
kwú⁾-ᶜts'z ᶜnéi méí²-₍ts'ang fuí⁾-ᶜkoí,
₍suí yap₂ ₍híú ₍t'ín-₍t'ong, ᶜnéi ₍sam
ᶜtsₐng ₍m tak₎ ₍on-lok₂, ₍yan-waí²
₍t'ín-₍t'ong ke⁾ sz², yat₎ ₍tí ₍tò kung²
ᶜnéi ₍sam ₍m ₍t'ung. ᶜNéi ₍m ₍tò
₍fún-ᶜhéi paí⁾ ₍chan ₍Shan ; yau² ₍m
oí⁾ ᶜk'öü ; ₍m ₍chung-yí⁾ ₍Ye-₍sò ke⁾
shín²-tò² ; kín⁾ ᶜShing⁾-₍shü ᶜmò méí² ;
ᶜkong fuk₎-₍yam, kín⁾ ₍m ᶜhò ₍t'eng† ;
kín⁾ ₍k'éi-t'ò ₍m ₍lau-₍sam : ᶜkòm
ᶜyöng* ko⁾ ₍sam haí² ₍o-₍tsò-ke⁾ (or
₍wú-₍tsò-ke⁾), tsau² ₍m yap₂ tak₎ ₍t'ín-
₍t'ong ₍lá. ᶜNéi yíú⁾ fuí⁾-ᶜkoí, tsau²
tak₎ Shing⁾-₍ling ᶜkòm-fá⁾ ᶜnéi ₍sam,
tsau² kíú⁾ tsò² ₍san ₍sam, yau² kíú⁾
tsò² tsoí⁾ ch'ut₎ shai⁾ kwo⁾.

He now invites you to-come. Perhaps
you fear self, so many sins wickednesses not enter can ; then must
repent-of sins ; change wickednesses ;
change-turn that [C.] heart (and)
bowels : afterwards then enter can.
Heaven's place one bit also is holy
pure matter. At that place live
ones, every one also is good man ;
therefore you not yet repent change,
although enter have heaven, your
heart absolutely not attain peace ;
because heaven's matters all also with
your heart not same. You not much
pleased worship true God ; further
not love him ; not like Jesus's holy
doctrine ; perceive holy book no taste ;
speak gospel (i.e. preaching) feel not
good to-hear ; feel prayer not detain
heart : so fashion, the heart is filthy
then not enter can heaven, 21. You
must repent change, then obtain Holy
Spirit convert your heart, then called
to-be new heart, also called to-be
again born over.

LESSON, XVIII.

ᶜNgo-téí²-ke⁾ ₍Shan ₍tong-yíú⁾ ᶜyau
₍nang ₍shöng-₍shí ₍pong-chò². Saí⁾
ᶜsíú ke⁾ nün² ᶜtsai, ₍shí-₍shí yíú⁾ ᶜlò-
ᶜmò ₍pong-chò².

Our God ought to-have power always
to-help. Tiny little tender children
always want (their) mothers to-help.

The blind always also need the assistance of their fellow men to lead them; the sick are always in need of the doctor's help.

We are in this world like little children; like the blind; like the sick: we are like little children—we need some one to protect us; we are like the blind—we need some one to lead us; we are like the sick—we need some one to watch over us. Who has power to help us? Our parents can help us in some matters; in some our teachers and friends; but they can not help us in all things.

They cannot always be with us. Even if they are beside us, yet they cannot always help us. How can they help us when they are asleep at night? How can they help us if we are far away from them? But we need one who can always help us, so that his mind is always present, his eye never asleep, his arms never weary. Is there such a one? Yes. God who is our Saviour is just such a one.

盲眼嘅時時佢亦要人幫
助眼拖都要病嘅人時
時拖都要醫生幫助。

我哋係呢個世界中好似
似細小嘅嫩好我哋個
盲人好似仔我一似人
好似細蚊要盲我似
保我仔哋好守助生
佑哋拖似看幫父係
一個一睇嘅母
人要有有事先
哋誰能事但
我呢嘅有哋唔
哋幫助幫助
嗰助嗰幫
朋友事嗰事
樣樣幫

不能常時同埋我哋或常
同埋我哋佢能亦半瞓呢
時幫助亦到我夜哋好
臉點能到我開哋佢呢
或者我哋離我嗰嗰常
遠又點佢一位唔心
但我哋幫就個處嗰總
時幫哋助要處救係
必要助時總唔主
瞓時手呢嘅
嘅哋嗰救
我嗰樣嘅
哋樣嘅。

ᵨMáng-ᶜngán-ke⁾ ᵨshí-ᵨshí yik₂ yíú⁾ ᵨyan ᵨpong-cho² ᵨt'o ᶜk'öü; ᶜyan peng²† ke⁾ ᵨyan ᵨshí-ᵨshí ᵨtò yíú⁾ ᵨyí-ᵨshang ᵨpong-cho².

ᶜNgo-téí² ᶜhaí ᵨni ko⁾ shaí⁾-káí⁾ ᵨchung ᶜhò ᶜts'z saí⁾ ᶜsíú ke⁾ nün² ᶜtsaí; ᶜhò ᶜts'z ᵨmáng ᵨyan; ᶜhò ᶜts'z peng²† ᵨyan: ᶜngo-téí² ᶜhò ᶜts'z saí⁾-ᵨman-tsaí—yíú⁾ yat₂ ko⁾ ᶜpò-yau² ᶜngo-téí²; ᶜhò ᶜts'z ᵨmáng ᵨyan—yíú⁾ yat₂ ko⁾ ᵨt'o ᶜngo-téí²; ᶜhò ᶜts'z peng²† ᵨyan—yíú⁾ yat₂ ko⁾ ᵨhon-ᶜshau ᶜngo-téí². Mat₂ ʳshuí* ᶜyau ᵨnang ᶜkòm ᵨpong-cho² ᶜngo-téí² ₒni ? ᶜYau ᵨti sz² fú²-ᶜmò ᶜwúí ᵨpong-cho²; ᶜyau ᵨti sz²ᵨsín-ᶜsháng ᵨp'ang-ᶜyau ᶜwúí ᵨpong-cho²; tán² ᵨm haí² yöng²-yöng² sz² ᶜwúí ᵨpong-cho².

Pat₂ ᵨnang ᵨshöng-ᵨshí ᵨt'ung-ᵨmáí ᶜngo-téí². Wák₂ ᵨt'ung-ᵨmáí ᶜngo-téí², yik₂ pat₂ ᵨnang ᵨshöng-ᵨshí ᵨpong-cho². ᶜK'öü tò⁾ pún⁾ ye² fan⁾ ᵨnam, ᶜtim ᵨnang ᵨpong-cho² ᶜngo-téí² ₒni ? Wák₂-ᶜche ᶜngo-téí² ᵨléí-ᵨhoí ᶜk'öü ᶜhò ᶜyün, yan² ᶜtím ᵨpong-cho² ᶜngo-téí² ₒni ? Tán² ᶜngo-téí² yíú⁾ yat₂ ᶜwaí* ᶜwúí ᵨshöng-ᵨshí ᵨpong-cho², ᶜkòm tsau² ᶜko ko⁾ ᵨsam pít₂ yíú⁾ ᵨshí-ᵨshí ᶜhaí shü⁾, ᶜngán ᶜtsung ᵨm fan, ᶜshau ᶜtsung ᵨm kwúí². ᶜYau ᶜkòm ke⁾ ᶜmò ₒni ? ᶜYau lok₀. ᵨShan tsik₂ haí² ᶜngo-téí² ke⁾ Kau⁾-ᶜchü, ᵨngám-ᵨngám haí² ᶜkòm ᶜyöng* ke⁾.

Blind always also want people to-help to-lead them; have sickness people always also want doctor to-help.

We in this [C.] world midst very like tiny small tender children; very like blind men; very like sick people: we very like children—want one [C.] protect us; very like blind men—want one [C.] to-lead us; very like sick men—want one [C.] watch over us. Who has power so to-help us, eh ? 53. There-are some matters father mother can help; some matters teacher (and) friends can help; but not is every-kind-of matters can help.

Not able always with us. If with us, also not able always to-help. They arrived midnight sleep sound, how able to-help us, eh ? 53. If we are-separated-from them very far, further how help us, eh ? 53. But we need one [C.] always to-help, so then that [C.] heart must-needs always at the-place, eye entirely not sleep, hands entirely not tired. Is-there such not, eh ? 53. There-is, 32. God just is our Saviour exactly is so fashion.

He is present with us at night the same as during the day. Whether at home or abroad, it is all the same: his eye does not sleep.

His arm is always strong. There is no place where he is not. In the Psalms, it is said, 'God is our refuge and strength; a very present help in trouble.' David also said, ''The Lord is the strength of my life; of whom shall I be afraid?'

Long ago David kept his flock of sheep; and a lion and a bear tried to get his sheep; but David was not afraid, because God helped him to kill those two fierce beasts. He was not even afraid of Goliath the Philistine, though he was a giant and a fierce man of war, because God helped him and caused him to vanquish Goliath. Everyone in this world, whoever he is, requires God to help him.

The Gentiles have many gods. They think one god attends to one place, and cannot help the people belonging to another place; but this is not wise, it is foolish.

Truly the gods of the Gentiles, no matter of what place, are not able to help their suppliants. No man, whoever he may be, is able to help us.

好出一樣，佢哋一齊跟住我哋，夜晚日好瞓嘅眼唔瞓。同頭一陣似眼唔瞓。埋我哋屋企唔瞓。我哋屋企唔瞓。佢似外佢嘅。

不我力神也無地話，佢力極話神使慌也，有詩篇有難時，神都幫助我，我'使慌也。佢手在，佢當嚟幫係幫助我、我'使野呢。

一佢因個怕高助，世切有捉怕死唔亞利亞幫亞神利亞人，一羣想捉唔怕打死唔烏為烏嘅人，因贏有嘅。牧一隻大鬧助惡獸人因贏烏嘅。大鬧一隻大獅，一但幫助惡士勇佢中所有神幫助。昔日大隻嘅羊，為兩非大令界要神幫。

估地處聰明嘅。佢筐第二唔係蠢啫。神一第唔係蠢啫。好理得嘅愚。多打幫助呢，係愚。有神打幫助呢，係愚。人一位唔人嘅，異邦人一方，嘅人明嘅。

論求都唔神唔所人嘅助所人嘅。人嘅神助唔論也人嘅。不能論唔得。真講異邦筐，邊佢嘅，幫助得。

ꞓK‘öü ye²-ꞓmán ₎t‘ung-₍mái ꞓngo-téi² haí² ꞌhò ꞓts‘z yat₎-ᵀt‘au* yat₎yöng². ꞓNgo-téi² ch‘ut₎ngoí² ꞌhò ꞓts‘z ꞌhaí uk₎-ꞓk‘éí-yat₎ yöng² : ꞓk‘öü-ke꞊ ꞓngáu ₍m fan꞊.

ꞓK‘öü ꞓshan ₍shí-₍shí ꞓyau lik₎. ₍Mò téi² pat₎ tsoí². Shing꞊-₍shü ₍Shí-₍p‘ín ꞓyan wá², ' ꞓNgo-téi² ₎tong wán²-nán² ₍shí, ₍Shan kik₎ lik₎ ₍laí ₍pong-eho².' Tái²-p‘ek₎† ₎tò wá², ' ₍Shan haí² ₍pong-cho² ꞓngo, ꞓngo ꞓshaí ₎fong mat₎-ꞓye ₀ni ? '

Sik₎-yat₎ Tái²-p‘ek₎† múk₎ ₍yöng ₍kw‘an ; ꞓyau yat₎ ehek₀ ₍sz, yat₎ ehek₀ ₍hung ꞓsöng ehuk₀ ꞓk‘öü-ke꞊ ₍yöng; tán² Tái²-p‘ek₎† ₍m p‘á꞊, ₎yan-waí² ₍Shan ₍pong-eho² ꞓk‘öü ꞌtá-₍sz ꞓko ꞓlöng chek₀ ok₀ shan꞊. ꞓK‘öü ₎tò ₍m p‘á꞊ ₍Fét-léí²-₍sz ₍yan, ₍Wú-léí²-₍á, ₍kò táí² ꞓyung ꞓmáng, ₎yan-waí² ₍Shan ₍pong-cho², ₍ling ꞓk‘öü ꞌtá-₍yengt ₍Wú-léí²-₍á. Shaí꞊-káí꞊ ₍chung ꞓsho ꞓyau ke꞊ ₍yan, yat₎-ts‘ít₀ ꞓíú꞊ ₍Shan ₍pong-cho².

Yí²-₍pong ₍yan ꞓyau ꞌhò ₎to ₍shan. ꞓK‘öü ꞌkwú yat₎ ꞏwaí* ₍shan ꞓtà-ꞓléí yat₎ tát₀ téí²-₎fong, ₍m ₍pong-cho² tak₎ taí² yí² shü꞊-ke꞊ ₍yan; tán² ₍ní-₍ti ₍m haí² ₍ts‘ung-₍ming-ke꞊, haí꞊ ₍yü-ch‘un che₎.

₍Chan ꞌkong Yí²-₍pong ₍yan-ke꞊ ₍shan, ₍m ₍lun ₍pín tát₀, pat₎ ₍nang ₍pong-cho² ꞓsho ₍k‘au ꞓk‘öü ke꞊. ₍M ₍lun mat₎ ꞏyan*, ₎tò ₍m ₍pong-cho² tak₎.

He at-night with us is very like day one fashion. We go outside very like at home one fashion : his eyes not sleep.

His arms always have strength. No spot not is. Holy Book, Psalms, does say, 'We meet-with distress (and) difficulty time, God extreme, strength come assist.' David also said, 'God does help me, I need fear what thing, eh ? 53.'

Former day David shepherded sheep flock; there was one [*C.*] lion, one [*C.*] bear wished to-catch his sheep; but David not fear, because God helped him to-strike to-death the two [*C.*] fierce animals. He also not fear Philistine man, Goliath, that great brave fierce, because God helped (him), caused him to-beat Goliath. World's midst whatsoever there-are of men, the-whole-of-them need God to help.

The Gentiles men have very many gods. They think one [*C.*] god attends-to one spot-of ground, not help able another place's people; but this not is elever, is stupid only, 7.

Truly speaking Gentile people's gods, not matter what spot, not able to-assist whoever begs them. Not matter what men, also not assist able.

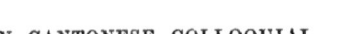

We need a God, who can help us at all times and every where, whether here or there; and there is only one God like that.—*The King's Highway.*

我哋要一位神、時時週圍都幫助我哋、或喺呢處、或喺個處、都幫助、嗽樣嘅神獨有一位啫。

LESSON, XIX.

A certain man had two sons: and the younger of them said to his father, 'Father, give me the portion of thy substance that falleth to me.'

有一個人、有兩個仔、個細仔對父親話、亞爸、搣我所應得嘅家業分過我喇。

And he divided unto them his living.

個父親就同兩個仔分開家業。

And not many days after, the younger son gathered all together, and took his journey into a far country; and there he wasted his substance with riotous living.

冇幾多日、個細仔聚埋所有嘅野、去好遠地方遊耍、喺個處好放蕩、花散佢嘅家業。

And when he had spent all, there arose a mighty famine in that country; and he began to be in want.

佢一啲都散清之時、個處地方有大饑荒、佢就有得使。

And he went and joined himself to one of the citizens of that country; and he sent him into his fields to feed swine.

嗽就去投靠個處地方一個人、個人打發佢去佢嘅田喂豬。

And he would fain have been filled with the husks that the swine did eat: and no man gave unto him.

佢想搣豬所食嘅豆殼嚟充饑、都冇人俾野佢食。

ᶜNgo-téí² yíú⁾ yat, ᶜwaí* ˻Shan, ˻shí-˻shí ˻chau-˻waí ˻tò ˻pong-cho² ᶜngo-téí², wák, ᶜhaí ˻ní shü⁾, wák, ᶜhaí ko⁾ shü⁾, ˻tò ˻pong-cho² ; ᶜkòm ᶜyöng* ke⁾ ˻Shan tuk, ᶜyau yat, ᶜwaí* che,.

We want a [C.] God always all-round, also help us. Perhaps in this place, perhaps in that place, also help; so fashion's God only have one [C.] only, 7.

LESSON, XIX.

ᶜYau yat, ko⁾ ˻yan ᶜyau ᶜlöng ko⁾ ᶜtsaí. Ko⁾ saí⁾ ᶜtsaí tuí⁾ fú²-˻ts'an wá², 'Á⁾-˻pá, ᶜk'áí ᶜngo ᶜsho ˻ying tak, ke⁾ ˻ká-yíp₂ ˻fan kwo⁾ ᶜngo ˻lá.'

There-was a [C.] man (who) had two [C.] sons. The small son to father said, 'Father, take I what ought to-obtain family property, divide to me, 21.'

Ko⁾ fú²-˻ts'an tsau² ˻t'ung ᶜlöng ko⁾ ᶜtsaí ˻fan-˻hoi ˻ká-yíp₂.

The father then for two [C.] sons divided family property.

ᶜMò ᶜkéí ˻tò yat, ko⁾ saí⁾ ᶜtsaí tsuí²-˻máí ᶜsho ᶜyan ke⁾ ᶜye, höü⁾ ᶜhò ᶜyün téí²-˻fong ˻yau-ᶜshá; ᶜhaí ko⁾ shü⁾ ᶜhò fong⁾-tong², ˻fá-ᶜsán ᶜk'öü-ke⁾ ˻ká-yíp₂.

Not very many days, the young son gathered together whatever had things, went very far place strolling; at that place very dissolute (and) squandered his family property.

ᶜK'öü yat, ˻ti ˻tò ᶜsán ˻ts'ing ˻chí ˻shí, ko⁾ shü⁾ téí²-˻fong ᶜyau táí² ˻kéí-˻fong ; ᶜk'öü tsau² ᶜmò tak, ᶜshaí.

He one atom even dissipated completely time, that spot-of place have great famine, he then not obtain (anything) to-spend.

ᶜKòm tsan² höü⁾ ˻t'au-k'áu⁾ ko⁾ shü⁾ téí²-˻fong yat, ko⁾ ˻yan ; ko⁾ ˻yan ᶜtá-fát₀ ᶜk'öü höü⁾ ᶜk'öü-ke⁾ ˻t'ín waí⁾ ₒchü.

So then went (and) threw himself (or depended on) that spot-of place one [C.] man; the man sent him to-go-to his fields, to feed the pigs.

ᶜK'öü ᶜsöng ᶜk'áí ˻chü ᶜsho shik, kc⁾ tau² hok₀ ˻laí ˻ch'ung ˻kéí: ˻tò ᶜmò ˻yan ᶜpéí ᶜye ᶜk'öü shik,.

He wished to-take the-pigs what eat beans husks in-order-to appease (his) hunger: also no man gave things to-him to-eat.

But when he came to himself he said, 'How many hired servants of my father's have bread enough and to spare, and I perish here with hunger! I will arise and go to my father, and will say unto him, "Father, I have sinned against heaven and in thy sight. I am no more worthy to be called thy son; make me as one of thy hired servants."'

佢醒悟咁，話，我父親處咁多工人，食嘅都有剩，但我喺呢處餓到要死。我要起身去到我父親處，對佢話，我得罪天，又得罪你，從今以後，唔敢做你嘅仔，俾我做一個工人罷喇。

And he arose and came to his father. But while he was yet afar off, his father saw him, and was moved with compassion, and ran, and fell on his neck, and kissed him.

佢就起身，離嗰處，歸去佢父親處。佢父親遠遠睇見佢，就可憐佢，走去抱住佢個頸，共佢親嘴。

And the son said unto him, 'Father, I have sinned against heaven, and in thy sight: I am no more worthy to be called thy son.'

個仔就對佢話，亞爸，我得罪天，又得罪你，從今以後，唔敢當叫做你嘅仔咯。

But the father said to his servants, 'Bring forth quickly the best robe, and put it on him; and put a ring on his hand, and shoes on his feet: and bring the fatted calf, and kill it, and let us eat, and make merry: for this my son was dead, and is alive again; he was lost, and is found.' 'And they began to be merry.'

佢父親就對嗰啲僕人話，即刻攞好衫嚟俾佢著，又攞隻戒指戴落俾佢戴，攞對鞋俾佢落腳著，又攞隻肥牛仔嚟劏死佢，等我哋食，快快樂樂。因為我個仔死咗又翻生，失咗又尋翻得首見。佢哋就快樂起嚟。

Ko' chaṹ² shí ᶜk'öü ᶜsing-ng²-ᶜhéi-laí
wá², ' ᶜNgo fú²-ts'an kòm' tò kung-
yan, ᶜk'öü löng-shik tò ᶜyau
shing² ; tán² ᶜngo ᶜhaí ni shü' ngo²
tò yíừ' ᶜsz lok₀. ᶜNgo tsöng ᶜhéi-
shan, höü' tò' ᶜngo fú²-ts'an shü',
töü' ᶜk'öü wá², " Á-pá, ᶜngo tak
tsuí² t'ìn, yan² tak tsuí² ᶜnéi.
Ts'ung kam ᶜyí hau², m ᶜkòm tong
tsò² ᶜnéi-ke' ᶜtsai ; ᶜpéi ᶜngo tsò² ᶜnéi
yat ko' kung-yan ᶜpá* lá." '
ᶜKòm tsau² ᶜhéi-shan, kwaí tò' ᶜk'öü
fú²-ts'an shü'. Chung² léi² ᶜhò ᶜyün,
ᶜk'öü fú²-ts'au t'ái-kín', tsau² ᶜho-lín
ᶜk'öü, ᶜtsau ts'ín höü', ᶜp'ò-chü² ᶜk'öü
ᶜkeng†, kung² ᶜk'öü ts'an-ᶜtsuí.
Ko' ᶜtsaí tsau² tuí'ᶜk'öü wá², ' Á-pá,
ᶜngo tak-tsuí² t'ìn, yau² tak tsuí²
ᶜnéi : ts'ung kam ᶜyí hau² m-kòm-
tong kíú' tsò² ᶜnéi-ke' ᶜtsaí lok₀.

ᶜK'öü fú²-ts'an töü' ko'-ti puk wá²,
'Tsik-hak ᶜlo chí' ᶜhò ke' ch'öng
shám ᶜpéi ᶜk'öü chök₀, ᶜlo káí'-ᶜchí
táí' lok ᶜk'öü ᶜshau-ᶜchí, ᶜlo háí
chök₀ lok ᶜk'öü kök₀. Láí ko'
chek₀ féi ngau-ᶜtsaí höü' t'ong,
ᶜtang ᶜngo-téi² fáí'-lok laí shik.
yan-waí² ᶜngo ni ko' ᶜtsaí ᶜsz-híú ;
yau² fán-sháng ; shat-híú, yau²
tak fán ká'.' 'ᶜKòm tsáu² ᶜk'öü-
téi² ᶜhéi-ᶜshau fáí'-lok.'

That period-of time he aroused (and)
said, 'My father so many work people,
their food also have remainder, but I
at this place starve also must die, 32.
I will arise, go to my father's place,
to him say, "Father, I have sinned
(against) heaven, further have sinned
(against) you. From now and in-
future, cannot presume to-be your
son ; let me be you one [C.] workman,
and-be-done-with-it, 21." '

So then (he) arose, homed to his father's
place. Still separated very far, his
father saw, then pitied him, ran for-
ward going, embraced his neck, with
him kissed.

The son then to him said, 'Father, I
have-sinned-against heaven, further
have-sinned-against you : from now
and in-future not presume to-be-
called to-be your son, 32.'

His father to the servants said, 'Immediately bring the best long robe,
give to-him to-wear, bring finger-ring
put down-on his finger, bring shoes
put down-on his feet. Seize that [C.]
fat calf, go-to slaughter, so-that we
may-be-joyful coming to-eat : because
my this [C.] son dead already, further
restored-to life ; lost already, again,
obtained back, 14.' 'So then they
began to-be-joyful.'

Now his elder son was in the field: and as he came and drew nigh to the house, he heard music and dancing, and he called to one of the servants, and enquired what these things might be.

And he said unto him, 'Thy brother is come; and thy father hath killed the fatted calf, because he hath received him, safe and sound.'

But he was angry, and would not go in: and his father came out, and intreated him.

But he answered and said to his father, 'Lo, these many years do I serve thee, and I never transgressed a commandment of thine: and yet thou never gavest me a kid, that I might make merry with my friends: but when this thy son came, which hath devoured thy living with harlots, thou killedst for him the fatted calf.'

And he said unto him, 'Son, thou art ever with me, and all that is mine is thine: but it was meet to make merry and he glad: for this thy brother was dead and is alive again; and was lost, and is found.'—'*Luke 15: 11-32.*'

但佢個大仔，喺田處，及至翻作嚟樂，將近到屋嘅聲，跳舞聽就嚇，聞作一個後生嚟問，叫係乜野事幹呢。

個後生對佢話，你細佬得翻嚟，你父親因為翻佢，冇病痛，所以劏嘵個隻肥牛仔。

個大仔就惱起嚟，唔肯入去，佢父親出嚟勸佢。

佢就答個父親話，我服事你咁多年，總冇背逆你嘅吩咐，你都未過我，曾俾一隻羊仔同埋，等我共朋友同個仔快樂。惟婦佢一隻吞噬你嘅家業，佢一到，你就為佢劏個隻肥牛仔喇咩。

個父親對佢話，我嘅仔，我係細嘵呀，你時時同我一齊，我都係個我所有嘅野，一的呢失嘵你嘅哩，但你又復生我，佬死嘵翻嘅，故此我又揾翻，應該歡喜快樂咩。

Tán² ʿkʻöü koʾ táí² ʿtsaí ʾhaí ͺtʻín shü²: kʻap₂ chiʾ ͺfán ͺlaí, ͺtsöng-kan² töʾ uk₂, ͺtʻeng†-ͺman tsok͵-ngok₂ ͺtʻíú- ʿmò-keʾ ͺshengt, tsau² kiúʾ yat₂ koʾ hau²-ͺsháng ͺlaí nian² ʿhá. ʻHaí² mat₂ ʿye sz²-konʾ ͺni?ʾ	But his that big son at field place: and until back came nearly to house, heard playing (and) music, dancing's sonnd. Then called one [C.] servant to come, asked a-bit, ʻIs what thing business, ch? 58.ʾ
Koʾ hau²-ͺsháng töü² ʿkʻöü wá², ʻʿNéí saíʾ-ʾlò ͺfán-ͺlaí; ʿnéí fú²-ͺtsʻan ͺyan- waí² tak₂ ͺfán ʿkʻöü, ʿmò peng²†- tʻungʾ, ʿsho-yíʾ ͺtʻong-ͺhíú koʾ chek₀ ͺféí ͺngau-ʿtsaí.ʾ	The ʻboy' to him said, ʻYour young brother back come; your father because obtain back him no illness (or) pain, therefore killed that [C.] fat calf.ʾ
Koʾ táí² ʿtsaí tsau² ʿnò ʿheí ͺlaí, ͺm ʿhang yap₂ höü²: ʿkʻöü fú²-ͺtsʻan chʻut₂ ͺlaí hünʾ ʿkʻöü.	The big son then anger arose came, not willing enter go: his father out came, remonstrated-with-him.
ʿKʻöü tsau² táp₀ koʾ fú²-ͺtsʻan wá², ʻʿNgo fuk₂-sz² ʿnéí kòmʾ ͺto ͺnín, ʿtsung-ʿmò puíʾ-yik₂ ʿnéí-keʾ ͺfan-fúʾ: ʿnéí ͺtò meí²-ͺtsʻang ʿpéí yat₂ chek₀ ͺyöng-ʿtsaí kwoʾ ʿngo, ʿtang ʿngo kung² ͺpʻaug-ʿyau ͺtʻung-ͺmáí fáíʾ- lok₂: ͺwaí haí² ʿnéí ͺni koʾ ʿtsaí, ͺtʻung kéíʾ-ʿfú ͺtʻan saíʾ keʾ ͺká-yíp₂ ʿkʻöü yat₂ tòʾ, ʿnéí tsau² waí² ʿkʻöü ͺtʻong koʾ chek₀ ͺféí ͺngau-ʿtsaí leʾ ͺme?ʾ	He then answered the father, saying, ʻI have-served you so many years not at all rebelled-against your orders: you also not yet give one [C.] kid (or young sheep) to me, so-that I with friends together rejoice: but it-is your [C.] son with harlots swallowed all your family property, he once arrived, you then, on-account-of him, slaughter the [C.] fat calf, (do you), eh? 26, 39.
Koʾ fú²-ͺtsʻan tuíʾ ʿkʻöü wá², ʻʿNgo-keʾ ʿtsaí áʾ, ʿnéí ͺshi-ͺshi ͺtʻung-ͺmáí ʿngo, ʿngo ʿsho ʿyau keʾ ʿye, yat₂-ͺti . ͺtò haí² ʿnéí-keʾ ͺle: tánʾ ʿnéí ͺni koʾ saíʾ-ʾlò ʿsz-ͺhíú yan² fuk₂-ͺsháng; shat₂-ͺhíú, yan² ʿwan-ͺfán keʾ: kwúʾ- ʿtsʻz ʿngo-téí² ͺying-ͺkoí ͺfún-ʿheí fáíʾ-lok₂ láʾ.ʾ	The father to him said, ʻMy son, 2, you always together-with me, I whatever have of things, even-to-the-least, also are yours, 24: but your this [C.] young brother dead again come to life; lost again found back: therefore we ought to-be-pleased joyful, 22.ʾ

LESSON, XX.

The Lord is my shepherd; I shall not want.

耶和華係我之牧人。我必不致缺乏。

He maketh me to lie down in green pastures: He leadeth me beside the still waters.

使我瞓在芳草之地。帶我歇在靜水之邊。

He restoreth my soul: He guideth me in the paths of righteousness for His name's sake.

令我靈魂復蘇，爲佢之名。引我直行義路。

Yea, though I walk through the valley of the shadow of death, I will fear no evil; for Thou art with me: Thy rod and Thy staff, they comfort me.

我雖經過陰翳險死之谷，亦唔怕受害，因爲你常在我側邊。你之棍，你之杖，必安慰我。

Thou preparest a table before me in the presence of my enemies.

在我敵人之前，爲我預備筵席。

Thou hast anointed my head with oil; my cup running over.

你也曾用油搽我頭，斟滿我隻杯。

Surely goodness and mercy shall follow me all the days of my life: and I will dwell in the house of the Lord for ever.—*Twenty-third Psalm.*

我在世咁耐，必有恩典憐恤跟隨我。要永遠住在耶和華殿裏。

LESSON, XX.

_ᶜYe-_ᶜwò-_ᶜwá hat² ^ᶜngo _ᶜchí muk_ᴐ-_ᶜyan; ^ᶜngo pit_ᴐ pat_ᴐ chí k'üt_ᴐ-fat_ᴐ.

Jehovah is my shepherd ; I certainly not arrive-at want.

^ᶜShai ^ᶜngo fan² tsoi² _ᶜfong-^ᶜts'o _ᶜchí-téí² : táí^ᴐ ^ᶜngo hit_ᴐ tsoi² tsing² ^ᶜshuí _ᶜchí _ᶜpin.

Makes me lie-down in fresh grass's ground : leads me to-stop in still water's side.

Ling² ^ᶜngo _ᶜling-_ᶜwan fuk_ᴐ-_ᶜsò : waí² ^ᶜk'öü-_ᶜchí ^ᶜmeng*, ^ᶜyan ^ᶜngo chik_ᴐ _ᶜháng yí²-lò².

Causes my soul to-revive : on-account-of his name, guides me straight to-walk righteousness road.

^ᶜNgo _ᶜsuí _ᶜking-kwo^ᴐ _ᶜYam-aí^ᴐ ^ᶜHim-^ᶜsz _ᶜchí Kuk_ᴐ, yik_ᴐ _ᶜm p'á shau² hoí²; yan-waí² ^ᶜnéí _ᶜshöng tsoí² ^ᶜngo chak_ᴐ-_ᴐpin : ^ᶜNéí-_ᶜchí kwan^ᴐ, ^ᶜnéí-_ᶜchí chöng², pit_ᴐ _ᶜon-waí^ᴐ ^ᶜngo.

I although pass through Infernal Shade (and) Danger of Death's Valley, also not fear suffer injury ; because You constantly at my side. Your rod, Your staff certainly comfort me.

Tsoí² ^ᶜngo tik_ᴐ-_ᶜyan _ᶜchí _ᶜts'ín, waí² ^ᶜngo yü²-péí² _ᶜyín-tsik_ᴐ.

In my enemy's presence, for me prepare feast.

^ᶜNéí ^ᶜyá-_ᶜts'ang yung² _ᶜyau _ᶜch'á ^ᶜngo _ᶜt'au; _ᶜcham ^ᶜmún ^ᶜngo chek_ᴐ _ᶜpúí.

You already use oil anoint my head ; pour full my [C.] cup.

^ᶜNgo tsoí² shaí^ᴐ ^ᶜkòm noí², pit_ᴐ ^ᶜyau _ᶜyan-tín _ᶜlín-sut_ᴐ _ᶜkan-_ᶜts'uí ^ᶜngo : yíú^ᴐ ^ᶜwing-^ᶜyün chü² tsoí² _ᶜYe-_ᶜwò-_ᶜwá tín²-^ᶜluí.

I in world so long must have favour, pity follow me : must eternally live in Jehovah's temple within.

LESSON, XXI.

God is our refuge and strength, a very present help in trouble. Therefore will not we fear, though the earth do change, and though the mountains be moved in the heart of the seas; though the waters thereof roar and be troubled, though the mountains shake with the swelling thereof.

神係我哋避難之所，與及我哋之力量。當患難時，極力嚟幫助。所以地雖移動。山雖離位倒在海心。我亦唔慌起。任從波浪大聲湧湧到山都搖動。

There is a river, the streams whereof make glad the city of God, the holy place of the tabernacles of the Most High. God is in the midst of her, she shall not be moved: God shall help her, and that right early.

有一條河，佢分支流出嚟，令神之邑歡喜，即聖係至上者所居之地。神住在其中，呢個邑是必唔郁動，天一光，神必嚟幫助佢。

The nations raged, the kingdoms were moved: he uttered his voice, the earth melted.

列邦發怒，列國搖動，主一發聲，地就消鎔。

The Lord of hosts is with us; the God of Jacob is our refuge.

萬軍之主耶和華同我哋，雅各之神，係我之堅城。

Come behold the works of the Lord. What desolations he hath made in the earth.

你哋嚟睇吓耶和華所行之事。睇佢點樣降災世間。

LESSON, XXI.

ₛShan haí² ᶜngo-téí² péí²-ₛnán ₛchí ᶜsho, ᶜyü-k'ap₂ ᶜngo-téí² ₛchí lik₂-löng², ₛtoug wán²-ₛnán ₛshí, kik² lik₂ ₛlaí ₛpong-cho². ᶜSho-ᶜyí téí² ₛsuí ₛyí-tung², ₛshán ₛsuí ₛléí ᶜwaí*, ᶜtò ᶜtsoí ᶜhoí ₛsam, ᶜngo yik₂ ₛm ₛfong; yam²-ₛts'ung ₛpo-long² táí² ₛshengț ᶜyung-ᶜhéi, ᶜyung tò⁾ ₛshán ₛtò ₛyíú-tung².

ᶜYan yat₂ ₛt'iú ₛho, ᶜk'öü ₛfan ₛchi ₛlau ch'ut₂ ₛlaí, ling² ₛShan ₛchi yap₂ ₛfún-ᶜhéi, tsik₂ haí² Chí⁾-shöng²-ᶜche ᶜsho ₛköü ₛchi shing⁾ téí². ₛShan chü² tsoí² ₛk'éí ₛchung. ₛNi-ko⁾ yap₂ shí²-pit₂ ₛm yuk₂-tung² : ₛt'ín yat₂ ₛkwong, ₛShan pít₂ ₛlaí ₛpong-cho² ᶜk'öü.

Lit₂ ₛpong fát₀-nò², lít₂ kwok₀ ₛyíú-tung² : ᶜChü yat₂ fát₀ ₛshengț, téí² tsau² ₛsíú-ₛyung.

Màn² ₛkwan ₛchí ᶜChü, ₛYe-ₛwò-ₛwá, ₛt'ung ᶜngo-téí² ; ᶜNgá-kok₀ ₛchí ₛShan, haí² ᶜngo ₛchí ₛkín ₛshengț.

ᶜNéí-téí² ₛlaí ᶜt'aí ᶜhá ₛYe-ₛwò-ₛwá ᶜsho ₛháng ₛchí sz². ᶜT'aí ᶜk'öü ᶜtim ᶜyong* kong⁾ ₛtsoí shaí⁾-ₛkán.

God is our refuge (péí²-ₛchí-ᶜsho) from-difficulties (and) our strength, while-in distress (and) difficulty time, utmost strength (He) comes to-help (us). Therefore earth although removed, mountains although separated-from (their) place, throw into sea heart, we also not fear ; allow the waves (with a) great sound rush up, rush till the-mountains even shake.

There-is a [C.] river, its divided streams flow out come, cause God's city to-be-pleased, just is Most High what live holy ground. God lives in its midst. This city certainly not move : heaven first light, God certainly come help her.

The-different nations got angry, the-different kingdoms moved : Lord as-soon-as uttered sound, earth then melted.

Myriad sovereigns' Lord, Jehovah, with us ; Jacob's God is our firm city.

You come look a-bit Jehovah what do's things. See He how fashion send-down calamities (on) earth.

He maketh wars to cease unto the end of the earth; He breaketh the bow and cutteth the spear in sunder; He burneth the chariots in the fire.

佢令全地停息爭戰,將弓拗折,將鎗整斷,搣火燒嗮啲車。

Be still, and know that I am God: I will be exalted among the nations, I will be exalted in the earth.

對世人話,你哋須當安靜,要知我係神,列邦之人,必尊崇我,我必受天下所尊崇。

The Lord of hosts is with us; the God of Jacob is our refuge.—*Forty-sixth Psalm.*

萬軍之主耶和華同我哋,雅各之神,係我之堅城。

LESSON, XXII.

There is therefore now no condemnation to them that are in Christ Jesus, who walk not after the flesh, but after the Spirit. For the law of the Spirit of life in Christ Jesus made me free from the law of sin and of death.

故此但凡心在基督耶穌,唔係從情欲,惟從聖神嘅,就唔定罪,因爲倚賴基督耶穌,受聖神得生嘅法,就脫用陷罪致死嘅法。

For what the law could not do, in that it was weak through the flesh, God, sending his own Son in the likeness of sinful flesh, and as an offering for sin, condemned sin in the flesh; that the ordinance of the law might be fulfilled in us, who walk not after the flesh, but after the Spirit.

律法因爲情欲,故此無力滅罪,惟上帝打發人罪自己之子,好似罪人,嚟贖人罪,致令消滅人身嘅罪,獨從我哋唔從情欲,聖神,成全律法嘅義。

ᶜK'öü ling² ₒtsʻün téi² ₒtʻing-sik₎ ₒcháng chín⁾ ; ₒtsöng ₒkung ᶜáu-chít₀, ₒtsöng ₒtsʻöng ᶜching-ᶜtʻün ; ᶜkʻái ᶜfo ₒshíú sái⁾ ₒti ₒchʻe.

Töü⁾ shaí⁾ ₒyan wá², ' ᶜNéi-téi² ₒsuí ₒtong ₒon-tsing², yiú⁾ ₒchí ᶜngo haí² ₒShan : lít₎ ₒpong ₒchí ₒyan, pít₎ ₒtsün-ₒshung ᶜngo, ᶜngo pít₎ shaü² ₒtʻiu há² ᶜsho ₒtsün-ₒshung.'

Mán² ₒkwan ₒchí ᶜChü, ₒYe-ₒwò-ₒwai, ₒtʻung ᶜngo-téi² ; ᶜNgá-kok₀ ₒchí ₒShan, haí² ᶜngo ₒchí ₒkín ₒshengt.

He causes the-whole earth to-cease-from wars ; take bow break-into-pieces, take spear make broken ; take fire burn all the chariots.

To world's people say, ' You even ought to-be-still, must know I am God : the several-countries' people must exalt me, I must receive heaven's under whatever exaltation.'

Myriad armies' Lord, Jehovah, with us ; Jacob's God is our firm city.

LESSON, XXII.

Kwú⁾-ᶜtʻsz táü²-ₒfán ₒsam tsoi² ₒKéi-tuk₎ ₒYe-ₒsò, ₒm haí² ₒtsʻung ₒtsʻing-yuk₎, ₒwai ₒtsʻung Shing⁾ ₒShan ke⁾, tsan² ₒm ting²-tsui². ᶜYan-waí² ᶜyi-láí⁾ ₒKéi-tuk₎ ₒYe-ₒsò, shan² Shing⁾ ₒShan tak₎ ₒsháng ke⁾ fát₀, tsan² tʻüt₀ lat₎ hám² tsui² chí⁾ ᶜsz ke⁾ fát₀.

Lut₀-fát₀ ₒyan-waí² ₒtsʻing-yuk₎, kwú⁾-ᶜtʻsz ᶜmò lik₎ mít₎ tsui², waí² Shöng²-tái⁾ ᶜtá-fát₀ tsz²-ᶜkéi ₒchí ᶜtsz, ᶜhò ᶜtʻsz tsui² ₒyan ᶜkòm ke⁾ ₒying-chong², ₒlai shuk₎ ₒyan tsui², ₒsiú mít₎ ₒyan ₒshan ke⁾ tsui² ; chí⁾ ling⁾ ᶜngo-téi² ₒm ₒtsʻung ₒtsʻing-yuk₎, tuk₎ ₒtsʻung Shing⁾ ₒShan, shing-ₒtsʻün lut₀-fát₀ ke⁾ yí².

Therefore whosoever heart (is) in Christ Jesus, not is follow lusts, but follow (the) Holy Ghost, then not condemned. Because relying-on Christ Jesus, receive Holy Spirit obtain life's law, then take off fall-into sin until death's law.

(The) law on-account-of lust, therefore no strength to-destroy sin, but (the) Supreme Ruler sent his own son, very like sinful man so likeness, in-order-to redeem men's sins, destroy man body's sin ; in-order-to cause us not to-follow lust, only to-follow (the) Holy Spirit, to-perfect the laws' righteousness.

For they that are after the flesh do mind the things of the flesh; but they that are after the Spirit the things of the Spirit. For the mind of the flesh is death; but the mind of the spirit is life and peace: because the mind of the flesh is enmity against God; for it is not subject to the law of God, neither indeed can it be: and they that are in the flesh cannot please God. But ye are not in the flesh, but in the Spirit, if so be that the Spirit of God dwelleth in you. But if any man hath not the Spirit of Christ, he is none of his. And if Christ is in you, the body is dead because of sin; but the Spirit is life because of righteousness.—'*Romans, VIII: 1—10.*'

情嘅、體貼情嘅、體必死、必情做嘅、以得上帝、你從聖神嘅略。

體貼神情、從聖事、必是人、是貼帝得嘅、所不能使上帝、你從聖神嘅心、而死、

欲情神嘅、神平、係服人、設你情欲有屬基督基督在你罪、因義而生。

嘅從事、貼情貼而嘅、敵亦情不欲歡住、唔但唔使肉身必因

因爲嘅欲體貼體生、欲仇法、從上帝嘅就神嘅、設個靈魂

從事貼情貼而嘅心、敵不欲喜。在從凡係基督雖魂必因

LESSON, XXIII.

We praise Thee, O God: we acknowledge Thee to be the Lord.

我哋讚美主、認爲萬有之主。

All the earth doth worship Thee: the Father everlasting.

主爲無始無終之父、通天下人無不敬拜。

ᵪYan-waí² ᵪts'ung ᵪts'ing-yuk₂ ke᾽, ᶜt'aí-t'íp₀ ᵪts'ing-yuk₂ ke᾽ sz᾽-ᵪts'ing; ᵪts'ung Shing᾽ ᵪShan ke᾽, ᶜt'aí-t'íp₀ Shing᾽ ᵪShan ke᾽ sz²-ᵪts'ing. ᶜT'aí-t'íp₀˙ ᵪts'ing-yuk₂ ke᾽ ᵪyan, shí² pít₂ ᶜsz; ᶜt'aí-t'íp₀ Shing᾽ ᵪShan ke᾽ ᵪyan, shí² pít₂ ᵪsháng, ᵪyí-ᶜch'e ᵪping-ᵪon: ᶜt'aí-t'íp₀ ᵪts'ing-yuk₂ ke᾽ ᵪsam haí² kung² Shöng²-taí᾽ tsö² ᵪch'au-tik₂; ᵪyan ᵪm fuk₂ Shöng²-taí᾽ ke᾽ fát₀, yik₂ pat₂ ᵪnang fuk₂ tak₂: ᶜsho-ᶜyí ᵪts'ung ᵪts'ing-yuk₂ ke᾽ ᵪyan pat₂ ᵪnang tak₂ Shöng²-táí᾽ ᵪfún-ᶜheí. Ch'ít₀-ᶜsz Shöng²-taí᾽ ke᾽ ᵪShan chü² tsoí² ᶜneí ᵪsam noí², ᶜneí tsau² ᵪm ᵪts'ung ᵪts'ing-yuk₂, pít₂ ᵪts'ung Shing᾽-ᵪShan. Tán²-ᵪfán ᶜmò ᵪKeí-tuk₂ Shing᾽-ᵪShan ke᾽, ᵪm haí² shuk₂ ᵪKeí-tuk₂ ke᾽ lok₀. Ch'ít₀-ᶜsz ᵪKeí-tuk₂ tsoí² ᶜneí ᵪsam, ᶜkòm ko᾽ yuk₂ ᵪshan ᵪsuí ᵪyan tsuí² ᶜyí ᶜsz; ᵪling-ᵪwan pít₂ ᵪyan yí² ᶜyí ᵪsháng.

Because follow lusts, patronise lust's incidents; follow Holy Spirit's, favour Holy Spirit's matters. Favour lusts' men, must certainly die; favour Holy Spirit's men, must certainly live, moreover peace: favour lust's heart is with Supreme Ruler being enemy; because not submissive Supreme Ruler's law also not able to-be-subject able: therefore follow lust's men not able to-obtain Supreme Ruler pleased. If Supreme Ruler's Spirit live in your heart within, you then not follow lusts, must follow Holy Spirit. Whosoever has-not Christ's Holy Spirit, not is belong-to Christ, 32. Supposing-that Christ in your heart, so that flesh body although on-account-of sin to die; (the) soul must on-account-of righteousness to live.

LESSON, XXIII.

ᶜNgo-teí² tsán᾽-ᶜmeí ᶜChü: ying² waí² mán² ᶜyau chí᾽ ᶜChü.

We praise the-Lord: acknowledge to-be myriad havings Lord (i.e. the Lord of all that there-is).

ᶜChü waí² ᵪmò ᶜch'í ᵪmò ᵪchung ᵪchí Fú²: ᵪt'ung ᵪt'ín-há² ᵪyan ᵪmò pat₂ king᾽ páí᾽.

The Lord is no beginning no ending's Father: throughout heaven's under people not (who do) not reverently worship.

To Thee all angels cry aloud: the heavens and all the powers therein.

天共天使，同天上有權能之人者，高聲讚美主。

To Thee cherubin and seraphin continually do cry, 'Holy, holy, holy, Lord God of Sabaoth;

基路冰同西拉冰，時時大聲稱讚主話，聖哉，聖哉，聖哉，天地萬物之主。

Heaven and earth are full of the majesty of thy glory.'

主之榮耀威嚴，充滿天地。

The glorious company of the apostles praise Thee.

所有榮耀嘅使徒，都讚美主。

The goodly fellowship of the prophets praise Thee.

衆聖先知，都讚美主。

The noble army of martyrs praise Thee.

所有捨命爲道之人，都讚美主。

The holy Church throughout all the world doth acknowledge Thee.

通天下聖教會，都尊奉主。

The Father of an infinite majesty; Thine honourable, true, and only Son;

極大威嚴嘅聖爻，你嘅至尊至眞獨一之聖子。

Also the Holy Ghost: the Comforter.

並安慰人心之聖靈。

Thou art the King of Glory, O Christ.

我之基督係大有尊榮之王。

Thou art the everlasting Son of the Father.

係聖爻無始無終之聖子。

When Thou tookest upon Thee to deliver man, Thou didst not abhor the Virgin's womb.

主呀，當你要拯救世人，你甘心爲童貞女所生。

_ᵥT'ín kung² _ᵥt'ín-sz' _ᵥt'ung _ᵥt'ín shöng²
ᶜyau _ᵥk'ün-_ᵥnang _ᵥchí _ᵥyan ᶜche, _ᵥkò
_ᵥsheng† tsán'-ᶜméi ᶜChü.

_ᵥKéi-lò²-_ᵥping _ᵥt'ung saí'-_ᵥláí-_ᵥping
_ᵥshí-_ᵥshí táí² _ᵥsheng† _ᵥch'íng-tsán'
ᶜChü, wá²:—'Shing'-_ᵥtsoí, shing'-
_ᵥtsoí, shing'-_ᵥtsoí, _ᵥt'ín téí² mán²
mat₂ _ᵥchí ᶜChü.

ᶜChü _ᵥchí _ᵥwing-yíú² _ᵥwaí-_ᵥyím _ᵥch'ung-
ᶜmún _ᵥt'ín téí².'

ᶜSho ᶜyau _ᵥwing-yíú² ke' sz'-_ᵥt'ò, _ᵥtò
tsán'-ᶜméi ᶜChü.

Chung' shing' _ᵥsín-_ᵥchí, _ᵥtò tsán'-ᶜméi
ᶜChü.

ᶜSho ᶜyau ᶜshe meng²† waí² tò² _ᵥchí
_ᵥyan, _ᵥtò tsán'-ᶜméi ᶜChü.

_ᵥT'ung _ᵥt'ín-há² shing' Káu'-wúí², _ᵥtò
_ᵥtsün-fung² ᶜChü.

Kik₂ táí² _ᵥwaí-_ᵥyím _ᵥti Shing' Fú²; ᶜNéi
ke' chí' _ᵥtsün, _ᵥchí-chan', túk₂ yat₂
_ᵥchí Shing' ᶜTsz.

Ping' _ᵥOn-waí' _ᵥyan _ᵥsam _ᵥchí Shing'
_ᵥLíng.

ᶜNgo-_ᵥchí _ᵥKéi-tuk₂ haí² táí² ᶜyau _ᵥtsün-
_ᵥwing _ᵥchí _ᵥWong.

Haí² Shing' Fú² _ᵥmò ᶜch'í _ᵥmò _ᵥchung
_ᵥchí Shing' ᶜTsz.

ᶜChü á', _ᵥtong ᶜNéi yíú' ᶜch'íng-kau'
shaí' _ᵥyan, ᶜNéi _ᵥkòm _ᵥsam waí²
_ᵥt'ung-_ᵥching ᶜnuí ᶜsho _ᵥsháng.

The heavens and angels with heaven above have influence and ability's people high sound praise the Lord.

Cherubin with Seraphin always loud sound praise (the) Lord, saying:—'Holy, holy, holy, heaven (and) earth myriad things' Lord.

(The) Lord's glory majesty fills-up heaven (and) earth.'

Whoever there-are glory's apostles, also praise the-Lord.

All holy prophets, also praise the-Lord.

Whoever there-are relinquish (their) lives on-account-of the-doctrine's people, also praise the-Lord.

Throughout heaven's under Holy Church, also honour (and) serve (the) Lord.

Greatest majesty's Holy Father; Your most exalted, most true, only one Holy Son.

And comforting men's hearts' Holy Spirit.

Our Christ is great, possessing exalted glory's King.

Is Holy Father's no beginning no ending Holy Son.

Lord, 2, when You wished to-rescue world's men, You readily by virgin what born.

When Thou hadst overcome the sharpness of death, Thou didst open the kingdom of heaven to all believers.

Thou sittest at the right hand of God, in the glory of the Father.

We believe that Thou shalt come to be our Judge.

We therefore pray Thee, help Thy servants, whom Thou hast redeemed with Thy precious blood.

Make them to be numbered with Thy saints in glory everlasting.

O Lord, save Thy people, and bless thine heritage.

Govern them, and lift them up for ever.

Day by day, we magnify Thee;

And we worship Thy name, ever world without end.

Vouchsafe, O Lord, to keep us this day without sin.

O Lord, have mercy upon us, have mercy upon us.

O Lord, let Thy mercy lighten upon us, as our trust is in Thee.

O Lord, in Thee have I trusted: Let me never be confounded.

主呀、你打勝死亡之後、就爲一切信道人開曉天國之門。

主呀、你坐在上主之右邊、享受聖父之榮耀。

我哋信主、必再降臨審問我哋。

主呀、你曾用寶血贖救世人、我哋現在求主拯救。

使我哋得列在聖徒之中、得享永遠榮耀。

主呀、我哋求主拯救主之百姓、賜福俾主之選民。

求主常常管束我哋、扶助我哋。

我哋日日稱主爲尊爲大。

我哋尊奉主之聖名、永世無盡。

我哋今日求主保佑、使我哋不犯罪。

求主可憐我哋、可憐我哋。

我哋獨倚賴主、求主可憐我哋。

我哋獨倚賴主、求主令我永不至於羞愧。

ᶜChü á⁾, ᶜnéi ᶜtá-ₗshing ᶜsz möng₂ ₍chí
hau², tsau² wai² yat, ts'ít₀ sun⁻-tò²-
ₗyan ₍hoí-ₗhiú ₍t'ín kwok₀ ₍chí ₍mún.

ᶜChü á⁾, ᶜNéi ᶜts'o*† tsoí⁾ Shöng²⁻ᶜChü
₍chí yau² pín², ᶜhöng-shau² Shing⁾
Fú² ₍chí ₍wing-yíú².

ᶜNgo-téi² sun⁾ ᶜChü, pít, tsoí⁾ ᶜkong⁾-
ₗlam ᶜsham-man² ᶜngo-téi².

ᶜChü á⁾, ᶜNéi ₍ts'ang ynng² ᶜpò hüt₀
shuk₂ kau⁾ shai⁾ ₍yan, ᶜngo-téi² yín²-
tsoí² ₍k'au ᶜChü ᶜeh'ing-kau⁾.

ᶜSz ᶜngo-téi² tak, lít₂ tsoí² shing⁾ ₍t'ò
₍chí ₍chung, tak, ᶜhöng ᶜwing-ᶜyün
₍wing-yíú².

ᶜChü á⁾, ᶜNgo-téi² ₍k'au ᶜChü ᶜeh'ing-
kau⁾ ᶜChü ₍chí pák₀-sing⁾, t'sz⁾ fúk,
ᶜpéi ᶜChü ₍chí ᶜsün ₍man.

₍K'au ᶜChü ₍shöng-₍shöng ᶜkwún-ch'uk,
ᶜngo-téi², ₍fú-cho² ᶜngo-téi².

ᶜNgo-téi² yat₂-yat₂ ₍ch'ing ᶜChü wai²
₍tsün, wai² tái² ;

ᶜNgo-téi² ₍tsün-fung² ᶜChü ₍chí Shing⁾-
ᶜmeng*†, ᶜwing shai⁾ ₍mò tsun².

ᶜNgo-téi² ₍kam-yat₂ ₍k'au ᶜChü ᶜpò-
yau², ᶜshai ᶜngo-téi² pat, fán²-tsuí².

₍K'au ᶜChü ᶜho-ₗlín ᶜngo-téi², ᶜho-ₗlín
ᶜngo-téi².

ᶜNgo-téi² túk₂ ᶜyí-lái² ᶜChü, ₍k'au ᶜChü
ᶜho-ₗlín ᶜngo-téi².

ᶜNgo-téi² túk, ᶜyí-lái² ᶜChü, ₍k'au
ᶜChü ling² ᶜngo ᶜwing pat, chí⁻-₍yü
₍sau-ᶜk'waí.

Lord, 2, You vanquished death's after,
then on-account-of one all believers
opened heaven's kingdom's door.

Lord, 2, You sat òn Superior Lord's
right side, to-enjoy receive Holy
Father's glory.

We believe the-Lord must again des-
cend-to-earth to-judge us.

Lord, 2, You already used (thy) precious
blood to-redeem save world's men, we
now beg the-Lord to-save (us).

Cause us to-obtain to-be-numbered in
holy disciples' midst, to-obtain to-
enjoy eternal glory.

Lord, 2, we beg the-Lord to-save the-
Lord's people, to-bestow happiness-on
the-Lord's chosen people.

(We) beg the-Lord constantly to-govern
us, to-assist us.

We day (by) day style the-Lord to-be
exalted, to-be great ;

We honour (and) serve the-Lord's holy
name eternally world without end.

We to-day beg the-Lord to-protect (us),
cause us not to-sin.

(We) beg (the) Lord to-have-pity-on
us, to-have-mercy-on us.

We only rely-on the-Lord, (we) beg
the-Lord to-have-pity-on us.

We only rely-on the-Lord, (we) beg
the-Lord to-cause us eternally not
to-arrive-at shame.

LESSON, XXIV.

'Let not your heart be troubled: ye believe in God, believe also in me. In my Father's house are many mansions; if it were not so, I would have told you; for I go to prepare a place for you. And if I go and prepare a place for you, I come again, and will receive you unto myself; that where I am, there ye may be also. And whither I go, ye know the way.' Thomas saith unto him, 'Lord, we know not whither thou goest; how know we the way?' Jesus saith unto him, 'I am the way, and the truth, and the life: no one cometh unto the Father, but by me.'

你哋我住先去倘地你個去條對處、得佢眞係處
你哋信爻所話爲若方、哋處之路、佢我個話哋理由呀。
心上嘅、倘過我去、我到你處、你話哋我呀、我
唔帝都中若你哋預爲定處、係哋知呀知到即係命人冇
使要好係哋預爲你翻嘇等處、哋知到、你到耶係命呀、到
愁信我多必我方、備接嘇所個嘛邊識對呀、唔得爻
你哋我住先去倘地你個去條對處

LESSON, XXIV.

'ᶜNéi-téi² ₍sam ₍m ᶜshai ₍yau-₍shau : ᶜnéi-téi² sun⁾ Shöng²-tai⁾, ₍tò yiü⁾ sun⁾ ᶜngo. ᶜNgo Fú²-ke⁾ ₍ka ₍chung ᶜyan ʿhò ₍to chü² ᶜsho: ʿtʿong-yök₎ ₍m hai², ᶜngo pít₎ ₍sin wá² kwo⁾ ᶜnéi-téi² ₍chí ; ₍yan ᶜngo höü⁾ wai² ᶜnéi-téi² yü²-péi² téi²-₍fong. ʿTʿong-yök₎ ᶜngo höü⁾ wai² ᶜnéi yü²-péi² téi²-₍fong, ᶜngo pít₎-ting² ₍fán ₍lai, tsip₍ ᶜnéi-téi² tò⁾ ᶜngo shü⁾ ; ᶜtang ᶜngo ʿhai ko⁾ shü⁾, ᶜnéi ₍tò ʿhai shü⁾. ᶜNgo ᶜsho höü⁾ ₍chí shü⁾, ᶜnéi-téi² ₍chí-tò⁾ ; ko⁾ ₍tʿiú lò², ᶜnéi ₍tò ₍chí-tò⁾.' ₍To-ᶜmá töü⁾ ᶜkʿöü wá², 'Chü á⁾, ᶜNéi höü⁾ ₍pín shü⁾, ᶜngo-téi² ₍m ₍chí-tò⁾ ; ʿtim shik₎ tak₎ ko⁾ ₍tʿiú lò² ₍ni ?' ₍Ye-₍sò töü⁾ ᶜkʿöü wá², 'ᶜNgo tsik₎ hai² ₍tʿiú lò² á⁾, ₍chan ᶜléi á⁾, ₍sháng-meng²* á⁾ : yök₎ ₍m hai² ₍yau ᶜngo, ᶜmò ₍yau tò⁾ tak₎ Fú² shü⁾ á⁾.'

'Your heart not need sorrow : you believe-in the-Supreme Ruler, also must believe-in me. My father's family midst have very many dwelling places ; if not was, I certainly first said to you to-know ; for I go for you to-prepare place. If I go on-account-of you to-prepare place, I certainly back come, to-receive you to my place ; so-that I at that place, you also at the-place. I what go place, you know ; the [C.] road, you also know.' Thomas to him said, 'Lord 2, You go what place, we not know ; how know able that [C.] road, eh ? 53.' Jesus to him said, 'I just am [C.] road, 2, true principle, 2, life, 2 : if not is from me, no man arrive able Father's place, 2.'

LESSON, XXV.

And Ruth the Moabitess said unto Naomi, 'Let me now go to the field, and glean among the ears of corn after him in whose sight I shall find grace.' And she said unto her, 'Go, my daughter.' And she went, and came and gleaned in the field after the reapers: and her hap was to light on the portion of the field belonging unto Boaz, * * *. And, behold, Boaz came from Bethlehem, and said unto the reapers, 'The Lord be with you.' And they answered him, 'The Lord bless thee.' * * *.

摩押女話、(我)就執阿管田執到嘅。* * * 伯人你和

女想去得也誰個下咪答喇、跟佢嘅田、* * * 利話哂、願耶穌賜

路去乜(啊)剩咪去間、剩嘅田、剛恒願耶穌賜

得田誰下話、路住嘅嗒波士對和答過

對嘅人嘅媳得收嘅嗒對和答過福

拿間、後穗呀去嘅穗、係波士正禾同願你。* * *

咪係（我）便拿只到人所士從嘅埋耶* * *

Then said Boaz unto Ruth, 'Hearest thou not, my daughter? Go not to glean in another field, neither pass from hence, but abide here fast by my maidens. Let thine eyes be on the field that they do reap, and go thou after them: Have I not charged the young men that they shall not touch thee? And when thou art athirst, go unto the vessels, and drink of that which the young men have drawn.'

波士你去咪埋喇。收我咪就人

對聽別離我佢割已欺去所

路我講嘅呢嘯就經負佢汲

話、唔田處、婢女係跟吩你哋

我執惟女係住若器嘅

女使遺係呢管哋年你飲

呀、(or 好)穗近處田去、人渴僕

LESSON, XXV.

‸Mò-áp͙ ꞈnöü Lò²-tak‸ töü⁾ ‸Ná-‸o-ꞈmaí wá², 'ꞈNgo ꞈsöng höü⁾ ‸t'ín-‸kán, yök‸-haí² (ꞈngo) tak‸ mat‸ ꞈshuí* ke⁾ ‸yan, (ꞈngo) tsaú² ꞈhaí (ꞈko) ko⁾ ‸yan hau²-pín² chap‸ ꞈk'öü shing²-há² ke⁾ mak‸-söü².' ‸Ná-‸o-ꞈmaí táp͙ wá², 'Sik‸-ꞈfú à⁾, chik͙-ꞈkwún höü⁾ ‸lá.' Lò²-tak‸ tsaú² höü⁾ to⁾ ‸t'ín-‸kán, ‸kan-chü² ‸shau-kot͙-ke⁾-‸yan, chap‸ ꞈk'öü shing²-há² ke⁾ söü²: ꞈk'öü ꞈsho tò⁾ ke⁾ ‸t'ín, ‸kong-‸ngám haí² ‸Po-‸sz ke⁾. * * *. ‸Po-‸sz ching⁾ ‸ts'ung Pak͙-léí²-‸hang ‸laí, töü⁾ kot͙-‸wo-ke⁾-‸yan wá², 'Yün² ‸Ye-‸wò-‸wá ‸t'ung-‸máí ꞈnéi-téí².' Chung² ‸yan táp͙ wá², 'Yün² ‸Ye-‸wò-‸wá t'sz⁾ fuk‸ kwo⁾ ꞈnéi.' * * *.

‸Po-‸sz töü⁾ Lò²-tak‸ wá², 'ꞈNgo ꞈnöü à⁾, ꞈnéi ‸t'engƚ ꞈngo ꞈkong. ‸M ꞈshaí (or ‸hò) höü⁾ pít‸ ‸yan-ke⁾ ‸t'ín chap‸ ‸waí söü²; ꞈmaí ‸léí-‸hoí ‸ni shü⁾, ‸waí haí² ‸kan-‸máí ꞈngo-ke⁾ ꞈp'éí-ꞈnöü ꞈhaí ‸ni shü⁾ ‸lá. ꞈK'öü-téí² chü² ꞈhaí ‸pín tát͙ ‸t'ín ‸shau-kot͙, tsaú² ‸kan-chü² ꞈk'öü-téí² höü⁾: ꞈNgo ꞈyí-‸king fán-fú⁾ ꞈshíú ‸nín ‸yan ꞈmaí ‸heí-fú² ꞈnéi. Yök‸ haí² ꞈnéi hot͙, tsaú² höü⁾ ꞈk'öü-téí² héí⁾-ꞈming, ꞈyam puk‸-‸yan ꞈsho k'ap‸ ke⁾ ꞈshuí.'

The Moabitess woman Ruth to Naomi said, 'I wish go field if (I) obtain anyone's grace, (I) then at (that) [C.] man behind pick-up (what) he leaves-behind of wheat. Naomi answered, said, 'Daughter-in-law (*it means also a grandson's or nephew's* wife), 2,' very-well-then go, 21. Ruth then went to (the) fields, followed reapers, picked-up they left-behind of ears-of-grain: she what arrived-at field exactly was Boaz's. * * *. Boaz exactly from Bethlehem came, to cutters-of-grain-men said, 'I-wish Jehovah (be) together-with you.' All the-people answered, said, 'May Jehovah bestow happiness upon you.' * * *.

Boaz to Ruth said, 'My daughter, 2, you listen to-me speaking. Not need (*or* do not) go another man's field to-pick-up left-behind ears-of-corn; do not go-away-from this place, but it is (that you) follow to-gether-with my maids at this place, 21. They live at what spot field reap, then follow them going: I already have-ordered the-few years men not to-insult you. If it is (that) you (are) thirsty, then go to-their vessels, drink slave-men what drawn water.'

Then she fell on her face, and bowed herself to the ground, and said unto him, 'Why have I found grace in thy sight, that thou shoudest take knowledge of me, seeing I am a stranger?'

路得嚟低頭、仆倒地處、對佢話、我係外人、做乜蒙你嘅恩德、致你顧恤我呢。

And Boaz answered and said unto her, 'It hath fully been shewed me, all that thou hast done unto thy mother-in-law since the death of thine husband: and how thou hast left thy father and thy mother, and the land of thy nativity, and art come unto a people which thou knewest not heretofore. The Lord recompense thy work, and a full reward be given thee of the Lord, the God of Israel, under whose wings thou art come to take refuge.'

波士夫答佢話、自你丈夫死後、凡你向你家婆所做嘅、並及你離開父母、同埋你生長平素個地方、嚟到你平素唔識嘅百姓處、呢的事我所知到嘅。願耶和華報賴你、以色列個神、你倚靠佢、投佢翼下、願佢大大賞賜。

Then she said, 'Let me find grace in thy sight, my lord; for that thou hast comforted me, and for that thou hast spoken kindly unto thine handmaid, though I be not as one of thine handmaidens.'

路得話、願蒙你嘅恩、主呀、你安慰我、用慈愛嘅說話對我講、我雖然唔係同你眾婢友一個。

And at meal-time, Boaz said unto her, 'Come hither, and eat of the bread, and dip thy morsel in the vinegar.'

到食飯嘅時候、波士夫喺呢處、喊你嚟、對路得話、你嚟食、攞的餅嚟食、點落醋中呀。

Lo^{2}-tak꜁ wúᵓ ꜀tai ꜀t'au, p'uk꜁ ᶜtò téí^{2} shüᵓ, töüᵓ ᶜk'öü wá^{2}, 'ᶜNgo haí^{2} ngoí^{2}-꜀pong keᵓ ꜀yan, tsò^{2} mat꜁ ꜀mung ᶜnéí keᵓ ꜀yan-tak꜁, chíᵓ ᶜnéí kwúᵓ-sut꜁ ᶜngo ꜀ni?'

Ruth bowed down (her) head, prostrated on earth place to him said, 'I am outside kingdom's person. Do why thanks-to your favour (to me and) regard-with compassion me, eh? 53.'

꜀Po-꜀sz táp꜀ ᶜk'öü wá^{2}, 'Tsz^{2}-꜀ts'ung ᶜnéí chöng^{2}-꜀fú ᶜsz hau^{2}, ꜀fán ᶜnéí böngᵓ ꜀ká-꜀p'o ᶜsho tsò^{2} keᵓ: pingᵓ ᶜnéí ꜀léí-꜀hoí tsz^{2}-ᶜkéí fú^{2}-ᶜmò, k'ap꜁ ᶜsho ꜀sháng-ᶜchöng keᵓ kwúᵓ ᶜt'ò, ꜀laí tòᵓ ᶜnéí ꜀p'ing-sòᵓ ꜀m ꜀söng shik꜁ keᵓ pák꜀-singᵓ koᵓ tát꜀: koᵓ-꜀ti sz^{2}, ꜀yan-téí^{2} ᶜyí-꜀king ᶜkong sáíᵓ kwoᵓ ᶜngo ꜀chí. Yün^{2} ꜀Ye-꜀wò-꜀wá chíúᵓ ᶜnéí ᶜsho tsò^{2} keᵓ ᶜshöng-pòᵓ ᶜnéí, ᶜnéí ꜀laí toᵓ ꜀ni shüᵓ ᶜyi-laí^{2} ᶜYí-shik꜁-lit꜁ keᵓ ꜀Shan ꜀Ye-꜀wò-꜀wá keᵓ yik꜁ há^{2}. Yün^{2} ᶜnéí ꜀ts'ung ᶜk'öü koᵓ shüᵓ tak꜁ táí^{2} ᶜshöng-t'szᵓ.

Boaz answered her saying, 'Since your husband died after, all you towards (your) mother-in-law what done: and you separate-from you-own father mother, and what born grown-up native land, come to you ordinarily not mutually acquainted people that spot: these matters people already spoken all to-me to-know. May Jehovah according-to you what have-done reward you (and) recompense you, you come to this place rely-on Israel's God Jehovah's wings under. May you from his that place obtain great reward.'

Lò^{2}-tak꜁ wá^{2}, 'Yün^{2} ꜀mung ᶜChü ꜀yan; ᶜngo ꜀söü-꜀yín ꜀m k'ap꜁ ᶜnéí chungᵓ ᶜp'éí, ᶜnéí ᶜking-꜀yín ꜀on-waíᵓ ᶜngo, yung^{2} ᶜyau-oíᵓ keᵓ shüt꜀-wá^{2} töüᵓ ᶜngo ᶜkong.'

Ruth said, 'I-wish (and) hope the-lord's favour; I although not equal-to your all maids, you have comforted me used friendly love's words to me to-talk.'

Tòᵓ-꜀híú shik꜁ fán^{2} keᵓ ꜀shí-hau^{2}, ꜀Po-꜀sz töüᵓ Lò^{2}-tak꜁ wá^{2}, 'ᶜNéí ꜀laí ꜀ni shüᵓ ᶜlo ꜀ti ᶜpeng† ꜀laí shik꜁, ᶜk'áí ᶜnéí fáíᵓ ᶜtím lok꜁ ts'òᵓ ꜀chung áᵓ.'

Arrived eat rice's time, Boaz to Ruth said, 'You come this place take some cake to-eat, take your piece dip down-into vinegar midst, 2.'

And she sat beside the reapers: and they reached her parched corn, and she did eat, and was sufficed, and left thereof.

路得就坐喺收割嘅人傍，波士就撴炴穀過佢食，佢食到飽，重有剩。

And when she was risen up to glean, Boaz commanded his young men, saying, 'Let her glean even among the sheaves, and reproach her not. And also pull out some for her from the bundles, and leave it, and let her glean, and rebuke her not.'

路得起身去執遺穗，波士吩咐啲少年人話，雖然佢喺禾捆中執啲穗都容佢，唔好羞辱佢，或喺禾捆中剩落俾佢執，特登遺落俾佢，唔好喝佢。

So she gleaned in the field until even; and she beat out that she had gleaned, and it was about an ephah of barley.

路得就喺田間執佢所遺嘅穗，直到挨晚，將佢有執嘅打曉，約有一哦咭大麥。

And she took it up, and went into the city: and her mother-in-law saw what she had gleaned. * * *.

佢就撴嚟帶入城去，俾家婆見佢所執嘅。* *

And her mother-in-law said unto her, 'Where hast thou gleaned to-day? and where wroughtest thou? blessed be he that did take knowledge of thee.'

佢家婆問佢話，今日你喺邊處執剩下嘅穗呢，你喺（邊）處做工呢，願顧恤你嘅得福咯。

And she shewed her mother-in-law with whom she had wrought, and said, 'The man's name with whom I wrought to-day is Boaz.'—'Ruth, 2: 2—19.'

路得就將自己喺邊個處做工，講過家婆知，話，我今日喺佢處做工個人名叫波士。

Lò²-tak, tsau² ʿhaí ₍shau-kot₀-ke²-₍yan ₍p'ong-₀pín ˢts'o*† lok, : ₍Po-₍sz tsau² ˢk'áí hong²-ke² kuk, ʿpéí kwo² ˢk'öü shik,, ˢk'öü shik, tò² ʿpáu, chung² ˢyau shing².

Lò²-tak, ʿhéí ₍shan höü² chap, ₍t'ín-₍kán-ke² ₍waí-söü², ₍Po-₍sz ₍fan-fú² ˢshíú-₍nín ₍yan, wá², 'ˢK'öü ₍söü-₍yín tsoí² ₍wo- k'wan ₍chung chap, ₍ti söü², ₍tò ₍yung ˢk'öü, ₍m ʿhò ₍sau-yuk, ˢk'öü. Wák, tsoí² ˢk'wan ₍chung mang² ch'ut,, ₍ti tak,-₍tang shing² lok,, yam²-₍ts'ung ˢk'öü chap,, ₍m ʿho hot₀ ˢk'öü.'

ʿKòm tsau² Lò²-tak, ʿhaí ₍t'ín-₍kán chap, ₍waí-söü², chik, tò² ₍áí-ˢmán ; ₍tsöng ˢk'öü ʿsho chap, ke² ʿtá-₍híú, yök, ˢyau yat, ˢyí-fát, táí²-mak,.

ˢK'öü tsau² ˢk'áí ₍laí táí² yap, ₍sheng† höü² : ʿpéí ₍ká-₍p'o kín² ˢk'öü ʿsho chap, ke². * * *.

ˢK'öü ₍ká-₍p'o man² ˢk'öü wá², '₍Kam-yat, (or ₍kam-mat,) ˢnéí ʿhaí ₀pín shü chap,-shing²-há²-ke²-söü² ₀ni ? ˢNéi ʿhaí (₀pín) shü tsò² ₍kung ₀ni ? Yün² kwú²-sut, ˢnéí-ke² tak, fuk, lok₀.

Lò²-tak, tsau² ₍tsöng tsz²-ʿkéí ʿhaí ₀pín ko² shü tsò² ₍kung, ʿkong kwo² ₍ká-₍p'o ₍chí, wá², 'ˢNgo ₍kam-yat, (or ₍kam-mat,) ʿhaí ˢk'öü shü tsò² ₍kung, ko² yan. ˢmeng*† kíú² ₍Po-₍sz.'

Ruth then at reapers side sat down : Boaz then took toasted (or parched) paddy gave to her to-eat, she ate until satisfied, still have remaining.

Ruth up (her) body went to-pick fields' midst left-behind ears-of-corn, Boaz ordered the-youths, saying, 'She although in grain sheaves midst pick-up some ears-of-corn, even allow her, not good insult her. Perhaps in sheaves middle pull out some purposely leave down, let her pick-up, do not restrain (or call-out-to) her.'

So then Ruth in field picked-up leavings-of the-ears-of-grain, straight to evening ; took she what picked, beaten-it approximately there-was one ephah-of barley.

She then took (it) in-order-to take into city to-go : give-to (her) mother-in-law to-see she what gleaned. * * *.

Her mother-in-law asked her, saying, 'To-day you at what place gleaned, eh ? 53. You at what place did work, eh ? 53. May showed-compassion-on you him obtain happiness, 32.'

Ruth then took herself at what person's place did work, told to (her) mother-in-law to-know, saying, 'I to-day at his place did-do work, that man's name is-called Boaz.'

LESSON, XXVI.

As I walked through the wilderness of this world, I lighted on a certain place where was a den, and I laid me down in that place to sleep; and, as I slept, I dreamed a dream. I dreamed, and behold, I saw a man clothed with rags, standing in a certain place, with his face from his own house, a book in his hand, and a great burden upon his back; I looked, and saw him open the book, and read therein; and, as he read, he wept, and trembled; and not been able to contain, he brake out with a lamentable cry, saying:— 'What shall I do?'

In this plight, therefore, he went home and refrained himself as long as he could, that his wife and children should not perceive his distress; but he could not be silent long, because that his trouble increased.

Wherefore at length he brake his mind to his wife and children; and thus he began to talk to them:—'O! my dear wife,' said he, 'and you the children of my bowels, I, your dear

世上猶如曠野、我行喺個地方、遇着一笪地方、有個巖喺地裏、我就喺個巖裏夢、夢着喺個好處、屋個開眼、流得眼淚、我就該應、夢見嘅一嘅、狼狽打慌、止唔得話、脊見驚禁喊、我止話呢。着住爛嘅衣服、企喺自己背部、手揸包書、自發點、佢手大部淚、睇己聲樣做呢。

佢情形嗰樣、勉強襟住、妻兒見佢、漸漸深、閂唔得住。後來因嘅、瓿漸漸深、閂唔住。歸去唔瓿、唔閂、想呀、忍唔住。

妻呀、至大親嘅哩、如今因個大、對賢妻共我係、事話、個啲事情、將一聲嘆、個仔呀、愛子呀、你哋、故此兒愛親。

LESSON, XXVI.

Shai꜄ shöng² ꜀yau-꜀yü k'wong꜄-꜄ye. ꜄Ngo ꜀hai ko꜄ shü꜄ ꜀háng, yü²-chök꜀ yat꜄ tát꜀ téi²-꜀fong ꜄yau ko꜄ ꜀ngám. ꜄Ngo tsoi꜄ ꜀ngám ꜄löü-꜀t'au fan꜄-chök꜀; tsau² fát꜀ ko꜄ mung². Mung² kin꜄ yat꜄ ko꜄ ꜀yan chök꜀ ꜀ti ꜀hò lán²-ke꜄ ꜀yi-fuk꜀, ꜄k'éi tsoi² yat꜄ shü꜄, ꜄k'öü mín꜄ pöü꜄ chü² tsz²-꜀kéi-ke꜄ uk꜀, ꜀shau ꜀chá pò² ꜀shü, pöü꜄-tsek꜀† ꜀me ko꜄ tái² ꜀páu-fük꜀; yaü꜄ kín꜄ ꜄k'öü ꜀tá-꜀hoi pò² ꜀shü ꜀t'ai; ꜀hò ꜀king-꜀fong, ꜀lau ꜄ngán-löü²; tsz²-꜀kéi ꜀m kam²-꜀chi-tak꜀-chü², tsau² fát꜀ ꜀shengt, tái² hám꜄, wá²:— '꜄Ngo ꜀ying-꜀koi ꜀tím ꜄yöng* tsò² ꜀ni?'

꜄K'öü ꜀ts'ing-꜀ying ꜀kòm ꜄yöng*, hau²-꜀loi höü꜄ ꜀kwai, ꜄mín-꜄k'öng kam²-chü²; ꜀yan-wai² ꜀m ꜄söng ꜀ts'ai ꜀yí kín꜄ ꜄k'öü-ke꜄ pai꜄-ai꜄ á꜄; tán² pai꜄-ai꜄ ꜄tsim-꜄tsím* ꜀sham ꜀m ꜄yan-tak꜀-chü².

Kwú꜄-꜀t'sz ꜀tsöng ko꜄-꜀ti sz²-꜀ts'ing töü꜄ ꜀ts'ai ꜀yí; t'án꜄ yat꜄ ꜀shengt, wá²:—'꜀Yín ꜀ts'ai á꜄, oi꜄ ꜀tsz á꜄, ꜄néi kung² ꜄ngo hai² chí꜄ ꜀ts'an-ke꜄ ꜀le. ꜀Yü-꜀kam ꜀yan ko꜄ tái²

The-world (is) like a-wilderness. I at that place walk, (and) came-across one spot-of ground, (where) there-was [C.] cave. I in cave inside slept; then dreamed [C.] dream. (In the) dream, (I) saw one [C.] man wearing some torn clothing, standing at one place, his face backed his own house, (his) hands held [C.] book, (his) back carried [C.] large bundle (of clothing); (I) also saw him open [C.] book, looking (at it) (*i.e.* reading to himself in it, not aloud); (he was) very frightened, (and) wept tears; himself not restrain able, then made noise loud crying, saying:—'I ought how fashion to-do, eh? 53.'

His aspect (being) so fashion, afterwards (he) went home, compelling (himself) to-restrain (himself); because (he did) not wish (his) wife (and) children to-see his sorrow, 2; but (the) distress gradually deepened, (and could) not (be) concealed able.

Therefore taking those matters (*or* incedents) to (his) wife (and his) children; sighing one sound (he) said:—'My-admirable wife, 2, myloved children, 2, you with me are

friend, am in myself undone by reason of a burden that lieth hard upon me; moreover, I am for certain informed that this our city will be burned with fire from heaven; in which fearful overthrow, both myself, with thee my wife, and you my sweet babes, shall miserably come to ruin; except (the which yet I see not) some way of escape can be found, whereby we may be delivered.' At this his relations were sore amazed; not for that they believed that what he had said to to them was true, but because they thought that some frenzy distemper had got into his head; therefore, it drawing towards night, and they hoping that sleep might settle his brains, with all haste they got him to bed.

敗寶火書要搵得嘅佢慌，但時啲心瞓
要得天災都早避嘅聞驚真，個早佢去，
我知被個咄大黙有聽異係啫，佢翻去佢，
我我必呢你唔知兒詫話癲望定催佢
住且是着我若生唔妻好說發晚，或急速催
磧而城，遇我略，一條但啫，就佢係將者速急
袱蟻個燒時，亡一呢，有講當佢色覺，就
包亡呢所之滅定角路嘅唔估天瞓嘅

But the night was as troublesome to him as the day; wherefore, instead of sleeping, he spent it in sighs and tears. So, when the morning was come, they would know how he did. He told them, worse and worse: he also set to talking to them again; but

但佢成晚都好似日頭唔短，天話又
嘅心中着唔安樂總嗟嘆到安樂
瞓得歇喺處長流淚。問安
嘆不人流眼見唔安
光家嚟眼見問唔
越耐越見人越安

ₒpáu-ṭuk₂ chăk₀ · chü² ⸢ₒngo, ⸢ₒngo
yíú⁾ pái²-ₒmong ₒlá; ₒyi-⸢ch‘e ⸢ₒngo
ₒchí-tak₂ · shat₂ ₒni ko⁾ ₒshengṭ,
shí²-pít₂ péí² ₒt‘ín ⸢fo ⸢sho ₒshíú;
yü²-chök₂ ₒni ko⁾ ₒtsoí-hoí²-ₒchí
ₒshi, ⸢ngo kung² ⸢néí-téí⁾ ₒtò yíú⁾
mít₂-ₒmong lòk₀; yök₂ ₒm táí²-⸢tsò
⸢wan ting² yat₂ ₒt‘íú ₒsháng lò², ⸢tím
péí² ⸢tak₂ ⸢lat₂ ₒni? Tán² ₒm ₒchí
⸢yau ⸢kòm-ke lò² ⸢mò che₂.’ ₒTs‘aí
ₒyí ₒt‘engṭ-ₒman ⸢k‘öü ⸢kòm ⸢kong,
tsau² ⸢hò ch‘á⁾-yí², ₒking-ₒfong; ₒm
tong² ⸢k‘öü shüt₀-wá² haí²ₒ|ₒchan, tán²
⸢kwú ⸢k‘öü haí² fát₀-ₒtín che₂. Ko⁾
ₒshí ₒt‘ín shik₂ ₒtsöng ⸢mán, mong²
⸢k‘öü ⸢tsò-ₒti fan⁾-kán⁾. Wák₂-⸢che
ting² ₒfán ⸢k‘öü sam; ⸢kòm tsau²
kap₂-ts‘uk₂ ₒts‘öü ⸢k‘öü höü⁾ fan⁾.

Tán² ⸢k‘öü ₒshengṭ ⸢mán ₒtò ⸢hò ⸢t‘sz
yat₂-⸢t‘an* ⸢kòm, sam ₒchung ₒm ₒon-
lok₂; ⸢tsung ₒm fan⁾-tak₂ chök₀: ⸢haí
shü⁾ ₒchöng ₒtse ⸢tün t‘án⁾, pat₂ hít₀
ₒlau ⸢ngán-löü². Tò⁾ ₒt‘ín-ₒkwong ₒká-
ₒyan ₒlaí ₒman on. ⸢K‘öü wá²:—‘ Yüt₂
noí², yüt₂ kín⁾ ₒm ₒon-lok₂;’ yan²

most nearly related, 24. Now on-account-of that large bundle weighing-
down me, I must be·ruined-and-
perish, 21; moreover I know for-
certain (that) this [C.] city will-
certainly by heavenly fire be-burned;
on-meeting-this [C.] calamity (at
that) time, I with you also must
be extinguished-and-ruined, 32; if
(we do) not very early find certain
one length-of life road, how avoid
able to-escape, eh? 53. But (I do)
not know (if) there-is such a-road
(or) not only, 7.’ (His) wife (and)
children hearing him so talk, then
very wondered, (and were) afraid;
(they did) not consider his words
to-be true, but thought he was
crazy only, 7. (At) that time the-
sky’s colour (was) near night.
(They) hoped (that by) him earlier
sleeping perhaps settled back (again
would get) his heart; so then with-
all-despatch (they) hurried him to-
go to-sleep.

But he the-whole night also (was) very
like day so; (his) heart midst (was)
not (at) peace; at-all not sleep able
to-complete: there (he was) long-
drawn-out sighs (and) short, sighs
without ceasing, shedding tears. At
dawn (the) family, came to-ask (of

they began to be hardened. They also thought to drive away his distemper by harsh and surly carriages to him: sometimes they would deride, sometimes they would chide, and sometimes they would quite neglect him. Wherefore he began to retire himself to his chamber, to pray for and pity them, and also to condole his own misery; he would also walk solitarily in the fields, sometimes reading, and sometimes praying: and thus for some days he spent his time.—'*Bunyan's Pilgrim's Progress.*'

講唔俾以笑唔入自家嘅己、或幾
話、總唔可恥、或自己中、一連
說佢嘅爲可恥、或總自己擗憐佢、自己田中、
佢以者有時、或佢自己擗憐佢獨自中、
啲聽、佢意思就罵佢以、一則可醒、每每去祈禱、
個啲意思待佢、翻嘅或怒佢。所以一則惡迷不每每出書、或祈禱、
日佢佢、意待佢翻嘅或怒佢。房中、罪痴迷不又(一個)出書、
撳過嘅情好佢理去己人祈禱。(一個)睇日都係嘅。

ᶜk'ái tsok⸴-yat⸴ ko²-ⲥti shütₒ-wá², ᶜkong kwo²ᶜk'öü-téí² ⲥt'engꝉ. ᶜK'öü-téí² ᶜtsung ⲥm ᶜts'oí ᶜk'öü, yí²-sz² ᶜyí-waí² ⲥm ᶜpéí ⲥts'ing-ᶜléí toí² ᶜk'öü, wák⸴-ᶜche ᶜho-ᶜyí ᶜhò ⲥfáu : ᶜkòm tsan²⁻ᶜyau ⲥshi ᶜch'í-síú² ᶜk'öü, wák⸴ nò²-má² ᶜk'öü, wák⸴ ᶜtsung ⲥm ᶜléí ᶜk'öü. ᶜSho-ᶜyi ᶜk'öü tsz²⁻ᶜkéí yap⸴ höü² ⲥfong ⲥchung : yat⸴ tsak⸴ paí²-aí² tsz²⁻ᶜkéí tsöü² okₒ ; yat⸴ tsak⸴ ᶜho-ⲥlín ⲥká ⲥyan ⲥch'í-ⲥmaí pat⸴ ᶜsing ; t'aí² ᶜk'öü-téí² ⲥk'éí-ᶜt'ò. Yau² ᶜmúí-ᶜmúí tuk⸴ tsz²⁻ᶜkéí (yat⸴ ko²) ch'ut⸴ höü² ⲥt'ín ⲥchung, wák⸴ ᶜt'aí ⲥshü, wák⸴ ⲥk'éí-ᶜt'ò : yat⸴ ⲥlín ᶜkéí yat⸴ ⲥtò haí² ᶜkòm.

his) welfare. He said :—'Still longer still-more (I) feel not at-peace ;' also (he) took yesterday those words (and) spoke to them to-hear. They at-all (would) not pay-attention-to (or heed) him, (the) intention (being) in-order-to not to-be courteous to him, perhaps (he) might (get) well again : so then there-were times (they) jeered-at him, or angrily scolded him, or at-all not attended-to him. Therefore he himself entered (and) went-into (his) room midst : on-one hand (he) was-sad (on-account-of) his-own sins (and) evil ; on-the-other hand (he) pitied (his) family people in-darkness (and) not awakened ; (and) on-behalf-of them (he) prayed. Again every-now-and-then, only himself out went to-the-fields midst, either to-look-at (his) book, or to-pray : in-one connected (series of) several days (he) even was (like) so.

LESSON, XXVII.

But now, in this Valley of Humiliation, poor Christian was hard put to it; for he had gone but a little way before he espied a foul fiend coming over the field to meet him: his name is Apollyon. Then did Christian begin to be afraid, and to cast in his mind whether to go back or to stand his ground. But he considered again that he had no armour for his back; and therefore thought that to turn the back to him might give him the greater advantage with ease to pierce him with his darts: therefore he resolved to venture and stand his ground; for, thought he, had I no more in mine eye than the saving of my life, it would be the best way to stand.

So he went on, and Apollyon met him. Now the monster was hideous to beheld: he was clothed with scales, like a fish (and they are his pride); he had wings like a dragon, feet like a bear, and out of his belly came fire and smoke; and his mouth was as the mouth of a lion. When he was come up to Christian, he beheld

基督徒嘅情形有幾從叫做亞督徒商量叮好佢前有頭但要扎頭一路行去。

徒在居謙谷處、佢行情形極苦、因爲見魔嘅時慌、遠忽然望走嚟、佢個驚慌、轉處話、田野走波淪好走翻倒嚇、後翻傷命、做亞中話、或企又想着若易全處、唔向前、心量抑呢。甲倘更保硬意、走受生好便得着背係想硬就立處、唔向

亞波淪對正（佢處）嚟惡緊佢嘅樣子、好兇惡、好醜怪、令人憎惡、亦令人驚慌。滿身都有鱗甲、佢反以爲體面、有翼好似龍嘅、對脚

LESSON, XXVII.

‚Kéi-tuk‚-‚t'ò tsoí² ‚Köü-‚hím Kuk‚ shü²,
ᶜk'öü-ke² ‚ts'ing-‚ying kik‚ ᶜfú, ‚yan-
waí² ‚háng ᶜmò ᶜkéi ᶜyün, fat‚-‚yín
mong²-kín² ‚Mo-ᶜkwaí, ‚ts'ung ‚t'ín-
ᶜye ᶜtsan ‚laí : ᶜk'öü-ke² ᶜmeng*
kíú² tsò² Á²-‚pò-‚lun. Ko² ‚shí ‚Kéi-
tuk‚-‚t'ò ‚sam ‚chung ᶜhò ‚king-
‚fong ; tsz²-ᶜkéi ‚shöng-löng² wá² :—
'ᶜTsau ‚fán-ᶜchün-‚t'au ᶜhò ‚á, yik‚-
wák² ᶜk'éi ᶜtò shü², ᶜtang ᶜk'öü ᶜhò
‚ni ?' Yau² ᶜsöng ᶜhá, wá² :—'ᶜNgo
‚ts'ín-pín² ᶜyan káp‚ chök‚ che‚,
han²-pín² ᶜmò tak‚ chök‚; ᶜt'ong-
yök‚ ᶜtsan ‚fán ᶜchün ‚t'au púí² pín²
kang²-yí² shau² ‚shöng lá² : tán²-haí²
‚söng ᶜpò-‚ts'ün ‚sháng-meng²†, ‚tong-
yíú² cháp‚-ngáng² ᶜk'éi shü², ‚m
‚fán ᶜchün-‚t'an, ᶜkòm tsan² láp‚-yí
höng² ‚ts'in yat‚ lò² ‚háng höü².'

Á²-‚pò-‚lun töü² ching² (ᶜk'öü shü²)
‚laí-ᶜkan. ᶜK'öü-ke² ᶜyöng* ᶜtsz
ᶜhò ‚hung-ok‚ ; ᶜhò ᶜch'au-kwáí²,
ling² ‚yan ‚tsang-wú², yik‚ ling²
‚yan ‚king-‚fong : ᶜmún shan ‚tò
ᶜyau ‚lun-káp‚, ᶜk'öü ᶜfán ᶜyí
waí² ᶜt'aí-mín² ; ᶜyau yik‚ ᶜhò
ᶜt'sz ‚lung ᶜkòm, töü² kök‚

Christian in Humiliation Valley place,
his circumstances (were) very bitter,
because walking not very far, suddenly
he saw the-devil, from field-wilds,
running coming : his name was-called
to-be Apollyon. That time Christian
heart middle very frightened ; with-
himself discussed, saying :—'To-run
back, turning the head, good, eh ? 1,
or stand at the-place, wait-for him
good, eh ? 53. Again he-thought a-
bit, saying :—'My front has armour
wearing only, 7, back not obtained
the-wearing ; if run back, (my) back
more easily receive wound, 22 : but
wishing to-protect entire (my) life,
(I) must firmly stand at-the-place,
not back turn head, so then (he)
decided facing before by-all the-way
(or one road) to walk going.
Apollyon towards straight him coming
(*i.e.* came straight on). His appearance (was) very fierce, very hideous,
causing men to-hate (him), also causing men to-be-afraid : full the-body
also had scales, he notwithstanding
considered (them) as (something)
to-be-proud-of ; further (he) had
wings very like dragon's such, (his)

him with a disdainful countenance, and thus began to question with him:—

APOLLYON.—'Whence came you? and whither are you bound?'

CHRISTIAN.—'I am come from the City of Destruction, which is the place of all evil, and am going to the City of Zion.'

APOLLYON.—'By this I perceive that thou art one of my subjects; for all that country is mine, and I am the prince and god of it. How is it, then, that thou hast run away from thy King? Were it not that I hope thou mayest do me more service, I would strike thee, now, at one blow, to the ground.'

CHRISTIAN.—'I was born, indeed, in your dominions, but your service was hard, and your wages such as a man could not live on,—"for the wages of sin is death," therefore, when I was come to years, I did as other considerate persons do, look out, if perhaps I might mend myself.'

有似裏好似肚好似個嘴嚟人嘅出火似熊獅子嘅好烟獅個時行起雙眼凸處嚟、到基督徒面前、話你從邊處嚟、想去邊處呢。

基督徒話、我從將亡城嚟、個處係萬惡嘅地方、如今想去聚邱山呀。

魔鬼話、聽你咁講、一定係我開嘅百姓、因我係個地方嘅王帝、個處嘅上帝、你點解離開我、走去別處呢、我若唔係想你再服事我、即刻就打死你咯。

基督徒話、我本來係你嘅百姓、但服事你好難、你嘅錢又做惡必長嘅別路、你又係定大人、做工唔夠養、因係報應、此明明有罪嘅工夫、之後死亡、個咁望、望益咯。

ᶜhò ᶜt'sz ₍hnng-₍yan ᶜkòm, ᶜt'ò
ᶜlöü ᶜyau ˙ ₍yín ᶜfo ch'ut₎ ₍laí ;
ko⁾ ₍tsöü ᶜhò ᶜt'sz ₍sz-ᶜtsz ᶜkòm.
Ko⁾ ₍shí ₍háng tò⁾ ₍Kéí-tuk₎-₍t'ò mín²
₍ts'ín, tat₎-ᶜhéí-₍shöng-ᶜngán, wá² :—
' ᶜNéí ₍ts'ung ₀pín shü⁾ ₍laí ; ᶜsöng
höü⁾ ₀pín shü⁾ ₀ni ? '
₍Kéí-túk₎-₍t'ò wá² :—' ᶜNgo ₍ts'ung ₍Tsöng-
₍mong ₍sheng† ₍laí, ko⁾ shü⁾ haí² mán²
ok₀ tsong²-tsöü² ke⁾ téí²-₍fong, ₍yü-₍kam
ᶜsöng höü⁾ ₍Sun ₍Shán á⁾.'
₍Mo-ᶜkwaí wá² :—' ₍T'eng† ᶜnéí ᶜkòm
ᶜkong, yat₎ ting² haí² ᶜngo-ke⁾
pák₀-sing⁾ ; ₍yan ko⁾ shü⁾ téí²-₍fong
haí² ᶜngo-ke⁾, ᶜngo haí² ko⁾ shü⁾
ke⁾ ₍wong, pák₀-sing⁾ ₍tò ₍tsün ᶜngo
waí² ₍Shöng²-taí⁾. ᶜNéí ₍yan-₍ho
₍léí-₍hoí ᶜngo höü⁾ pít₀ shü⁾ ₀ni ?
Yök₂ ₍m haí² ᶜsöng ᶜnéí tsoí² fuk₂-
sz² ᶜngo, tsau² tsik₎-hak₎ ᶜtá-ᶜsz
ᶜnéí lok₀.'
₍Kéí-túk₎-₍t'ò wá² :—' ᶜNgo ᶜpún-₍loí
haí² ᶜnéí-ke⁾ pák₀-sing⁾, tán² fnk₎-
sz² ᶜnéí-ke⁾ ₍kung-₍fú ᶜhò ₍nán tsò²,
₍kung-₍ts'ín yau² ₍m kau ᶜyöng-
ᶜhau ; ₍yan-waí² tsò² ᶜnéí-ke⁾ ₍kung-
₍fú, ₍k'öü haí² tsöü²-ok₀-ke⁾ sz², hau²-
₍loí ₍chí pò⁾-ying⁾ pít₎-ting² haí² ᶜsz-
₍mong ; kwú⁾-ᶜt'sz ᶜngo ᶜchöng-taí²,
tsau² hok₂ ko⁾-₍ti ₍ts'ung-₍ming-ke⁾
₍yan, sz⁾ pín² kòm⁾ mong², mong²
ᶜyau pít₎ lò² ling² ᶜngo tak₎ yik₎ lok₀.'

pair of-feet like bear's such, stomach
within had smoke (and) fire issuing-out
come ; the snout very like lion's such.

That time walked-up to Christian's face
before, glaring (at him he) said :—
'You from what place come ; wish
to-go what place, eh ? 53.'

Christian said :—' I from About-to-be
Destroyed City come, that is myriad
evils gathering's place, now wish
to-go-to Zion Hill, 2.'

The Devil said :—' Hearing you so speak,
to-a certainty (you) are (one of) my
people ; because that place-of ground
is mine, I am that place's prince,
the-people also exalt me as Supreme
Ruler. You why separate from-me,
(and) go another place, eh ? 53. If
not was wishing you again to-serve
me, then immediately strike-to-death
you, 32.'

Christian said :—' I originally was (one
of) your people, but serving your
work very hard to-do, wages further
not enough to-support-life ; because
doing your work, all is sin (and)
evil's business, afterwards's recompence
certainly is death ; therefore I grown-
up, then copied those intelligent
people, four sides so looked, (and)
saw there-was another path (which)
would-cause me to-obtain profit, 32.'

APOLLYON.—'There is no prince that will thus lightly lose his subjects, neither will I as yet lose thee: but since thou complainest of thy service and wages, be content to go back; what our country will afford, I do here promise to give thee.'

魔鬼話、爲王嘅、點肯俾百姓逃走呢、我亦唔放你去、若係你話工夫難做、工錢又少、同本國中所有嘅物件、我都俾過你。

CHRISTIAN.—'But I have let myself to another, even to the King of Princes; and how can I, with fairness, go back with thee?'

基督徒話、我已經應承別個主人咯、卽係萬王之王嘅、我依理點跟得你翻去呢。

APOLLYON.—'Thou hast done in this according to the proverb, "changed a bad for a worse:" but it is ordinary for those that have professed themselves his servants, after a while to give him the slip, and return to me. Do thou so too, and all shall be well.'

魔鬼話、俗語有講、你引磚引玉蠢自己、每每有幾舊做、凡係做佢僕人嘅、過一陣仍舊離開、忽然歸向我哩、你照樣做也好、就好嘅。

CHRISTIAN.—'I have given him my faith, and sworn my allegiance to him; how, then, can I go back from this, and not be hanged as a traitor?'

基督徒話、我已經同佢立約、盡忠佢、誓願如今、若係背約、豈唔係有應得嘅背逆罪咩。

ₗMo-ᶜkwaí wa² :—'Waí² ₗWong ke²,
ᶜtím ᶜhang ᶜpéi pák₀-sing² ₗt'ò-ᶜtsáu
₀ni ? ᶜNgo shí²-pít₂ ₗm fong² ᶜnéi
höü². yök₂ haí² ᶜnéi p'a² ᶜngo
ₗkung-ₗfú ₗnán tsò², ₗkung-ₗts'ín
yan² ᶜshíu, ᶜnéi chik₀-ᶜkwún ₗt'ung
ᶜngo ₗfán höü² ᶜpún kwok₀ ; ᶜngo
kwok₀ ₗchung ᶜsho ᶜyau ᶜhò mat₂-
ᶜkín* ₗtò ᶜpéi kwo² ᶜnéi.'

ₗKéi-tuk₂-ₗt'ò wá² :—ᶜNgo ᶜyí-ₗking
ₗying-ₗshing pit₂ ko² ᶜchü-ₗyan, tsik₂
haí² Mán² ₗWong-ke² ₗWong lok₀ ;
ₗyí ᶜléi ₗlai lun², yau² ᶜtím ₗkan tak₂
ᶜnéi ₗfán höü² ₀ni ?'
ₗMo-ᶜkwaí wá² :—'Tsuk₂ ᶜyü ᶜyau
ᶜkong :—" P'án ₗchün ᶜyan yuk₂ :"
ᶜnéi ᶜkòm ᶜyöng* tsò², haí² ₗp'án
yuk₂ ᶜyan ₗchün ₗlá. Tsò² mat₂
ᶜkòm ₗyü-ch'un ₀ni ? ᶜMúi-ᶜmúi
ᶜyau ᶜhò ₗto ₗyan, tsz²-ᶜkéi wá²
haí² ₗKéi-tuk₂-ke² ₗshan-puk₂ ; kwo²
ᶜmò ᶜkéi ᶜnoi*, fat₂-ₗyín ₗléi-ₗhoi
ᶜk'öü, ₗying-kau² ₗkwai höng² ᶜngo.
ᶜNéi yik₂ chíú ᶜkòm tsò² tsau²
ᶜhò ₗle.'

ₗKéi-tuk₂-ₗt'ò wá² :—'Ngo ᶜyí-ₗking
ₗt'ung ᶜChü láp₂ yök₂, shaí² kwo²
yün², yíú² tsun²-ₗchung ke² ; ₗyü-
ₗkam yök₂ haí² pöü²-yik₂ ᶜk'öü, ᶜhéi
ₗm haí² ᶜyau ₗying-tak₂ ke² tsöü²
ₗₗme ?'

The Devil said :—' Those-who-are princes,
how willing to-let (their) people run
away, eh ? 53. I certainly not let you
go : if it-is (that) you fear my work
difficult to-do, wages further too-little,
you, well ! *(it is almost impossible to
render this in English)* with me back
go (to your) original country ; My
country midst whatever have good
things also give to you.'

Christian said :—' I already promised
another [C.] master, just is Myriad
Princes' Prince, 32 ; according-to
principle coming-to speak, again how
follow able you back go, eh ? 53.'

Devil said :—' Proverb does say.—
" Casting-away a-brick to-attract a-
jadestone :" you so fashion do is
casting-away a-jadestone to-attract a-
brick, 22. Do what so stupid, eh ? 53.
Always there-are very many people
themselves say they-are Christ's servants ; passed-over not very long, suddenly separate-off from-him, after-the
old-style, return face-towards me. You
also according-to so do, then good, 24.'

Christian said :—' I already with Lord
established a-covenant, sworn have
an-oath, must be-entirely honest ;
now if it-is-that-I-do rebel-against
him, will it-not be that-I-have me-
rited guilt, eh ? 39.'

APOLLYON.—'Thou didst the same to me, and yet I am willing to pass by all, if now thou wilt yet turn again and go back.'

魔鬼話、你既係嗽背逆我、又肯跟我做呢、講我今日、雖然你若翻去、我亦唔怪你。

CHRISTIAN.—'What I promised thee was in nonage; and, besides, I count the Prince under whose banner now I stand, is able to absolve me; yea, and to pardon also what I did as to my compliance with thee. And besides, O thou destroying Apollyon! to speak truth, I like his service, his wages, his servants, his government, his company and country, better than thine; and, therefore, leave off to persuade me further: I am his servant, and I will follow him.'

基督徒話、我從前應承你嘅話、係前時年少、如今全住我主嘅、乃係執行嗽、因嗽我唔解得你免呀、縱使必依赦淪、我主前能波知得、況且亞你呢個害人嘅魔鬼、老實講、我見佢嘅工夫、佢嘅工錢、佢嘅僕、佢嘅政、佢嘅國、都比你好、所以你唔好講多、我決意要從佢。

APOLLYON.—'Consider, again, when thou art in cool blood, what thou art like to meet with in the way that thou goest. The knowest that, for the most part, his servants come to an ill end, because they are transgressors against me and my ways. How many of them have been put to shameful deaths! And,

魔鬼話、你行呢條路、好多苦難嚇、你當細心想、得僕好知、受逼害呀、你估服事主嘅法嘅、佢嘅僕好多到死哩、其中死嘅事佢、犯我得罪我、唔少呀。

ˌMo-ʿkwaí wǎ² :—ʿʿNéi kéíʾ haí² ʿkòm ʿkong, tsò² matˌ ˌkam-yatˌ yau² pöüʾ-yikˌ ʿngo ₒni ? ˌSöü-ˌyín, ʿnéi yökˌ haí² ʿhang ˌkan ʿngo ˌfán höüʾ, ʿngo yikˌ ˌm kwáíʾ ʿnéi.ʾ

ˌKéí-tukˌ-ˌtʿò wǎ² :—ʿ ʿNgo ˌtsʿung-ˌtsʿín ˌying-ˌshing fukˌ-sz² ʿnéi, ˌyan haí² síuʾ ˌshí ʿlün* tsok₀ ʿlünᵒ waí² cheˌ ; ˌyü-ˌkam ʿngo ʿsho fukˌ-sz² keʾ, ʿnái haí² ˌTsʿün-ˌnang-keʾ ʿChü ; tsungʾ-ʿsz ʿnéi chapˌ-chüʾ ʿngo, hiú² takˌ ʿChü pítˌ ʿwúí ʿkái-tʿüt₀ ʿngo, ʿngo ˌtsʿung-ˌtsʿín ˌyí ʿnéi ˌháng ok₀, ʿngo ʿChü yikˌ ˌnang sheʾ-ʿmínkeʾ. Hoí² ˌyan-keʾ Áʾ-ˌpo-ˌlun áʾ, ʿngo shatˌ-tsoíʾ wǎ² ʿnéi ˌchi, ʿngo kínʾ ʿChü ʿpéí-káuʾ ʿnéi ʿhò takˌ ˌto, ʿkʿöü kwok₀ ˌchung-keʾ ˌkʿwaí-ʿköü, ˌkung-ˌfú, kung-ʿtsʿín*, ˌshan-pukˌ, chingʾ-ling², ʿngo ˌto ˌfún-ʿhéi ; ʿnéi ˌm ʿshaí ˌto ʿkong ; ʿngo haí² ʿChü-keʾ ˌshan-pukˌ, ʿngo kʿüt₀-yíʾ yiúʾ ˌtsʿung ʿkʿöü keʾ lok₀.ʾ

ˌMo-ʿKwaí wǎ² :—ʿʿNéi ˌháng ni ˌtʿiú-lò², ʿwúí yü²-chökˌ ʿhò ˌto ʿfú nán² káʾ, ʿnéi ˌtong saíʾ-ˌsam ʿsöng ʿhá chíʾ ʿhò. ʿNéi ʿChü-keʾ pukˌ takˌ tsöü² ʿngo, fán² ʿngo-keʾ fát₀, ʿhò ˌto ˌm takˌ ʿhò ʿsz keʾ ; ʿnéi ˌchí-tòʾ ˌle. ˌKʿéi ˌchung ʿyau ˌti shau² pikˌ-hoí² ˌyí-ʿsz-keʾ, yikˌ ˌm ʿshíu áʾ. ʿNéi ʿkwú fukˌ-sz² ʿkʿöü,

---

Devil said:—'You since do so speak, what thing to-day also rebel-against me, eh ? 53. Notwithstanding (which), you if-are willing follow me back go, I also not blame you.'

Christian said:—'I formerly promised serve you because it was (that) I was in-my-young time (and) unregulated acts (and) disordered doings only, 7 ; now I whom serve, is the-Almighty Lord. If-indeed you seize me, I-think my-Lord certainly can let-free me. I formerly according-to you do evil, my-Lord also able to-forgive. Injuring men Apollyon, 2, I certainly say to-you to-know, I see Lord compared-with you good able much, his kingdom midst's customs, work, wages, servants, official orders, I also am-pleased-with ; you not need more to-speak ; I am Lord's servant, I am-determined must follow him, 32.'

Devil said:—'You walking this length-of road may meet very many bitter troubles, 14, you onght carefully think a-bit in-order to-be-well. Your Lord's servants obtaining guilt-against me, breaking my laws, very many not able good die ; you know, 24. Them amongst there-are some-who suffer persecution to-death also not

besides, thou countest his service better than mine, whereas he never came yet from the place where he is, to deliver any that served him out of their hands: but as for me, how many times, as all the world very well knows, have I delivered, either by power or fraud, those that have faithfully served me, from him and his, though taken by them; and so will I deliver thee.'

CHRISTIAN.—'His forbearing at present to deliver them is on purpose to try their love, whether they will cleave to him to the end: and as for the ill end thou sayest they come to, that is most glorious in their account; for, for present deliverance, they do not much expect it, for they stay for their glory, and then they shall have it, when their Prince comes in his and the glory of the angels.'

APOLLYON.—'Thou has already been unfaithful in thy service to him; and how dost thou think to receive wages of him?'

CHRISTIAN.—'Wherein, O Apollyon, have I been unfaithful to him?'

見僕盡主、就嚟嘅、救
未臣有嘅、我翻知嚟嘅救
咩、嘅係你住、救人所係
我佢若被捉救眾人亦係
事過手。
服過我嘅盡係如今
好過嚟離服佢力哪我
佢脫心或盡呢哩你呀。

刻想冇主以嘅僕後榮嚟、榮光
即為心從得反前臣日嘅落榮
因嘅肯唔僕眼嘅主望住天得
主係主底話臣救主係住天亦得
唔係嘅
我僕愛到佢至能係單乘個臣僕、
話臣有佢從在幸、唔望主共嘅
基督徒佢睇從在榮難、想福、共嘅
救試又唔死為苦所嘅光主呀。

呢個忠賞唔
服事得係佢嘅
你唔算得望
已經重望咩。
又話、邊樣唔
魔鬼主、心賜。
基督徒話、我有邊樣唔
忠心呢。

ʿhò kwo' fuk₂-sz² ʿngo ₍me? Méi²
kín' ʿk'öü ₍lai kau'-kwo' ʿk'öü-ke'
₍shan-puk₂, t'üt₀ ₍léi ʿngo ʿshau:
yök₂ hai² ʿyau tsun² ₍sam fuk₂-sz²
ʿngo, péi² ʿnéi-ke' ʿChü, wák₂ ʿk'öü-
ke' puk₂ chuk₀-chü², ʿngo tsau²
tsun² lik₂, tsun² ₍mau, kan' ʿk'öü
₍fán-₍lai. ₍Ni-₍ti hai² chung' ₍yan
ʿsho ₍chí ke' ₍le. ʿNgo ₍yü-₍kam
yik₂ hui² ₍lai kau' ʿnéi á'.'

₍Kéi-tuk₂-₍t'ò wá² :—'ʿNgo ʿChü ₍m
tsik₀-hak₂ kau' ʿk'öü ₍shan-puk₂,
hai² ₍yan-wai² ʿsöng shi' ʿk'öü ʿyau
oi' ʿChü-ke' ₍sam ʿmò: yau² 't'ai
ʿk'öü tò'-'tai ʿhang ₍ts'ung ʿChü ₍m
₍ts'ung: chi' ₍yü wá² ₍m tak₂ ʿhò
ʿsz, tsoi² ʿk'öü-ke' ₍shan-puk₂ ʿfán
ʿyí-wai² ʿwing-hang'; ₍nang kau'
ʿngán-₍ts'ín-ke' ʿfú-₍nán, ₍m hai²
ʿChü-ke' ₍shan-puk₂ ʿsho ʿsöng
mong², ₍tán hai² mong² yat₂-hau²-ke'
fuk₂. ʿChü ₍shing-chü² ʿk'öü-ke'
wing₂-₍kwong, kung² ko'-₍ti ₍t'ín-sz'
lok₂ ₍lai, ʿChü-ke' ₍shan-puk₂ yik₂
tak₂ ₍wing-₍kwong á'.'

₍Mo-ʿkwai yau² wá² :—'ʿNéi fuk₂-sz² ₍ni
ko' ʿChü ʿyí-₍king ₍m sün' tak₂ hai²
₍chung ₍sam lok₀; chung² ʿmong²
tak₂ ʿk'öü-ke' ʿshöng-t'sz' ₍me?'

₍Kéi-tuk₂-₍t'ò wá² :—'ʿNgo ʿyau ₍pín
yöng² ₍m ₍chung ₍sam ₍ni?'

few, 2. You think serve him better
than serving me, eh? 39. Not-yet
seen him come to-save his servants,
to-deliver from my hands: If it-is
(that you) have entire heart to-serve
me, by your Lord, or his servants
caught, I then to-the-extreme-of
strength, to-the-extreme-of plans save
(them) back come. This is all men
what know, 24. I now also am
come to-save you, 2.'

Christian said:—'My Lord not immediately save his servants, is because
wish to-try them have love Lord's
heart (or) not; further to-see (whether) they to-the bottom are-willing
to-follow the-Lord, (or) not to-follow ·
as to saying not able (to-have-a)
good death, it-is-to his servants
changed to-be glory; able to-save-
from eyes before difficulties not is
Lord's servants what wish hope-for,
only is hope future's happiness. Lord
in-his glory, with those angels, down
come, Lord's servants also obtain
glory, 2.'

Devil further said:—'You serve this
[*C.*] Lord already not reckon obtain
have sincere heart, 32; still look
to-obtain his reward, eh? 39.'

Christian said:—'I have what kind not
faithful heart, eh? 53.'

APOLLYON.—'Thou didst faint at first setting out, when thou wast almost choked in the Gulf of Despond. Thou didst attempt wrong ways to be rid of thy burden, whereas thou shouldest have stayed till thy Prince had taken it off. Thou didst sinfully sleep, and lose thy choice thing. Thou wast, also, almost persuaded to go back at the sight of the lions. And when thou talkest of thy journey, and of what thou hast heard and seen, thou art inwardly desirous of vain glory in all that thou sayest or doest.'

魔鬼話，你初死心在意大，懶嘅替主着而個兩翻路，若貪出，始在懶嘅替唔且部隻轉，所講名嚟。呢鬱略、祆脫法犯書。爭及聞知嘅意，行憂惰包解嘅據子，與所人嘅聲，條泥又應你子罪，又嘅行嘅時思。話爭就所等靠解，曉個走條你有露，魔鬼路中你該反嚟，失見就呢事時流。

CHRISTIAN.—'All this is true, and much more which thou hast left out; but the Prince whom I serve and honour is merciful, and ready to forgive. But, besides, these infirmities possessed me in thy country, for there I sucked them in; and I have groaned under them, being sorry for them, and have obtained pardon of my Prince.'

基督徒話，你實你所講有及，心嘅。先嘅惡樣，自就住嘆，所重講主罪。我嚟做一今我曾嘅人事，學喜野磧嗟，如事未事赦惡中歡好磧嗟，你服肯嘅國時食罪自免，係惡所悲呢你陣似個怨赦，確嘅我慈且在個好被埋主，別但中而日因事，我已得。

₋Mo-ᶜkwaí wä² :—ᶜ ᶜNéí ᶜch'í-₋ch'o ₋háng ₋ni ₋t'íú lò², ₋cháng ₋ti ᶜsz tsoí² ᶜYau-wat, ₋Naí ₋chung, tsau² ₋sam ᶜlán, yí² to²-lok₀. Yan² ᶜnéí ᶜsho ₋me ke² tát² ₋pán-fük₂, ₋ying-₋koí ᶜtang ᶜChü t'aí² ᶜnéí ᶜkáí-t'üt₀, ᶜnéí ᶜfán k'án²-₋ chök₀ ₋m 'hò ke² fát₀-ᶜtsz ₋laí ᶜkáí. ₋Yí-ᶜch'e ₋t'ám fan² fán²-tsöü², shat,-₋híú ko² pò² ₋p'ang-köü² ₋shü. Yan² kin² ko² ᶜlöng chek₀† ₋sz-ᶜtsz, ₋cháng ₋ti tsau² ᶜtsau fán-ᶜchün-₋t'au. ₋Yü-k'ap₂ ₋háng ₋ni ₋t'íú lò², ᶜsho kin², ᶜsho ₋man-ke² sz², ᶜnéí yök₂ ᶜkong kwo² ₋yan ₋chí, ₋shí-₋shi ᶜyan ₋t'ám ₋meng†-₋sheng† ke² yí²-sz², ₋lan-lò²-ch'ut,-₋laí.'

₋Kéí-tuk,-₋t'ò wä²:—ᶜ ᶜNéí ₋yü-₋kam ᶜsho ᶜkong ke², k'ok₀ haí² shat, sz², ᶜngo chung² ᶜyan pít, ₋ti ok₀, ᶜnéí méí²-₋ts'ang ᶜkong-k'ap₂ ; tán² ᶜngo ᶜsho fuk₂-sz²-ke² ᶜChü ₋sam ₋chung ₋ts'z-₋péí ᶜhang she² ₋yan tsöü²-ke². Yí-ᶜch'e ₋ni-₋ti ok₀ sz², ᶜngo sin-yat₂ tsoí² ᶜnéí kwok₀ ₋chung hok₀-₋laí-ke², ₋yan ko² chan² ᶜshí*, ₋fún-ᶜhéí tsò² ok₀ sz², ᶜhò ᶜt'sz shik₂ ᶜhò ᶜye yat, yöng² ; ᶜngo péí² ko²-₋ti tsöü² chák₀-chü², tsz²-ᶜkéí ₋máí-yün², tsz²-ᶜkéí ₋tse-t'án², tsau² tak, ᶜChü she²-ᶜmín lok₀.

Devil said:—'You beginning walk this [*C.*] road, wanted a-little-of dying in Despond Mud midst, then heart lazy, intention indolent, 32. Further you what carry-on-back big bundle-of-clothing, ought to-wait-till Lord for you undo, you on-the-contrary depend-upon not good means in-order-to undo. Moreover coveting sleep, sinned, lost that [*C.*] proof-book. Further seeing those two [*C.*] lions, wanted a-little-of just running back. And walking this [*C.*] road whatever you-have-seen, whatever-you-have heard matters, you if spoke to people for-them-to-know, constantly have coveted good-reputation's mean-ing, inadvertently-disclosed.'

Christian said:—'You now what say, truly is a-real matter, I still have other evils you not-yet spoken about ; but I whom serve Lord (*i.e.* the Lord whom I serve) heart middle compassionate, willing to-forgive men (their) sins. Moreover these evil things I former-day in your country midst learned-come, because that [*C.*] time pleased to-do evil matters, very like eat good things one same ; I by those sins pressed-down, self cherish ill-will, self groaned, then obtained Lord forgive, 32.'

Then Apollyon broke out into a grievous rage, saying, 'I am an enemy to this Prince; I hate his person, his laws, and people; I am come out on purpose to withstand thee.'

個時亞波淪忽然大怒，話，我就係你嘅仇敵，極憎惡佢，極憎惡佢嘅律法同佢嘅百姓，我如今出嚟正係要阻止你。

CHRISTIAN.—'Apollyon, beware what you do; for I am in the King's highway, the way of holiness; therefore take heed to yourself.'

基督徒話，呀路（亞波淪）呀，你要子細呀，我如今在主嘅聖潔大路之中，即係潔路，故此你自己要打黙呀。

Then Apollyon straddled quite over the whole breadth of the way, and said:—'I am void of fear in this matter. Prepare thyself to die; for I swear by my infernal den, that thou shalt go no further; here will I spill thy soul.'

個時亞波淪橫截住路，話，我唔怕死喺呢件野，你願稱呢命，我必要喺呢處誓過唔俾你過去，我指陰府放你過嘅去得，一定要攞你條命，若放你過，唔怕死咯。

And with that he threw a flaming dart at his breast; but Christian had a shield in his hand with which he caught it, and so prevented the danger of that.

前，籤傷。佢主嘅胸受，割信，好彩，鏢掟袖，基督徒擋住個牌，嗷就。

Then did Christian draw, for he saw it was time to bestir him: and Apollyon as fast made at him, throwing darts as thick as hail; by the which, notwithstanding all that Christian could do to avoid it,

惡唔聖淪似雜，兇就將亞波淪鏢好似雨一樣，基督徒雖，佢咁死，袖攻，拔出嚟，盡力神寶劍，基督徒見佢咁企喺處等死，好

Ko[,] ₍shí Á[,]-₍po-₍lun fat₍-₍yín táí²-nò² ⁵héí ₍laí wá²:—‘ ⁵Ngo tsau² haí² ⁵néí ⁵Chü-ke⁷ ₍ch‘au-tik₍; kik₍ ₍tsang-wú⁷ ₍⁵k‘öü-ke⁷ lüt₍-fát₀₀, kik₍ ₍tsang-wú⁷ ⁵k‘öü-ke⁷ pák₀-sing⁷ ; ₍ngo ₍yü-₍kam ch‘ut₍, ₍laí, ching⁷ haí² yíú⁷ ⁵cho-⁵chí ⁵néí.'

₍Kéí-tuk₍-₍t‘ò wá²:—‘ ⁵Néí yíú⁷ ⁵tsz-saí⁷ á⁷ ; ⁵ngo ₍yü-₍kam tsoí² ⁵Chü-ke⁷ táí² lò² ₍chi ₍chung, tsik₍ haí² shing⁷ kít₀-ke⁷ lò² ; kwú⁷-⁵t‘sz ⁵néí tsz²-⁵kéí yíú⁷ ⁵tá ⁵tím á⁷.'

Ko[,] ₍shí Á[,]-₍po-₍lun ₍wáng-tsít₍-chü² lò², ₍m ⁵péí ₍Kéí-tuk₍-₍t‘ò kwo⁷ wá²:—‘ ⁵Ngo p‘á⁷ mat₍ ⁵ye ₍ni ? ⁵Ngo pít₍ yíú⁷ ⁵néí ⁵sz tsoí² ₍ni shü⁷ ; ₍ngo shaí² ₍híú yün⁷ lok₀, yök₍ fong⁷ ⁵néí kwo⁷ höü⁷, ₍m ch‘ing tak₍ waí² ₍Yam-fú-ke⁷ ₍Wong ; ⁵haí ₍ni shü⁷ yat₍ ting² yíú⁷ ⁵lo ⁵néí ₍t‘íú meng²*.

⁵Kòm tsau² ⁵k‘áí tsau²-₍píú kat₍ ⁵k‘öü ₍hung-ts‘ín ; ₍Kéí-tuk₍-₍t‘ò ₍ning sun⁷ ⁵Chü-ke⁷ ₍t‘ang ₍p‘áí tong⁷ chü², ⁵hò ⁵ts‘oí ⁵mò ₍shan² ₍shöng.

₍Kéí-tuk₍-₍t‘ò kín⁷ ⁵k‘öü kòm⁷ ₍hung-ok₀, ₍m ⁵hò ⁵k‘éí shü⁷ ⁵tang ⁵sz, tsau² ₍tsöng Shing⁷-₍Shan ⁵pò kím⁷ pat₍ ch‘ut₍: Á[,]-₍po-₍lun tsun² lik₍ ₍laí ₍kung, tsau²-₍píú ⁵hò ⁵t‘sz lok₍ ⁵yü yat₍ yöng² ; ₍Kéí-tuk₍-₍t‘ò ₍söü

That time Apollyon suddenly great anger rise come, said :—‘ I just am your Lord's enemy ; extremely hate his laws, extremely hate his people ; I now am-out come just is want to-hinder you.'

Christian said :—‘ You must be-careful ; 2 ; I now in Lord's main road's midst, just is holy pure road ; therefore you must be-prepared, 2.'

That time Apollyon across stopped the-road, not let Christian pass, saying :—‘ I afraid-of what thing, eh ? 53. I certainly want you to-die in this place ; I sworn have an-oath, 32, if let you pass away, not entitled can be Hades's Prince ; at this place to-a certainly must take your [*C.*] life.'

So then with sleeve-dart to-stab his breast ; Christian took trusting-in the-Lord's rattan shield, (and) warded (it off), very fortunate not receive injury.

Christian seeing him so fierce, not good stand at-the-place waiting-for death, then took the-Holy Spirit precious sword, drawing (it) out : Apollyon with-his-whole strength come-on to-attack, sleeve-dart very like falling

Apollyon wounded him in his head, his hand, and foot. This made Christian give a little back; Apollyon, therefore, followed his work amain, and Christian again took courage, and resisted as manfully as he could. This sore combat lasted for above half a day, even till Christian was almost quite spent; for you must know that Christian, by reason of his wounds, must needs grow weaker and weaker. Then Apollyon, espying his opportunity, began to gather up close to Christian, and wrestling with him, gave him a dreadful fall; and with that, Christian's sword flew out of his hand.

頭脚手但擋抵力出
此故咯傷受有都面
越淪波亞。後退輕輕
奮再徒督基。前土發
共力氣盡出、神精起
足戰苦塲呢。戰大佢
氣嘅徒督基、日半有
因咯嗞有都啲爭、力
候時個呢到、傷受爲
淪波亞。咯弱軟然自
前子勢個呢趁
地落佢攞、佢住攬
曉跌覺不徒督基時個
劍。把

Then said Apollyon:—'I am sure of thee now!' And with that he had almost pressed him to death, so that Christian began to despair of life. But, as God would have it, while Apollyon was fetching of his last blow, thereby to make a full end of this good man, Christian nimbly reached out his hand for his sword, and caught it, saying:—'Rejoice not against me, O mine enemy: when I fall, I shall arise!;' and with that gave him a deadly

命條你今如、話淪波亞
盡就、手我在死唔重
嘅徒督基、佢住壓力
知誰。咯生得望唔就
值適、典恩帝上得佢
想、手隻起遞淪波亞
手伸徒督基、佢死打
劍把己自着摩、摩一
聲大佢、淪波亞剌就
喜歡咁咪你、敵仇、話

ᶜch'ŭt, lïk, ᶜtaí tong², tán² ᶜshaŭ, kök𝒸, ₫t'aŭ, mín², ₫tò ᶜyaŭ shaŭ² ₫shöng lok𝒐. Kwú²-ᶜt'sz ₫heng†-₫heng*† (NOTE.— This is very peculiar : when the two words occur together, the first is put down into the 下平) t'öü² haŭ²; Á²-₫po-₫lun yüt₂-fät𝒐 ᶜshöng-₫ts'ín. ₫Kéi-tŭk,-₫t'ò tsoí² ᶜfan ᶜhéi ₫tsing-₫shan, ch'ŭt, tsun² héi²-lik₂, kung² ᶜk'öü taí² chín². ₫Ni ₫eh'ŏng ᶜfú chín² tsuk, ᶜyaŭ pún² yat₂, ₫Kéi-tŭk,-₫t'ò-ke² héi²-lik₂, ₫cháng ₫ti ₫tò ᶜmò saí² lok𝒐; ₫yan-waí² shaŭ² ₫shöng, tò² ₫ni ko² ₫shí-haŭ², tsz²-₫yín ᶜyün-yök₂ lok𝒐. Á²-₫po-₫lun ch'an² ₫ni ko² shaí²-tsz, tsan²ᶜshöng-₫ts'ín ᶜlám chü² ᶜk'öü, ᶜung ᶜk'öü lok₂ téí²; ko² ᶜshí ₫Kéi-tŭk,-₫t'ò pat,-kok𝒐 tít𝒐-₫hiú ᶜpá kím².

Á²-₫po-₫lun wä²:—'₫Yü-₫kam ᶜnéi ₫t'íú meng²* chung² ₫m ᶜsz tsoí² ᶜngo ᶜshaŭ?' Tsan² tsun² lik₂ át𝒐-chü² ᶜk'öü, ₫Kéi-tŭk,-₫t'ò ᶜkòm tsan² ₫m mong² tak, ₫sháng lok𝒐. ᶜShöü-₫chí ᶜk'öü tak, Shöng²-taí² ₫yan-ᶜtíu, shik,-chik₂, Á²-₫po-₫lun taí² ᶜhéi chek𝒐 ᶜshaŭ, ᶜsöng ᶜtá ᶜsz ᶜk'öü, ₫Kéi-tŭk,-₫t'ò ₫shan ᶜshaŭ yat, ᶜmo, ᶜmo chök𝒐 tsz²-₫kéi ᶜpá kím², tsan² kat, Á²-₫po-₫lun, ᶜk'öü taí² ₫sheng† wä²:— '₫Ch'an-tïk₂, ᶜnéi ᶜmaí kòm² ᶜfún-ᶜhéi,

of-rain one same; Christian although exerting (his) strength to-ward-off, but hands, feet, head, face even have receive wounds, 32. Therefore lightly retire back; Apollyon still-more advanced. Christian again roused-up (his) energy, (and) exerted all (his) vigour together-with him (had) a-great battle. This [C.] bitter fight fully had half a-day, Christian's vigour wanted-but a-little-of even (being) none at-all, 32; because (he) had-received wounds arrived-at this [C.] time, consequently weak, 32. Apollyon availed (himself)-of this [C.] opportunity, then (stepped) up-for-ward, (and) putting-his-arms-round him, pushed him down-to the-ground; at-that time Christian inadvertently let-fall [C.] sword.

Apollyon said:—'Now your [C.] life still not die in my hands?' Then (he) expended-all (his) strength (and) pressed him, Christian (being) so then not hope to-be-able to-live, 32. Nevertheless he obtaining God's favour, just-then Apollyon lifted up [C.] hand, wishing to-strike to-death him, Christian stretched-out (his) hand with-one feel, by-feeling got-hold-of his-own [C.] sword, then stabbed Apollyon, he great sound said:—

thrust, which made him give back, as one that had received his mortal wound. Christian perceiving that, made at him again, saying :—'Nay, in all these things we are more than conquerors through Him that loved us.' And with that Apollyon spread forth his dragon's wings, and sped him away, that Christian for a season saw him no more.—'*Pilgrim's Progress*.'

我雖跌倒重可以起
得身嘅。亞波淪撒開
手，好似受重傷嘅。基
督徒趁呢個勢子，再
上前迫佢，話，托賴愛
我嘅主，令我打贏呀。
亞波淪就展開對翼，
急急飛去。

LESSON, XXVIII.

But there were three of those that came from the land of Doubting, who after they had wandered and ranged the country awhile, and perceived that they had escaped, were so hardy as to thrust themselves, knowing that yet there were in the town some who took part with Diabolus—I say, they were so hardy as to thrust themselves into Mansoul. (Three, did I say ? I think there were four). Now to whose house shonld these Doubters go, but to the house of an old Diabolonian in Mansoul, whose name was Evil-Questioning; a very great enemy he was to Mansoul, and a great doer among Diabolonians there. Well, to this Evil-

過曉幾個月，魔王有四
個至大膽嘅疑兵，靜
中揾倒機會入人靈
城，一直嚟到邪辨嘅屋
跡，因邪辨係魔王嘅
老僕役，大有威勢嘅。
邪辨當時出去迎接
佢哋，而且供應添，住
下冇耐，邪辨就問佢埋
四人話，你哋係同唔
一個城地方嚟嘅係
係呢。四人答話，唔係
呀，同省嘅啫，有一個
話，我係思疑全能王
處嚟嘅，又一個話，我

ᶜngo ˌsöü tít₀-ᶜtò, chung² ᶜho-ᶜyí ᶜhéi-
tak,-ˌshan-ke². Á²-ˌpo-ˌlun sá²-ˌhoi
ᶜshan, ᶜhò ᶜt'sz shau² ᶜch'ung ˌshöng
ᶜkòm. ˌKéi-tuk,-ˌt'ò ch'an² ˌni ko²
shaí²-ᶜtsz, tsoí² ᶜshöng-ˌts'ín ˌchöü
ᶜk'öü, wá² :—' T'ok₀-láí² oí² ᶜngo-ke²
ᶜChü ling² ᶜngo ᶜtá-ˌyengᵀ á². Á²-
ˌpo-ˌlun tsau² ᶜchín ˌhoi töü² yik₂,
kap,-kap, ˌféí höü².

'Enemy, you don't-be so pleased, I
although fall, still may rise.' Apollyon threw-out (his) hands very like
(he) had-received serious wound so.
Christian embracing this [C.] opportunity, again advancing pursued him,
saying :—'Relying-upon loving me
Lord (who has) caused me to-get-the-
victory, 2.' Apollyon then spreading
open (his) pair-of wings, quickly flew
away.

LESSON, XXVIII.

Kwo² ˌhíú ᶜkéi ko² yüt₂, ˌMò-ᶜWong
ᶜyau sz' ko² chí-táí² ᶜtám ke² ˌYí-
ˌping, tsing² ˌchung ᶜwan-ᶜtò ˌkéi-
wúí² yap₂ ˌYan-ˌling-ˌsheng†, yat,
chik₂ ˌlaí-tò² ˌTs'e-pín² uk,-ᶜk'éi ;
ˌyan ˌTs'e-pín² haí² ˌMo-ᶜWong-ke²
ᶜlò puk₂-yik₂, táí² ᶜyau ˌwaí-shaí²-
ke². ˌTs'e-pín² ˌtong-ˌshi ch'ut, höü²
ˌying-tsíp₀ᶜk'öü-téí² ; ˌyí-ᶜch'e ˌkung-
ying² ˌt'ím. Chü²-ᶜhá ᶜmò ᶜnoí,*
ˌTs'e-pín² tsau² man² ᶜk'öü sz' ˌyan
wá²:—ᶜNéi-téí² haí² ˌt'ung-ˌmáí yat,
ko² ˌsheng† téí²-ˌfong ˌlaí-ke² ˌm
haí² ˌni ?' Sz' ˌyan táp₀ wá² :—' ˌM
haí² á², ˌt'ung ᶜsháng-ke² che,.'
ᶜYau yat, ko² wá² :—ᶜNgo haí²
ˌSz-ˌyí ˌTs'ün-ˌnang ˌWong shü² ˌlaí
ke',' Yau² yat, ko² wá² :—ᶜNgo

(After) passed (were) several [C.] months,
Devil-Prince had four [C.] greatest
courage Doubter-soldiers, secretly
found opportunity to-enter Mansoul
City, one straight came-to Evil-Questioning house ; because Evil-Questioning was Devil-Prince's old servant,
(he was) great (in) having authority
(or power). Evil-Questioning at-that
time out went to-greet them ; moreover succoured also. (They had)
lived (there) not long, (when) Evil-
Questioning then asked them (the)
four men, saying :—'You are with
together one [C.] city's place come
(or) not is, eh ? 53.' Four men answering, said :—'(We) not are 2, (we
are) same province only, 7.' There-

Questioning's house, as was said, did these Diabolonians come; (you may be sure that they had directions how to find the way thither); so he made them welcome, pitied their misfortune and succoured them with the best that he had in his house.—Now after a little acquaintance, (and it was not long before they had that), this old Evil-Questioning asked the Doubters if they were all of a town; he knew that they were all of one kingdom. And they answered, 'No, nor of one shire neither; for I,' said one, 'am an Election-doubter;' 'I' said another, 'am a Vocation-doubter;' then said the third, 'I am a Salvation-doubter;' and the fourth said he was a Grace-doubter.—'Well,' quoth the old gentlemen, 'be of what shire you will, I am persuaded that you are down, boys; you have the very length of my foot, are one with my heart, and shall be welcome to me.' So they thanked him, and were glad that they had found themselves an harbour in Mansoul. Then said Evil-Questioning to them:—'How many of your company might there be that came with you to the siege of Mansoul? And they answered:—'There were but ten thousand

係思疑救主處嘅、又一個話我係思疑得救處嘅、又一個話我係思疑賜恩處嘅。邪辨話、你哋所出嘅地方雖係有別、但頗共我同心、我真係歡喜你哋喺呢處住囉。個四人就感謝佢、話我哋十分歡喜喺呢個城咁好地方住呀。邪辨問話、先時有幾多人同你哋嚟打人靈城呢、答話、一萬思疑兵、一萬五千流血兵、但可惜個啲流血兵俱被以馬內利捉清咯。邪辨話、一萬疑兵係好多叮、點解你哋咁細膽唔敢前攻打仇敵呢、答話、因爲我哋大元帥至先逃走呀。邪辨問話、嗰個懦弱元帥係乜誰呢、答話、就係不信囉。佢從前做過人靈城府尹嘅、你唔好話

haí² ˏSz-ˏyi Kau²-ᶜChü shü² ˏlaí ke² ; '
yau² yat, ko² wá² :—' ᶜNgo haí² ˏSz-
ˏyí Tak,-kau² shü² ˏlaí ke² ; ' yau² yat,
ko² wá² :—' ᶜNgo haí² ˏSz-ˏyí Ts'z²-
ˏyan shü² ke².' ˏTs'e-pín² wá² :—
' ᶜNéí-téí² ᶜsho ch'ut, ke² téí²-ˏfong,
ˏsöü haí² ᶜyau pít, tán² ᶜp'o kung²
ᶜngo ˏt'ung ˏsam ; ᶜngo ˏchan haí²
ˏfún-ᶜheí ᶜnéí-téí² ᶜhaí ˏni shü² chü²
lo².' Ko² sz² ˏyan tsau² ᶜkòm-tse²
ᶜk'öü, wá² :—' ᶜNgo-téí² shap,-ˏfan
ˏfún-ᶜheí ᶜhaí ˏni ko² ˏshengt, kòm²
ᶜhò téí²-ˏfong chü² á².' ˏTs'e-pín²
man², wá² :—' ˏSín-ˏshi ᶜyau ᶜkéí ˏto
ˏyan ˏt'ung ᶜnéí-téí² ˏlaí ᶜtá Yau-
ˏling-ˏshengt ˏni ? ' Táp. wá² :—
' Yat, mán² ˏSz-ˏyí ˏping, yat, mán²
ᶜng ˏts'ín ˏLau-hüt. ˏping ; tán² ᶜho
sik, ko²-ˏti ˏLan-hüt. ˏping, ˏk'öü
péí² ˏYí-ᶜmá-noí²-léí² chuk. ˏts'íng
lok..' ˏTs'e-pín² wá² :—' Yat, mán²
ˏYí ˏping haí² ᶜhò to ˏá. ᶜTím ᶜkáí
ᶜnéí-téí² kòm² saí ᶜtám, ˏm ᶜkòm
ᶜshöng-ˏts'ín ˏkung-ᶜtá ˏch'au-tik,
ˏni ? ' Táp.-wá² :—' ˏYan-waí² ᶜngo-
téí² Táí²-ˏyün-shöü² chi² ˏsín ˏt'ò-ˏtsau
á².' ˏTs'e-pín² man², wá² :—' ᶜKo-
ko² no²-yök, ˏYün-shöü² haí² mat,-
ᶜshöü* ˏni ? ' Táp. wá² :—' Tsau²
haí² Pat,-sun² lo². ᶜK'öü ˏts'ung-
ˏts'ín tsò²-kwo² ˏYan-ˏling-ˏshengt
ᶜFú-ᶜwan-ke². ᶜNéí ˏm ᶜhò wá²

was one [C.] said :—' I am (a) Doubter
(of the) Almighty Prince place come ; '
again one [C.] said :—' I am Doubter
(of) Saviour place come ; ' again one
[C.] said :—' I am Doubter (of)
Salvation place come ; ' again one
[C.] said :—' I am Doubter (of)
Giving Grace place come.' Evil-
Questioning said :—' You what out-
come place, although there-is having
difference, but considerable together-
with me united heart. I really am
delighted (for) you (to be) at
this place to-live, 31. Those four
men then thanked him, saying :—
' We (are) ten parts pleased in this
[C.] city, such (a) good place
to-live, 2.' Evil-Questioning asked,
saying :—' Formerly were how many
men with you came to-assault Mansoul City, eh ? 53.' (They) answering, said :—' One myriad Doubter-
soldiers, one myriad five thousand
Flow-Blood soldiers ; but alas those
Flow-Blood soldiers all by Emmanuel
were-taken completely, 32.' Evil-
Questioning, said :—' Ten-thousand
Doubter-soldiers are very many, 1.
How (is it to be) explained you (had)
so small courage (and did) not dare
to-go-forward to-fight (your) enemies,
eh ? 53.' (They) anwering, said :—

Doubters in all, for the rest of the army consisted of fifteen thousand Bloodmen. These Bloodmen,' quoth they, 'border upon our country, but, poor men, as we hear, they were every one taken by Emmanuel's forces.' 'Ten thousand!' quoth the old gentlemen, 'I'll promise you that is a round company. But how came it to pass, since you were so mighty a number, that you fainted, and durst not fight your foes?' 'Our general,' said they, 'was the first man that did run for it.' 'Pray,' quoth their landlord, 'who was that your cowardly general?' 'He was once the Lord-Mayor of Mansoul,' said they. 'But pray call him not a cowardly general, for whether any from the east to the west had done more service for our Prince Diabolus, than has my Lord Incredulity, will be a hard question for you to answer. But had they catched him, they would for certain have hanged him, and we promise you hanging is but a bad business.'

佢懦弱呀，因爲自東至西，自南至北，都冇一個人學得翻佢咁忠心順服魔王嚹，倘若佢被以馬內利捉住，是必吊死佢咯，噉樣走生重好過被吊死哩。

ˤk'öü no²-yök͵ á'; ͵yan-waí² tsz²
͵tung chí' ͵saí, tsz² ͵nám chí' pak͵,
͵tò ˤmò yat͵ ko' ͵yan hok͵ tak͵ ͵fán
ˤk'öü kòm' ͵chung-͵sam shun²-fuk͵
Mò-͵Wong ká'. ͨT'ong-yök͵ ˤk'öü
péí² ˤYí-ˤmá-noí²-léí² chuk͵-chü²,
shí²-pít͵ tíú' ˤsz ˤk'öü lok͵ ˤkòm
ͨyöng* ͨtsau-͵sháng chung² ˤhò kwo'
péí² tíú' ˤsz ͵le.'

'Because our generalissimo at-the-
very first ran away, 2.' Evil-Questioning asked, saying :—'That [C.]
cowardly general was who, eh ? 53.'
(They) answering, said :—'(It) just
was Unbelief, 31. He formerly was
[NOTE.—The meaning of this 做
tsò² might perhaps be better rendered
by "acted as," but without any sense
of an acting appointment in it].
Mansoul's Civil-Governor.' [NOTE.—
Williams in his Tonic Dictionary
gives this term 府尹 ͨfú-ˤwan as
Mayor of Peking, but as is well
known there is no such office as
that corresponding to Mayor amongst
Western people : this rendering in
Williams is therefore only a adap-
tive one. Mayers gives it in his
"Chinese Government" in one case
as Governor of (the Imperial Pre-
fecture of) 順天府 *Shun²-͵t'in ͨfú*,
and in the other case where it
is used as "Civil Governor" in one
of the Manchurian provinces. It is
perhaps the best and only term which
could be used in this connection, and,
at all events, conveys the idea of
Mayor as well as such an idea can be
conveyed to a Chinese mind, ignorant
of Western ideas]. You (must) not
(*i.e.* not good) say he (was) weak, 2 ;

Then said the old gentleman :—'I wonld that all the ten thousand Doubters were now well armed in Mansoul, and myself at the head of them, I would see what I could do.' 'Ay,' said they, 'that would be well if we could see that; but wishes, alas! what are they?' And these words were spoken aloud. 'Well,' said old Evil-Questioning, 'take heed that you talk not too loud, you must be squat and close, and must take care of yourselves while you are here, or I'll assure you, you will be snapped.' 'Why?' quoth the Doubters. 'Why?' quoth the old gentlemen! 'Why, because both the Prince and Lord Secretary, and their captains and soldiers, are all at present in town; yea, the town is as full of them as ever it can hold. And besides, there is one whose name is Willbewill, a most cruel enemy of ours, and him the Prince has

邪辨話、我若統帶個一必佢好係句辨喇呦內軍呀。萬疑兵、我絕滅羅。答話、佢就想到呢聲、邪辨講喇、被我若係重喺處空講大聲、咪咁大聲講喇、呦喇、但你如今呢講聲、恐怕有人知到、你呦就唔得嘅嗎、個時有人捉你呦呀。答話、因乜緣故呢、邪辨話、你呦唔知咩。因爲以馬內利嘅保惠師、共總兵士、都住滿城裏呀。更有一個人、名叫主大意嘅、佢係我呦至對頭、以馬內利命佢把守城門、又吩咐佢

because from east to west, from south to north, also not one [*C.*] man imitate able again him so honestly submissive-to Devil-Prince, 14. If he by Emmanuel caught certainly hanged to-death, 32. So fashion (he) ran-for-his-life still better than by hanging to-death, 24.'

Evil-Questioning said :—' I, if command-lead that one myriad Doubter-soldiers, Mansoul certainly by me utterly-destroyed (*or* exterminated), 31.' (They) answering said :—'They if were still at (this) place good, 21 ; but you now emply wish (*i.e.* a fruitless wish) it-is having what profit, eh ? 53.' (They) speaking (when it) arrived (at) this sentence of words was (with a) very loud sound. Evil-Questioning, said :—' Hullo ! Don't (with) so loud (a) sound speak, 21, fear afraid have man know you at this place, you then not be-able to-be-straight (*i.e.* it will be bad for yon), 22 ; at-that time have man come catch you, 2.' (They) answering, said :—' On-account-of what reason, eh ? 53.' Evil-Questioning said :—' You not know, eh ? 53. Because Emmanuel's (the) Comforter, together-with captains (and) soldiers even live (so as to make) full (the) city inside, 2.

ₛTs'e-pín² wá² :—' ᶜNgo yök₂ ᶜt'ung-táí² ᶜko yat₂ mán² ₛYí-ₛping, ₛYan-ₛJing-ₛsheng† shi²-pít₂ péí² ᶜngo mít₂-tsüt₂ lo².' Táp₀ wá² :—' ᶜK'öü-téí² yök₂ haí² chung² ᶜhaí shü tsau² ᶜbò ₗlá ; tán² ᶜnéí ₗyü-ₗkam ₗhung ᶜsöng, haí² ᶜyau mat₂ yik₂ ₀ni ?' ᶜKong tò² ₗni köü² shüt₀-wá² haí² ᶜhò táí² ₛshengt. ₛTs'e-pín² wá² :—' ₗWaí, ᶜmaí kòm² táí² ₛshengt ᶜkong ₗlá, ᶜhung p'á² ᶜyau ₗyan ₗchí-tò² ᶜnéí-téí² ᶜhaí ₗni shü², ᶜnéí-téí² tsau² ₗm̄ tak₂ tím² ke² lá ; ko² ₗshí ᶜyau ₗyan ₗlaí chuk₀ ᶜnéí-téí² á².' Táp₀ wá² :— ' ₗYan mat₂ ₗyün-kwú² ₀ni ?' ₗTs'e-pín² wá² :—' ᶜNéí-téí² ₗm ₗchí ₗme ? ₗYan-waí² ᶜYí-ᶜmá-noí²-léí² ke² ᶜPò-waí²-₋sz, kung² ᶜtsung-ₗkwan ₗping-sz², ₗtò chü² ᶜmún ₗshengt ᶜlöü á². Kang² ᶜyan yat₂ ko² ₗyan, ᵀmeng*† kiú² ᶜChü-yi ke², ᶜk'öü haí² ᶜngo-téí² chí-táí² töü²-ₗt'au. ᶜYí-ᶜmá-noí²-léí² ming² ᶜk'öü ᶜpá-ᶜshau ₛshengt ₗmún ; yau² ₗfan-fú² ᶜk'öü

made Keeper of the Gates, and has commanded him, that with all the Diligence he can, he should look for, search out, and destroy all, and all manner of Diabolonians. And if he lighted upon you, down you go, though your heads were made of gold.' And now to see how it happened; one of the Lord Willbe-will's faithful soldiers, whose name was Mr. Diligence, stood all this while listening under old Evil-Ques-tioning's eaves, and heard all the talk that had been betwixt him and the Doubters that he entertained under his roof.

The soldier was a man that my Lord had much confidence in, and that he loved dearly, and that both because he was a man of courage, and also a man that was unwearied in seeking after Diabolonians to apprehend them. Now this man, as I told you, heard all the talk that was between old Evil-Questioning and these Diabo-lonians; wherefore what does he but goes to his Lord, and tells him what he had heard.—'And sayest thou so, my trusty?' quoth my Lord. 'Ay,' quoth Diligence, 'that I do, and if your Lordship will be pleased to go with me, you shall find it as I have

盡力搜尋我哋勤滅，倘被佢捉住你哋，任你頭殼好似金咁堅固，佢都要斬嚹。

講緊說話之時，主意有個忠心差役，名叫殷勤，啱啱喺門前經過，側耳聽喥佢哋所講，呢個殷勤爲人極好膽量，主意十分重用佢，常常命佢日夜盤查城中奸細。如今佢聽喥呢個惡人議論，佢即刻去報過主意知，主意答話，係真嘅咩，殷勤話，真係嘅呀，你若同我去，就必見

tsun² lik₂ ʿsau-₍ts'am ʿngo-téí² ʿtsíú-
mít₂. ʿT'ong péí² ʿk'öü chuk₀-chü²
ʿnéí-téí², yam² ʿnéí ₍t'au-hok₀ ʿhò
ʿt'sz ₍kam kòm⁾ ₍kín-kwú⁾, ʿk'öü ₍tò
yíú⁾ ʿchám ká⁾.'

Besides have one [*C.*] man, name
called Will-be-will, he is our greatest
enemy. Emmanuel command him
guard city gates; again direct him
exert strength, search-for us (and)
exterminate (us). If by him caught
you, let your head very like gold so
strong, he also want chop, 14.'

ʿKong-ʿkan shüt₀-wá² ₍chí ₍shí, ʿChü-
yí⁾ ʿyau ko⁾ ₍chung-₍sam ₍ch'áí-yik₂,
ʿmeng*† kiü⁾ ₍Yan-₍k'an, ₍ngám-
₍ngám ʿhaí ₍mún ₍ts'ín ₍king-kwo⁾,
chak₂ ʿyí ₍t'eng† saí⁾ ʿk'öü-téí² ʿsho
ʿkong. ₍Ni ko⁾ ₍Yan-₍k'an waí² ₍yan
kik₂ ʿhò ʿtám-löng², ʿChü-yí⁾ shap₂-
₍fan chung²-yung² ʿk'öü, shöng²-
ʿshöng* míng² ʿk'öü yat₂ ye² ₍p'ún-
₍ch'á ₍sheng† ₍chung ₍kán-saí⁾. ₍Yü-
₍kam ʿk'öü ₍t'eng† saí⁾ ₍ni ko⁾ ok₀
₍yan ʿyí-lun²; ʿk'öü tsik₂-hak₂ höü⁾
pò⁾ kwo⁾ ʿChü-yí⁾ ₍chí. ʿChü-yí⁾ táp₀
wá² :—'Haí² ₍chan ke⁾ ₍me?' ₍Yan-
₍k'an wá² :—'Chan⁾ haí² ke⁾ á⁾. ʿNéí
yök₂ ₍t'ung† ʿngo höü⁾, tsau² pít₂ kín⁾

Speaking words' time Will-be-will have
[*C.*] faithful lictor, name called Diligence, just-exactly at door before pass,
inclined (his) ear, heard all they what
talk. This [*C.*] Diligence as (a) man
(was of) very good courage, Will-be-
will fully reposed-confidence (in) him,
constantly commanded him day (and)
night investigate city interior bad-
charaters. Now he head all this
[*C.*] wicked man deliberate; he immediately went reported to Will-be-
will to-know. Will-be-will answering,
said :—'Is true, eh? 39.' Diligence
said :—'True is, 2. You if with me
go, then must see them, 32.' Will-

said.' 'And are they there?' quoth my Lord: 'I know Evil-Questioning well, for he and I were great in the time of our apostacy. But I know not now where he dwells.'—'But I do,' said this man; and if your Lordship will go, I will lead you the way to his den.' 'Go,' quoth my Lord, 'that I will. Come, my Diligence, let us go find them out.'—So my Lord and his man went together the direct way to his house. Now his man went before to show him his way, and they went till they came even under old Mr. Evil-Questioning's wall. Then said Diligence:—'Hark! my Lord, do you know the old gentlemen's tongue when you hear it?' 'Yes' said my Lord, 'I know it well, but I have not seen him many a day. This I know, he is cunning; I wish he doth not give us the slip.' 'Let me alone for that,' said his servant, Diligence.—'But how shall we find the door?' quoth my Lord. 'Let me alone for that too,' said his man. So he had my Lord Willbewill about, and showed him the way to the door. Then my Lord, without more ado, broke open the door, rushed into the house, and caught them all five

佢呲咯。主意話，呢個邪辨重喺處咩，從前我共佢做過朋友，但如今一向唔知佢落在何方囉。殷勤話，我知得佢腳跡叮，等我帶你去喇。兩人於是嚟到邪辨嘅屋，企在門外，靜靜聽佢裏面講話。殷勤話，邪辨嘅聲音，你認得出唔呢。主意話，認得咯，獨係唔見佢幾年啫。佢說話極之狡猾嘅，你要小心至好，怕佢嚟逃避呀。殷勤話，唔使憂處，我是必小心，兩人即時撞破邪辨嘅門，入去捉住佢五個人，拉佢困入監，變過誠人看守。到第朝，主意所做，聞知主意所做，就好歡喜，唔係有捉倒疑兵，捉倒邪辨喜，實因捉倒邪辨，因爲呢個邪辨攪擾人靈城百姓，係好多次陷害明哲之事，因爲大歡呀，常時百姓亦明哲

ᶜk‘öü-téi² lok₀.’ ‘Chü-yí’ wá² :—‚Ni
ko’ ‚Ts‘e-pín² chung² ᶜhai shü’ ‚me ?
‚Ts‘ung-‚ts‘ín ᶜngo kung² ᶜk‘öü tsò²-
kwo’ ‚p‘ang-ᶜyau ; tán’ ‚yü-‚kam yat‚-
höng’ ‚m ‚chí ᶜk‘öü lok‚ tsoí² ‚ho
‚fong lo’.’ ‚Yan-‚k‘an wá² :—‘ ᶜNgo
‚chí-tak‚ ᶜk‘öü kök₀-tsik‚ ‚á ; ᶜtang
ᶜngo táí’ ᶜnéí höü’ ‚lá.’ ᶜLöng ‚yan
‚yü-‚shí ‚laí tò’ ‚Ts‘e-pín² ke’ uk‚, ᶜk‘éí
tsoí² ‚mún ngoí², tsing²-ᶜtsing* ‚t‘eng†
ᶜk‘öü ᶜlöü-mín² ᶜkong-wá². ‚Yan-
‚k‘an wá² :—‘ ᶜTs‘e-pín²-ke’ ‚sheng†-
‚yam, ᶜnéí yíng² tak‚ ch‘ut‚ ‚m ₀ni ?’
ᶜChü-yí’ wá² :—ᶜYíng²-tak‚ lok₀, tuk‚
haí² ‚m kín’ ᶜk‘öü ᶜkéí ‚nín che‚.
ᶜK‘öü shüt₀-wá² kik‚ ‚chí ᶜkáu-wát‚
ke’ ; ᶜnéí yíú’ ᶜsíú-‚sam chí’ ᶜhò, p‘á’
ᶜk‘öü ᶜwúí ‚t‘ò-péí² á’.’ ‚Yan-‚k‘an
wá² :—‘ ‚M ᶜshaí ‚yau-löü², ᶜngo shí²-
pít‚ ᶜsíú-‚sam.’ ᶜLöng ‚yan tsik‚-‚shí
chong² p‘o’ ‚Ts‘e-pín² ke’ ‚mún, yap‚
höü’, chuk₀-chü² ᶜk‘öü ᶜng ko’ ‚yan,
‚láí ᶜk‘öü k‘wan’ yap‚ ‚kám‚ ‚káu kwo’
‚sheng†‚yan hon-ᶜshau. Tò’ taí² ‚chíú,
‚Ming-chít₀ man² ‚chí ᶜChü-yí ᶜsho
tsò² ‚chí sz², tsau² ᶜhò ‚fún-ᶜhéí ; ‚m
haí² ‚yan-waí² chuk₀-ᶜtò ‚Yí-‚píng ᶜyau
kòm’ táí² ‚fún-ᶜhéí, shat‚ ‚yan chuk₀-
ᶜtò ‚Ts‘e-pín² á’ ; ‚yan-waí² ‚ni ko’
‚Ts‘e-pín² shöng²-‚shí ᶜkáu-ᶜyíú ‚Yan-
‚ling-‚sheng† pák₀-sing’. Yík‚ haí²
ᶜhò ‚to t‘sz’ hám²-hoí’ ‚Ming-chít₀.

be-will, said :—‘This [C.] Evil-
Questioning still at place, eh? 39.
Formerly I with him was friend;
but now all-along not know he descend in what place, 31.’ Diligence
said :—‘I know his haunts (*lit.* foot-
prints), 1 ; wait I take you go, 21.’
Two men hereupon came to Evil-
Questioning’s house, standing at door
outside, quietly heard him inside, talking words. Diligence said :—‘Evil-
Questioning’s voice, you recognise
can out not, eh? 53.’ Will-be-will,
said :—‘Recognise can, 32, only it-is
not seen him several years only, 7.
His words extremely crafty ; you need
(to-be) careful in-order-to be-well (for)
fear he he-able to-escape, 2.’ Diligence
said :—‘(You) not need be-anxious,
I will-certainly (be) careful.’ Two
men immediately smashed (*i.e.* rushed
against and broke) open Evil-Questioning’s door, in went, caught them
five [C.] men, drew them (away) con-
fined within gaol, handed-over to city
men to-watch. Arrived next morning Understanding heard knew Will-
be-will what done matter, then very
pleased ; not is on-account-of catch-
ing Doubter-soldiers have so great
pleasure, really because caught Evil-
Questioning, 2 ; because this [C.]

together, even as Diligence, his man, had told him. So my Lord apprehended them, and led them away, and committed them to the hand of Mr. True-man, the gaoler, and commanded, and he did put them in ward. This done, my Lord Mayor was acquainted in the morning with what my Lord Willbewill had done over night, and his Lordship rejoiced much at the news, not only because there were Doubters apprehended, but because that old Evil-Questoning was taken; for he had been a very great trouble to Mansoul, and much affliction to my Lord Mayor himself. He had also been sought for often, but no hand could ˙ever be laid upon him till now.

主意共本城百姓,搵佢好耐,都唔搵得着,如今捉倒佢,眞係好彩咯。

Well, the next thing was to make preparation to try these five that by my Lord had been apprehended, and that were in the hands of Mr. True-man, the gaoler. So the day was set, and the Court called and come together, and being seated, the prisoners were brought to the bar.—My Lord Willbewill had power to have slain them when at first he took them, and that without any more ado, but he thought it at this

於是定曉一個日期,審判呢五個人。到期個日,城中長老嚟到按察司衙門聚集,誠人就拉五個犯人到公案,主意本來有權立時釘死佢五個人,但想警戒衆仇敵,俾佢知到驚慌。故此拉佢哋去審,紳衿長老,仍

ʽChü-yí⁚ kung⁚ ʽpún-ͺshengt pák₀-sing⁚ ʽwan ⁚kʽöü ʽhò noí⁚ ͺtò ͺm ʽwan tak⸴ chök₀ ; ͺyü-ͺkam chuk₀-ʽtò ⁚kʽöü ͺchan haí⁚ ʽhò ʽtsʽoí lok₀.

Evil-Questioning constantly embroiled this-city's people, also is very many times insnared Understanding. Will-be-will with (the) city people, search-for him very long also not find able completed; now caught him really is very fortunate, 32.

ͺYü-ͺshí ting⁚-ͺhiú yat⸴ ko⁚ yat₂-ͺkʽéí, ʽsham-pʽún⁚ ͺni ⁚ng ko⁚ ͺyan. Tò⁚ ͺkʽéí ko⁚ yat⸴, ͺshengt ͺchung ʽchöng-ⁱlò ͺlaí tò⁚ On⁚-chʽát₀-ͺsz ͺngá-ʽmún* tsöü⁚-tsáp⸴, Shengt-ͺyan tsau⁚ ͺlaí ⁚ng ko⁚ fán⁚-ͺyan tò⁚ ͺkung-on⁚. ʽChü-yí⁚ ⁚pún-ͺloí ⁚yau ͺkʽün láp⸴-ͺshí ͺtengt-⁚sz ⁚kʽöü ⁚ng ko⁚ ͺyan, tán⁚ ʽsöng ʽking-káí⁚ chung⁚ ͺchʽan-tik⸴, ʽpéí ⁚kʽöü ͺchí-tò⁚ ͺking-ͺfong ; kwú⁚-ʽtʽsz ͺlaí ⁚kʽöü-téí⁚ höü⁚ ʽsham. ͺShan-ͺkʽam ʽchöng-ⁱlò, ͺying-

Here-upon fixed one [C.] date to-try these five [C.] men. Arrived-at date that day city's midst elders came to Chief Justice's Court met, City men then pulled-in five [C.] prisoners (criminals) to Judge's-bench. Will-be-will really-and-truly had (the) power immediately nail to-death those five [C.] men, but wished to-warn all (the) enemies, let them know be-frightened; therefore brought them away to-trial. Gentry elders again

time more for the honour of the Prince, the comfort of Mansoul, and the discouragement of the enemy, to bring them forth to public judgment. But, I say, Mr. True-man brought them in chains to the bar, to the town-hall for that was the place of judgment. So to be short, the jury was panelled, the witnesses sworn, and prisoners tried for their lives; the jury was the same. * * *.

And first, old Questioning himself was set to the bar; for he was the receiver, the entertainer and comforter of these Doubters, that by nation were outlandish men; then he was bid to hearken to his charge, and was told that he had liberty to object, if he had ought to say for himself. So his indictment was read; the manner and form here follows:—
'Mr. Questioning, Thou art here indicted by the name of Evil-Questioning, an intruder upon the town of Mansoul, for that thou art a Diabolonian by nature, and also a hater of the Prince Emmanuel, and one that hast studied the ruin of the town of Mansoul. Thou art also here indicted for countenancing the King's enemies, after wholesome laws made to the contrary: For, (1), Thou hast

然揀從前個十二位
公義人做同審官。
＊＊＊

明哲就先叫邪辨開喺
審、因佢係做窩家、窩
藏個四個疑兵喺自
己屋、行正就問佢話、
邪辨呀、有人告你、話
你係魔王黨羽、極憎
惡以馬內利、常時喺
人靈城謀反、想傾覆
滿城百姓。又話你暗
中窩藏外來賊匪、即
係個四個疑兵、一則、
你平素思疑人靈城
真理、二則、你想接一
萬疑兵入城、你嘅樣
行爲、有罪有呢。

꜁yín ꜂kán ꜁ts'ung-꜁ts'ín ko꜄ shap꜇-yí꜅ ꜃wai* ꜀kung-yí꜅ ꜁yan tsò꜅ ꜁t'ung ꜂sham-꜀kwún. * * *.

selected formerly those twelve righteous men to be jurors. * * *.

꜁Ming-ch'ít˳ tsau꜅ ꜀sín kíú꜄ ꜁Ts'e-pín꜅ ꜀hoí ꜁laí ꜂sham; ꜀yan ꜃k'öü haí꜅ tsò꜅ ꜀wo-꜀ká, ꜀wo-꜁ts'ong ko꜄ sz꜄ ko꜄ ꜁Yí-꜀ping ꜂hai tsz꜅-꜂kéí uk꜆; ꜁Háng-ching꜄ tsau꜅ man꜅ ꜃k'öü, wá꜅ :—꜁Ts'e-pín꜅ á꜄, ꜃yau ꜁yan kò꜄ ꜃néí, wá꜅ ꜃néí haí꜅ ꜀Mo-꜁Wong ꜂tong-꜃yü, kik꜆ ꜀tsang-wú꜄ ꜃Yí-꜃má-noí꜅-léí꜅, shöng꜅-꜁shí ꜂haí ꜁Yan-꜁ling-꜁sheng† ꜁mau-꜂fán, ꜂söng ꜀k'ing-fuk꜆ ꜃mún ꜁sheng† pák˳-sing꜄. Yau꜅ wá꜅ ꜃néí òm꜄ ꜀chung ꜀wo-꜁ts'ong ngoí꜅ ꜁loí ts'ák˳-꜀féí, tsik꜆ haí꜅ ko꜄ sz꜄ ko꜄ ꜁Yí-꜀ping: yat꜆ tsak꜆, ꜃néí ꜁p'ing-sò꜄ ꜀sz-꜁yí ꜁Yan-꜁ling-꜁sheng† ꜀chan ꜃léí; yí꜅ tsak꜆, ꜃néí ꜂söng tsíp˳ yat꜆ mán꜅ ꜁Yí-꜀ping yap꜇ ꜁sheng†. ꜃Néí ꜂kòm ꜃yöng* ꜁háng-waí꜅ ꜃yau tsöü꜅ ꜃mò˳ ˳ni?'

Understanding just first called Evil-Questioning out in-order-to try; because he was being harbourer-of-bad-characters, and secreted those four [C.] Doubter-soldiers in his-own house; Do-right then asked him, saying:—'Evil-Questioning, 2, have man prosecute you, saying, you are Devil-Prince adherent, extremely hate Emmanuel, constantly in Mansoul plotting, wishing to-overthrow (the) whole city's people. Further say you dark midst harbour (from the) outside (those that) come (as) thieves, just is those four [C.] Doubter-soldiers: in-the-first place, (you) formerly doubted Mansoul's true doctrine; in-the-second place, you wished to-receive a myriad Doubter-soldiers into (the) city. You so fashion conduct (yourself) have guilt not, eh? 53.'

questioned the truth of her doctrine and state; (2), In wishing that ten thousand Doubters were in her; 3. In receiving, in entertaining, and encourging of her enemies, that came from their army unto thee. What sayest thou to this indictment; art thou guilty, or not guilty?'

'My Lord,' quoth he, 'I know not the meaning of this indictment, forasmuch as I am not the man concerned in it; the man that standeth by this charge, accused before this bench, is called by the man of Evil-Questioning, which name I deny to be mine, mine being Honest-Inquiring. The one indeed sounds like the other; but I trow your Lordship knows, that between these two there is a wide difference; for I hope that a man, even in the worst of times, and that too amongst the worst of men, may make an honest inquiry after things without running the danger of death.'

邪辨答話、我唔明白你講乜野、你問乜誰呢、我名唔係叫邪辨、係叫明察啫、意思大不相同哩、但凡審事要眞實至好、切勿糊塗亂做嚟、想歸眞嘅人、要被拉去受死咩。

Then spake my Lord Willbewill, for he was one of the witness:—'My Lord, and you the honourable bench, and magistrates of the town of Mansoul, you all have heard with your ears, that the prisoner at the bar has denied his name; and so

主意就對明哲共十二位公義人話、你哋聽聞呢個惡人自己改名哩、話呢件案唔關佢事啝、但我已經識佢三十年咁耐、知實

‿Ts‘e-pín² táp。 wá² :—‘Ngo ‿m ‿ming-
pák。 ⸢néí ⸢kong mat, ⸢ye. ⸢Néí
man² mat, ⸢shöü* 。ni ? ⸢Ngo ⸢meng*†
‿m haí² kiú⸲ ‿Ts‘e-pín², haí² kiú⸲
‿Ming-ch‘át。 che,. Yí⸲-sz⸲ táí² pat,
‿söng‿-t‘ung ‿le. Táu²-‿fán ⸢sham-sz²
⸢yíú ‿chan shat, chí⸲ ⸢hò, ts‘ít。 mat,
‿wú-‿t‘ò ⸢lün* tsò² ká⸲. ⸢Söng ‿kwaí
‿chan ke⸲ ‿yan, yíú⸲ péí² ‿láí höü⸲
shau² ⸢sz ‿me ? ’

Evil-Questioning answering, said :—‘ I
not understand you speak what thing.
You asking what person, eh ? 53.
My name not is called Evil-Questioning, is called Honest-Inquiring
only, 7. Meaning great not agree,
24. Whosoever tries-matters must-
truly really (try) in-order-to-be good,
urgently not muddled confused do,
14. (He who) wishes to-be (a) true
man, must be dragged away receive
death, eh ? 39.’

⸢Chü-yí⸲ tsau² töü⸲ ‿Ming-ch‘ít。 kung²
shap,-yí⸲ ⸢waí* ‿kung-yí²-‿yan, wá²:—
⸢Néí-téí² ‿t‘eng†-man² ni ko⸲ ok。
‿yan tsz²-⸢kéí ⸢koí ⸢meng* ‿le, wá²,
‿ni kín⸲ on⸲ ‿m kwán ⸢k‘öü sz² wo⸲ ;
tán² ⸢ngo ⸢yí-‿king shik, ⸢k‘öü ‿sám-
shap, ‿nín kòm⸲ noí² ; ‿chí shat,

Will-be-will then to Understanding together-with the twelve [C.] jurors
said :—‘ You hear this [C.] wicked
man himself alters name, 24, saying,
this [C.] case not concern his business
so-he-says, 64 ; but I already known
him thirty years so long, know cer-

thinks to shift from the charge of the indictment. But I know him to be the man concerned, and that his proper name is Evil-Questioning. I have known him, my Lord, above this thirty years; for he and I (a shame it is for me to speak it) were great acquaintance, when Diabolus, that tyrant, had the government of Mansoul; and I testify that he is a Diabolonian by nature, an enemy to our Prince, and hater of the blessed town of Mansoul. He has in times of rebellion, been at and lain in my house, my Lord, not so little as twenty nights together; and we did use to talk then (for the substance of talk) as he, and his Doubters have talked of late; true, I have not seen him many a day. I suppose that the coming of Emmanuel to Mansoul, has made him to change his lodgings as this indictment has driven him to change his name; but this is the man, my Lord.'

Then said the Court unto him :—'Hast thou any more to say?'

'Yes,' quoth the old gentlemen, 'that I have; for all that as yet has been said against me, is but by the mouth

佢名叫邪辨。從前魔王據佔城裏之時，我同佢相交極厚，佢性情至憎惡以馬內利，共人靈城百姓，極之熱心順服魔王。舊時佢不歇探望我，如今我好耐唔見佢面咯，因以馬內利入城個時，佢改名搬去別處呀。

行正就對邪辨話，你重有乜野說話講呢。

邪辨答話，有呀，人嘅懍告訟我，係至唔公道

ᶜk'öü ᶜmeng* kíú⟩ ꞓTs'e-pín². ꞓTs'ung-
ꞓts'ín ꞓMo-ꞓwong köü⟩-chím⟩ ꞓsheng†
ᶜlöü ꞓchí ꞓshí, ꞓngo ꞓt'ung ᶜk'öü
ꞓsöng-ꞓkáu kik₂ ᶜhau. ᶜK'öü sing⟩-
ꞓts'ing chí⟩ ꞓtsang-wú⟩ ᶜYí-ᶜmá-noí²-
léi², kung² ꞓYan-ꞓling-ꞓsheng† pák₀-
sing⟩, kik₂ ꞓchí yít₂ ꞓsam shun²-fuk₂
ꞓMo-ꞓWong. Kau²-ꞓshí ᶜk'öü pat₂-
hít₀ t'ám⟩-mong² ᶜngo ; ꞓyü-ꞓkam
ᶜngo ᶜhò noí² ꞓm kíú⟩ ᶜk'öü mín²
lok₀ ; ꞓyan ᶜYí-ᶜmá-noí²-léi² yap₂
ꞓsheng† ko⟩ ꞓshí, ᶜk'öü ᶜkoí ᶜmeng*
ꞓpún höü⟩ pít₀ shü⟩ á⟩.

tainly his name called Evil-Questioning. Formerly Devil-Prince took-possession of-City interior's time, I with him mutually kept company-with extremely thick. His disposition most hate Emmanuel together-with Mansoul's people, extremely ardent heart submissive-to Devil-Prine. Old-time he unceasingly visited-and-saw me ; now I very long not see his face, 32 ; because Emmanuel entered city that time, he altered (his) name, moved away-to another place, 2.

ꞓHáng†-ching⟩ tsán² töü⟩ ꞓTs'e-pín²
wá² :—'ᶜNéi chung² ᶜyau mat₂ ᶜye
shüt₀-wá² ᶜkong ₀ni ? '
ꞓTs'e-pín² táp₀, wá² :—' ᶜYau á⟩.
ꞓYan ᶜkòm ᶜyöng* ko⟩-tsung²
ᶜngo, haí² chí⟩ ꞓm ꞓkung-tò²

Do-right then to Evil-Questioning said :—'You still have what thing words speak, eh ? 53.'

Evil-Questioning answering, said :—'Have 2. People so fashion prosecute me is most not just : only is

of one witness, and it is not lawful for the famous town of Mansoul, at the mouth of one witness, to put any man to death.'

Then stood forth Mr. Diligence, and said:—'My Lord, as I was upon my watch such a night at the head of Bad Street in this town, I chanced to hear a muttering within this gentlemen's house; then thought I what is to do here? So I went up close, but very softly, to the side of the house to listen, thinking, as indeed it fell out, that there I might light upon some Diabolonian conventicle. So, as I said, I drew nearer and nearer; and when I was got up close to the wall, it was but a while before I perceived that there were outlandish men in the house; but I did well understand their speech, for I have been a traveller myself. Now hearing such language, in such a tottering cottage as this old gentlemen dwelt in, I clapt mine ear to a hole in the window, and there heard them talk as followeth:—This old Mr. Questioning asked these Doubters what they were, whence they came, and what was their business in these parts? And they told him to all these questions, yet he did

嘅、獨係一個人做証、你就想殺我囉咩。

殷勤起身話、我都係做証人呀、於是對明哲話、先幾晚我查街、行到穢市個處側邊嘅屋、我聽聞幾個外江佬、喺佢屋裏講話、我當時仆倒佢門辨嘅聽、但我聽聞佢說話、亦明白佢聲音。佢就問個四個人話、你咃係乜人、由邊處嚟嘅、想做乜野事、佢咃就逐一逐二把來歷講嗤過邪辨知。邪辨又問佢咃先時打仗、帶有幾多疑兵嚟、佢咃答話、一萬、嗷就大家同講打仗之事。邪辨就話、點解唔出力攻打人靈城呢、又怪責佢元帥不信懦弱、又話自己倘若統帶個萬疑兵、是必打

ke² : tuk⟨-haí² yat⟨ ko² ⟨yan tsò²
ching². ⁵Néí tsan² ⁵söng shát₀ ⁵ngo
lo² ⟨me ? ʼ

⟨Yan-⟨kʻan ⁵héí-⟨shan wá² :—ʻ ⁵Ngo ⟨tò
haí² tsò² ⁵néí ching²-⟨yan á². ⟨Yü-
⟨shí töü² ⟨Ming-chʻít₀ wá :—ʻ ⟨Sín ⁵kéí
⁵mán ⁵ngo ⟨chʻá ⟨káí ⟨háng tò²
Waí² ⁵Shí ko² shü² chak⟨-₀pín-ke²
uk⟩, ⁵ngo ⟨tʻengt-man² ⁵yau ⁵kéí ko²
ngoí²-⟨kong ⁵lò, ⁵haí ⁵kʻöü uk⟩ ⁵löü
⁵kong wá² ; ⁵ngo ⟨tong ⟨shi pʻuk⟩-tò²
⁵kʻöü ⟨mún lá². ⟨laí ⟨tʻengt. Tán²
⁵ngo ⟨tʻengt-man² ⁵kʻöü shüt₀-wá² ;
yik⟩ ⟨ming-pák₀ ⁵kʻöü ⟨shengt-⟨yam.
⁵Kʻöü tsau² man² ko² sz² ko² ⟨yan
wá² :—ʻ ⁵Néí-téí² haí² mat⟩ ⁵yan* ; ⟨yau
₀pín shü² ⟨laí ke² ; ⁵söng tsò² mat⟩
⁵ye sz² ? ⁵Kʻöü-téí² tsau² chuk⟩ yat⟩
chuk⟩ yi² ⁵pá ⟨loí-lik⟩ ⁵kong sáí²
kwo² ⟨Tsʻe-pín² ⟨chí. ⟨Tsʻe-pín² yau²
man² ⁵kʻöü-téí² : ʻ ⟨Sín-⟨shí ⁵tá-chöng²
táí² ⁵yau ⁵kéí ⟨to ⟨Yí-⟨ping ⟨laí ? ʼ
⁵Kʻöü-téí² táp₀ wá² :—ʻ Yat⟨ mán².ʼ
⁵Kòm tsau² táí²-⟨ká ⟨tʻung ⁵kong
⁵tá-chöng² ⟨chí sz². ⟨Tsʻe-pín² tsan²
wá² :—ʻ Tim ⁵káí ⟨m chʻut⟩ lik⟩
⟨kung-⁵tá ⟨Yan-⟨ling-⟨shengt ₀ni ? ʼ
Yau² kwáí²-chak⟩ ⁵kʻöü ⟨Yün-
shöü² Pat⟨-sun², no²-yök⟩, yau²
wá² tsz²-⁵kéí ⁵tʻong-yök⟩ ⁵tʻung-táí²
⁵ko mán² ⟨Yí-⟨ping shí²-pít⟩ ⁵tá

one [*C.*] man is witness. You just
wish kill me, 31, 39.ʼ

Diligence got-up, said :—ʻ I also am
being you (against) witness, 2.ʼ At-
that time to Understanding said :—
ʻ Before (this) several nights, I-search-
ed (the) streets, walked to the-Filth
Market, that place sideʼs house, I
heard have several [*C.*] from-another-
province fellows in his house inside
speaking words ; I at-the-time crouch
down his door crack in-order-to hear ;
but I hear their words also understood their speech. He then asked
those four [*C.*] men, saying :—ʻ You
are what men ; from what place
come, wish to do what thing matter ? ʼ
They then item by item took (their)
antecedents talk all to Evil-Questioning to-know. Evil-Questioning again
asked them :—ʻ Formerly fighting
lead have how many Doubter-soldiers
come ? ʼ They answering, said :—ʻ One
myriad.ʼ Then just the-whole (of
them) together talked fightingʼs matter. Evil-Questioning then said :—
ʻ How explain not exert strength
assault Mansoul, eh ? 53.ʼ Again
reprimanded their generalissimo, Unbelief, cowardly. Further say himself

entertain them. He also asked what numbers there were of them; and they told him ten thousand men. He then asked them why they made not more manly assault upon Mansoul; and they told him: so he called their general 'coward,' for marching off when he should have fought for his Prince. Further, this old Evil-Questioning wished, and I heard him wish, Would all the ten thousand Doubters were now in Mansoul, and himself at the head of them. He bid them also to take heed and lie quiet, for, if they were taken, they must die, although they had heads of gold.'

Then said the Court:—'Mr. Evil-Questioning, here is now another witness against you, and his testimony is full: (1) He swears that you did receive these men into your house, and that you did nourish them there, though you knew that they were Diabolonians, and the King's enemies. (2) He swears that you did wish ten thousand of them in Mansoul. (3) He swears that you did give them advice to be quiet and close, lest they were taken by the King's servants. All which manifesteth that thou art a Diabolonian; for hadst

勝人靈城、又禁止佢
哋、唔好講咁大聲、恐
被外人聽見、就嚟捉
我哋呀。

話、呢個人
你第一
個疑兵、但
個人係
嘅仇敵。第二你
萬疑兵管帶。
個四個
大聲、但
就係顯
魔王黨羽

行正對邪辨
如今証你
窩藏呢四
你亦知個四
本城嘅仇
想得一萬
第三你禁止
人講話、唔好
呢幾樣行為
明你係做
憑據嘅。

‸shing ‸Yan-‸ling-‸shengʈ; yan² kam²-
‵chí ‵k‘öü-téí², " ‸M ‵hò ‵kong kòm²
táí² ‸sheugʈ, ‵hung péí² ngoí² ‸yan
‸t‘engʈ-kín² tsau² ‸lai chuk₀ ‵ngo-
téí² á²." ·

supposing commanded-and-led that
myriad Doubter-soldiers certainly
conquer Mansoul City; further (he)
forbid them :—" Not good to-talk so
loud sound, for-fear by outside men
hearing then come catch us, 2." ·

‸Hángʈ-ching² töü² ‸Ts‘e-pín² wá² :—
· ‸Ni-ko² ‸yan ‸yü-‸kam ching² ‵néí,
wá² :—‵N‸i, táí²-yat₅, ‸wo-ts‘ong ‸ni
sz² ko² ‸Yi-‸ping, tán² ‵néí yik₅ ‸chí-
ko² sz² ko² ‸yan haí² ‵pún ‸shengʈ-
ke² ‸ch‘au-tik₅. Taí² yí², ‵néí ‵söng
tak₅ yat₅ mán² ‸Yi-‸ping ‵kwún-táí².
Taí² ‸sám, ‵néí kam²-‵chí ko² sz²
ko² ‸yan ‵kong wá², " ‸M ‵hò táí²
‸shengʈ ;" tán² ‸ni ‵kéí yöng² ‸hángʈ-
waí² : tsau² haí² ‵hín-‸ming ‵néí haí²
tsó² ‸Mo ‸Wong ‵tong-‵yü ‸p‘ang-
köü² lá².'

Do-right to Evil-Questioning, said :—
'This [C.] man now witness-against
you, saying :—You firstly, harbour
these four [C.] Doubter-soldiers,
but you also knew those four
[C.] men were this city's enemies.
Secondly, you wished to-get a myriad
Doubter-soldiers to lead. Thirdly,
you restrained those four [C.] men,
speaking words, " Not good loud
sound ;" but these several kiuds of
actions just does make-clear you
are being Devil-Prince partizan
evidence, 22.'

thou been a friend to the King, thou wouldest have apprehended them.'

Then said Evil-Questioning :—'To the first of these I answer, the men that came into mine house were strangers, and I took them in, and is it now become a crime in Mansoul for a man to entertain strangers? That I did also nourish them is also true, and why should my charity be blamed? As for the reason why I wished ten thousand of them in Mansoul, I never told it to the witnesses, nor to themselves. I might wish them to be taken, and so my wish might mean well to Mansoul, for aught that any yet knows. I did also bid them take heed that they fell not into the Captain's hands; but that might be because I am unwilling that any man should be slain, and not because I would have the King's enemies, as such, escape.'

My Lord Mayor then replied :—'That though it was a virtue to entertain strangers, yet it was treason to entertain the King's enemies. And for what else thou hast said, thou dost by words but labour to evade, and defer the execution of judgment. But could there be no more proved

邪辨答話、有遠客嘞到我家、我迎接佢住、嘅咩、嘅行爲、係着唔嘅咩、人你好做仁愛事緣故、唔唔知我因也係城又得一萬疑兵罰佢想或著我刑我叫裏者呢。就係主意咇唔定備、咪被忍見佢咇防實因不城裏捉倒死我想人受得唔躲仇敵係避得呀。

明哲對佢話、欵待遠客以係着嘅喇、但欵待反馬內利仇係謀羽所咯、你係敵王黨羽咯。何以你應魔受死疑越況你重該王藏兵、加要受窩該疑受死藏兵喇。死喇。

ₑTs'e-pín² táp₀ wá² :—'ᶜYau ᶜyün hák₀ ₑlaí tò' ᶜngo ₑká, ᶜngo ₑying-tsíp₀ ᶜk'öü chü², ᶜkòm ke' ₑháng-waí², haí² ₑm chök₀ ke' ₑme ? ₑYan ₑm ᶜhò tsò² ₑyan-oí' sz² ₑme ? ᶜNéí yan² ₑm ₑchí ᶜngo ₑyan mat₍ ₑyün-kwú' ᶜsöng tak₍ yat₍ mán² ₑYí-ₑping ᶜhaí ₑsheng† ᶜlöü. Wák₎-ᶜche ᶜngo ᶜsöng ₑying-fat₍ ᶜk'öü-téí² ₑm ₑting ₀ni. Tsau² haí² ᶜngo kiú' ᶜk'öü-téí² ₑfong-péí² ᶜmaí péí² ᶜChü-yí chuk₀-tò' ; shat₍ ₑyan ᶜngo pat₍ ᶜyan kín' ₑyan shau²-ᶜsz, ₑm haí² ᶜsöng ₑsheng†-ᶜlöü ₑch'au-tik₍ tak₍ ᶜto-péí² á'.

Evil-Questioning answering, said :—
'Have distant guests come to my family I received them to-dwell such conduct is not correct, eh ? 39. Men not better do benevolent matters, eh ? 39. You further not know I on-account-of what reason wished to-obtain one myriad Doubter-soldiers in city interior. Perhaps I wished to-punish them not certain, 53. Just is I told them to-be-on-their-guard not allow Will-be-will catch really ; because I cannot endure to-see people suffer death, not is wish city interior's enemies to-obtain to-escape, 2.

ₑMing-ch'it₀ töü' ᶜk'öü wá² :—' ᶜFún-toí² ᶜyün hák₀ haí² chök₀ ke' ₑlá ; tán² ᶜfún-toí² ᶜYí-ᶜmá-noí²-léí² ₑch'au-tik₍ haí² ₑmau-ᶜfán lok₀. ᶜNéí haí² ₑMo-ₑWong ᶜtong-ᶜyü, ᶜsho-ᶜyí ᶜnéí ₑying-ₑkoí shau²-ᶜsz lok₀ ; ₑho-fong' ᶜnéí chung² ₑwo-ₑts'ong ₑYí-ₑping, yüt₍ ₑká yíú' shau² ᶜsz ₑlá.'

Understanding to him said :—'To-entertain distant guests is right, 21 ; but to-entertain Emmanuel's enemies is rebellion, 32. You are Devil-Prince partizan, therefore you ought to-suffer death, 32 ; how-much-more (is this the case when) you besides harbour Doubter-soldiers, more add

against thee, but that thou art a Diabolonian, thou must for that die the death by the law; but to be a receiver, a nourisher, a countenancer, and a harbourer of others of them, yea, of outlandish Diabolonians; yea, of far, on purpose to cut off and destroy our Mansoul; this must not be borne.'

Then said Evil-Questioning :—'I see how the game will go; I must die for my name, and for my charity.'

And so he held his peace.

邪 辨 話、我 因 仁 愛 心 要
受 死、嗽 就 冇 法 囉。

行 正 叫 佢 企 開。

LESSON, XXIX.

Let us first take the doctrines of filial piety and fraternal affection, and discourse of them in the hearing of all you people. Well, what then is filial piety? It is great indeed! In heaven above, in earth below, and among men placed between, there is not one that excludes this doctrine. Well, how is this proved? Because filial piety is the breath of harmony. Observe the heavens and the earth! If they did not harmonize, how could they produce and nourish so great multitudes of creatures? If

先 撋 呢 個 孝 弟 嘅 道 理、
講 過 你 哋 衆 百 姓 聽、
點 樣 係 孝 呢、呢 個 孝
順 嘅 道 理、好 關 係、上
係 天、下 係 地、中 間 係
人、冇 一 個 離 得 呢 啲
理 嘅、做 乜 嗽 講 呢、因
爲 孝 順 係 一 團 嘅 和
氣、你 睇 天 地 若 係 唔
和、點 樣 生 養 得 咁 多
人 物 出 嚟 呢、人 若 係
唔 孝 順、就 失 嘵 天 地

(that it is necessary that you) must suffer death, 21.

꜀Ts'e-pín² wá² :—'꜀Ngo ꜀yan ꜀yan-oí꜒ ꜀sam yíú꜒ shau² ꜀sz, ꜀kòm tsau² ꜀mò fát꜀ lo꜒.'
꜀Háng†-ching꜒ kíú꜒ ꜀k'öü ꜀k'éí ꜀hoí.

Evil-Questioning, said :—'I on-account-of benevolent heart must suffer death so then no means (of-escaping), 39.' Do-right told him to-stand off.

LESSON, XXIX.

꜀Sín ꜀k'áí ꜀ní ko꜒ hán꜒ taí² ke꜒ tò²-꜀léí ꜀kong kwo꜒ ꜀néí-téí² chung꜒ pák꜀-sing꜒ ꜀t'eng†. ꜀Tím ꜀yöng* haí² hán꜒ ꜀ni? ꜀Ni ko꜒ háu꜒-shun²-ke꜒ tò²-꜀léí ꜀hò ꜀kwán-haí². Shöng² haí² ꜀t'ín, há² haí² téí², ꜀chung-꜀kan haí² ꜀yan, ꜀mò yat꜒ ko꜒ ꜀léí tak꜒ ꜀ni-꜀ti ꜀léí ke꜒. ꜀Tsò² mat꜒ ꜀kòm ꜀kong ꜀ni? ꜀Yan-꜀waí² háu꜒-shun² haí² yat꜒ ꜀t'ün-ke꜒ ꜀wo héí. ꜀Néí ꜀t'aí ꜀t'ín téí² yök꜒ haí² ꜀m ꜀wo, ꜀tím ꜀yöng* ꜀sháng ꜀yöng tak꜒ kòm꜒ ꜀to ꜀yan mat꜒ ch'ut꜒ ꜀laí ꜀ni? ꜀Yan yök꜒ haí² ꜀m háu꜒-shun², tsau² shat꜒-꜀híú ꜀t'ín téí²

First explain this [C.] Filial-piety's (and) Fraternal-affection's doctrine, tell to you all people to-hear. How fashion is Filial-piety, eh? 53. This [C.] Filial-piety's doctrine very important. Above is heaven, below is earth, middle is man, not one [C.] separate-can-from this doctrine. Do what so speak, eh? 53. Because Filial-piety is one whole harmonious breath. You see heaven earth, if is not harmonious, how fashion produce nourish able so many men things out come, eh? 53, [sháng-ch'ut-laí,

man do not practice filial piety, he loses [his resemblance to] the harmony of nature—how then can he be accounted man?

Let us now take the ardent affection of the heart, and the yearnings of the bowels of your parents towards you, and enlarge on them a little—When you hung in their tender embrace were you hungry? You, yourselves knew not to eat food;—Were you cold? You yourselves knew not to put on clothes. Your aged father and mother observed the features of your face, and listened to the sound of your voice. Did you smile? They were delighted. Did you weep? They when unhappy. Did you begin to walk? They followed at your heels, step by step. If you had the least degree of illness, then their sorrow was inexpressible. Tea was not tea; rice was not rice to them [That is they did not relish them: or know the taste.] They waited [with anxiety] till you recovered; then their minds were composed. Their eyes were intent on you, watching your growth from year to year. You have no conception of how many anxious toils they bore, and of how many painful apprehensions

嘅和氣咯、點重成個
人呢。

如今且將爹母愛痛你
哋嘅心腸講一講、你
哋在懷抱個時候、餓
呢、自己唔曉食飯、冷
呢、自己唔曉着衫、你
嘅老母、睇住你嘅面
貌、聽住你嘅聲音、你
笑呢、就歡喜、你喊呢、
就憂愁、你走動呢、就
步步跟住你、你若係
暑暑有啲病啫、就憂
愁到了不得、茶不成
茶、飯不成飯、等到你
身子好曉、嗷致安心
眼看、看一年、大一年、
不知受過多少辛苦、
受過多少驚慌、養你
教你、到你成人長大、
替你娶妻生子、望你
讀書成名、替你創家
立業、邊一件事、唔關
爹母嘅心、呢個恩典
係報得盡嘅咩、你若

ke^ɔ ₍wo heí^ɔ lok。—ᶜTím chung²
₍shengᵗ ko^ɔ ₍yan ₀ni?

₍Yü-₍kam ᶜch'e ₍tsöng fü²-ᶜmò oí^ɔ-
t'ung^ɔ ᶜnéí-téí² ke^ɔ ₍sam-₍ch'öng,
ᶜkong yat, ᶜkong. ᶜNéí-téí² tsoí²
₍wáí ᶜp'ò ko^ɔ ₍shí-₍hau, ngo² ₀ni,
tsz²-ᶜkéí ₍m ᶜwúí shik, fán². ᶜLang
₀ni, tsz²-ᶜkéí ₍m ᶜwúí chök。₍shám.
ᶜNéí-ke^ɔ ᶜlò-ᶜmò ᶜt'aí-chü² ᶜnéí-ke^ɔ
mín²-máu^ɔ, ₍t'engᵗ-chü² ᶜnéí-ke^ɔ
₍shengᵗ-₍yam. ᶜNéí síú^ɔ ₀ni, tsau²
₍fún-ᶜheí. ᶜNéí hám^ɔ ₀ni, tsau² ₍yau-
₍shau. ᶜNéí ᶜtsau-tung² ₀ni, tsau²
pò²-pò² ₍kan-chü² ᶜnéí. ᶜNéí yök,
haí² lök,-ᶜlök* ᶜyau ₍ti peng²ᵗ che,,
tsau² ₍yau-₍shau tò^ɔ ᶜlíú-pat,-tak,.
₍Ch'á pat, ₍shengᵗ ₍ch'á; fán² pat,
₍shengᵗ fán²: ᶜtang tò^ɔ ᶜnéí ₍shan-
tsz ᶜhò-₍híú, ᶜkòm chí^ɔ ₀on ₍sam.
ᶜNgán hon^ɔ, hon^ɔ yat, ₍nín, táí^ɔ
yat, ₍nín. Pat, ₍chí shau²-kwo^ɔ ₍to-
ᶜshíú ₍san-ᶜfú, shau²-kwo^ɔ ₍to ᶜshíú
₍king-₍fong. ᶜYöng ᶜnéí, káu^ɔ ᶜnéí
tò^ɔ ᶜnéí ₍shengᵗ ₍yan ᶜchöng táí², t'aí^ɔ
ᶜnéí ᶜts'öü (or ts'öü^ɔ) ᶜtsaí ₍sháng ᶜtsz.
Mong^ɔ ᶜnéí tuk, shü ₍shengᵗ meng²ᵗ.
T'aí^ɔ ᶜnéí ch'ong^ɔ ₍ká láp, yíp,. ₀Pín
yat, kín² sz² ₍m ₍kwán fú²-ᶜmò-
ke^ɔ ₍sam? ₀Ni (ko^ɔ) ₍yan-ᶜtín haí²
pò^ɔ tak, tsun² ke^ɔ ₍me? ᶜNéí yök,

to produce]. Man, if (it is that
he) is not Filial, then lost heaven
earth's harmonious breath, 32.—How
still become a [*C.*] man, eh? 53.

Now further take father's, mother's
ardent-love of you (with their) heart
(and) bowels (of affection), talk one
talk. You in bosom embraced, that
time hungry, 53, yourself not able
eat rice. Cold, 53, yourself not
able to-put-on clothes. Your mother
looked-at your countenance, heard
your voice. You smile, 53, then
happy. You cry, 53, then unhappy
You run move, 53, then step [by]
step follow you. You if it-is (that
you are) a-little having little illness
only, then unhappy till finish not
able [= exceedingly, very]. Tea
not become tea [to their taste]; rice
not become rice [to their taste]: wait
until your body bettered, then only
peaceful heart. Eyes looking, look
one year, big one year. Not know
sustain more less troubles, sustain more
less fears-frights. Being you-up, teach
you until you become (a) man (and)
become big, on-behalf-of you get (a)
wife to-bear children. Hope you
study books establish a-name. On-
behalf-of you created (a) family
(and) established property. Which

they endured, in nourishing and in educating you. When you grew up to manhood, they gave you a wife to bear you a son. They waited in expectation, that your learning should raise you to fame. They strove to lay by a little property to enable you to set up in life. Now, which of all these things, did not require the heart of a father and mother? Can this kindness be ever fully rewarded? If you are not aware of the kindness of your parents, you have only to consider for a moment the heartfelt tenderness with which you treat your own children, and then you will know. The ancients said well, 'Bring up a child, then you will know the kindness of a father and mother.'

But if you indeed know the kindness of your parents, why do you not go and exercise filial piety towards them? For filial piety is not a thing difficult to practise. In ancient times, in order to display filial affection some slept on the ice, some cut the thigh, and one buried her own child. This kind of service it would be difficult to imitate; nor is it necessary thus to act in order that it may be denominated filial piety. It only

係唔曉得你父母嘅
恩，且將你待仔女嘅
心腸想一想，就曉得
咯，古人有話，養子方
知父母恩。

既係知到父母嘅恩咯，
做乜唔去孝順佢呢，
呢個孝順，亦唔係做
唔嚟嘅事，卽如古時
之人，有臥冰求鯉嘅，
有割股奉親嘅，有埋
兒養親嘅，噉樣嘅事
就難學咯，亦不必定
要噉樣做，致叫做孝，
但要心心念念擒在

haí² ₌m ˋhíú tak, ˢnéi fú²-ˢmò keˋ
₌yan, ˋch'e ₌tsöng ˢnéi toí² ˋtsaí ˢnöü
keˋ ₌sam ₌ch'öng ˋsöng yat, ˋsöng,
tsaú² ˋhíú tak, lok.。 ˋKwú ₌yan ˢyau
wá², ' ˢYöng ˋtsz ₌fong ₌chí fú²-ˢmò
₌yan.'

one [C.] matter not appertain-to
father mother's heart ? This kindness is rewarded able to-the-full,
eh ? 39. You if it-is (that you do)
not understand able your father's
mother's kindness, further take you
towards sons daughters that heart
bowels think one think, then understand able, 32. Ancient men have
said, 'Bring-up child, then know
father mother's kindness.'

Keˋ haí² ₌chí-tòˋ fú²-ˢmò-keˋ ₌yan lok.。,
tsò² mat, ₌m höü'ˋ háu'-shun² ˢk'öü
.ni ? ₌Ni koˋ háu'-shun², yik, ₌m
haí² tsò² ₌m ₌laí keˋ sz² Tsik,-₌yü
ˋkwú-₌shí ₌chí ₌yan, ˢyau ngò² ₌ping
₌k'au ˢléí keˋ, ˢyau kot。ˋkwú fung²
₌ts'an keˋ, ˢyau ₌máí ₌yí ˢyöng
₌ts'an keˋ. ˋKòm ᶜyöng* keˋ sz²,
tsaú² ₌nán hok, lok。; yik, pat,
'pit,-ting² yíúˋ ˋkòm ᶜyöng* tsòᶜ²
ˋchí kíú' tsòᶜ² háu' Tán² yíú'
₌sam-₌sam ním²-ním², ₌chaí tsoí²

Already is know father's (and) mother's
kindness, 32, do what not go filial-
piety them, eh ? 53. This [C.] filial-
piety also not is do not come matter
[tsò-m-laí = cannot be done]. For
instance ancient times' men have
sleep ice begging carp, have cut
thigh presented-to parent, have buried
child to-nourish parent. Such kind
of. matter, just difficult to-copy, 32 ;
also not really-certainly need so
fashion do before (or in order to)

requires the heart and thoughts placed on your parents, then all will be well. If you really would recompense their kindness, you must leave nothing undone that your powers can accomplish for the comfort and service of the aged. Better that you yourself should have little to eat and to use, and have sufficiency to give them to eat and to use; and [thus] lessen their toils. You must not gamble, nor drink wine; you must not go and fight with persons; you must not privately hoard up money for youself, or love your own wife and children, and overlook your father and mother. What if your external motions should not exactly accord, that will by no means impede the business; internal sincerity alone is required; then you will be successful. Suppose [for example] you can give them only daily coarse vegetables and dry rice: yet cause them to eat these with pleasure:—this then is filial piety and obedience.

We shall therefore take this principle and extend its application to other things. Thus, [to give a few instances] if in your conduct, you be not correct and regular, this is throwing contempt upon your own

爻母身上就好。你果然想報恩，就自己力量做得嘅，必要去奉承兩個老人家。寧可自己少啲使、少啲食，俾够佢使、俾够佢食，替佢做辛苦嘅事。唔好去賭錢、飲酒，唔好去共人打架，唔好暗中私自積埋錢銀，痛自己老婆仔女，不顧爻母。縱使外邊有乜禮文唔，都誠實，單要心裏誠實就好，即如每日粗茶淡飯，只要令佢歡歡喜喜嘅食，便是孝順咯。

開忽不唔忽輕推理道個呢將樣嘅，就如舉動之間，就係輕忽爻母嘅遺體，便為不孝咯，替朝廷做事，唔……端端正正，

fú²-ᶜmò ₋shan shöng², tsau² ᶜhò. ᶜNéi-
téí² ᶜkwo-₋yín ᶜsöng pò² ₋yan, tsau²
tán²-₋fán tsz²-ᶜkéí lik₋-löng² tsò² tak₋
₋laí ke², pít₋ yíú² höü² fung²-₋shing
ᶜlöng ko² ᶜlo-₋yan-₋ká. ₋Ning-ᶜho tsz²-
ᶜkéí shik₋ ᶜshíú-₋ti, ᶜshaí ᶜshíú-₋ti, ₋tò
ᶜpéí kau² ᶜk'öü shik₋, ᶜpéí kau² ᶜk'öü
ᶜshaí ; t'áí² ᶜk'öü tsò² ₋san-ᶜfú ke² sz².
₋M ᶜhò höü² ᶜtò ᶜts'ín*, ᶜyam ᶜtsau ;
₋m ᶜhò höü² kung² ₋yan ᶜtá-ká² ; ₋m
ᶜhò òm² ₋chung ₋sz tsz² tsik₋-₋máí
₋ts'ín*-ᶜngan*, t'ung² tsz²-ᶜkéí ᶜlò-
₋p'ò, ᶜtsaí, ᶜnöü, pat₋ kwú² fú²-ᶜmò.
Tsung²-ᶜsz ngoí² ₋pín ᶜmò-mat₋ ᶜlaí
₋man, ₋tò pat₋ ₋fong sz² ; ₋tán yíú²
₋sam ᶜlöü ₋shing-shat₋, tsau² ᶜhò.
Tsik₋-₋yü ᶜmúí-yat₋ ₋t'so ts'oí² ᶜt'ám
fán² : chik₋ yíú² ling² ᶜk'öü ₋fún-₋fún-
ᶜhéí-ᶜhéí ₋lai shik₋ :—pín² shí² háu²-
shun² lok₋.

ᶜKòm ᶜyöng*, ₋tsöng ₋ni ko² tò²-ᶜléí
₋t'uí-₋hoí ᶜkong. Tsau² ₋yü ᶜköü-
tung² ₋chí ₋kán, ₋m ₋tün-₋tün-ching²-
ching², tsau² haí² ₋hing-fat₋ fú²-ᶜmò-
ke² ₋waí ᶜt'aí :—pín² waí² pat₋ háu²
lok₋. T'aí² ₋ch'íú-₋t'ing tsò² sz², ₋m

---

be-called act filially. But must-have
heart heart thoughts thoughts placed
on parents' body above, then good.
You really wish to-recompense grace,
then whatever own ability do can
come, certainly must go (and) do whatever the two [C.] old persons (like
in order to please them). Rather
self eat lesser (amount), use lesser
(amount), also give sufficient them
to-eat, give sufficient them to-use ;
on-behalf-of them do hard matters.
Don't go gamble-with money, drink
spirits ; don't go with people fight ;
don't dark midst secretly self ac-
cumulate together money, love own
wife, son, daughter, not look-after
father, mother. Although outward
side not much formalities, also not
impede the-business ; only require
heart interior sincere, then good.
Supposing each day coarse vegetables,
tasteless rice, the-only (thing you)
must (do is) to-cause them very-
very-pleased come to-eat :—that is
filial-piety, 32.

So fashion take this [C.] doctrine extend (it) out to-speak. For-instance
actions' midst, not very-very-upright,
just is despise parents' left (to you)
body :—that is not filial, 32. On-
behalf-of (the) Government do mat-

bodies, which were handed down to you from your parents : this is not filial piety. When doing business for the government, if you do not exhaust your ideas, and exert your strength ; or if, in serving the prince, you be unfaithful, this is just the same as treating your parents ill :—this is not filial piety. In the situation of an officer of government, if you do not act well, but provoke the people to scoff and rail ; this is lightly to esteem the substance handed down to you from your parents :—this is not filial piety. When associating with friends, if, in speech or behaviour you be insincere ; this casts disgrace on your parents :—this is not filial piety. If you, soldiers, when the army goes out to battle, will not valiantly and sternly strive to advance ; but give persons occasion to laugh at your cowardice ; this is to degrade the progeny of your parents :—this also is not filial piety. In the present age there are very many disobedient children. If their parents speak a word to them, they instantly put on a surly face ; if their parents scold them, they pertly answer again—if called to the east, they go to

盡心竭力，事君不忠，
即待父母不好，做官嘅，
便是不孝咯，引百姓笑
罵，嘅係將父母遺體
待慢咯，就是不孝咯。
在朋友之前，說話做
事唔真實，便羞辱父
母，亦係不孝咯，若係
你哋做兵丁嘅，土陣
出戰之時，唔肯奮勇
爭先，令人笑你軟弱，
嘅就係將父母嘅遺
體作賤咯，亦係不孝
咯。如今世上忤逆嘅
仔，極多，父母話佢一
句，佢就反面，父母罵
佢一聲，佢就應嘴叫
佢去東，佢反去西，更
有啲自己老婆仔女
都飽飽煖煖，父母反
抵飢受餓，自己惹出
禍嚟，連累父母受氣，
自己犯嘵事，連累父
母上官入府。

tsun² ‿sam k‘ít꜀ lik‿; sz² ‿kwan pat‿ ‿chung, tsik‿ toí² fú²-⸜mò ‿m ⸜hò yat‿ yöng²:—pín² shí² pat‿ háu⁾ lok꜀. Tsò² ‿kwún ke⁾, yök‿-haí² ‿m ⸜hò, yan⁾ pák꜀-sing⁾ síú⁾ má²; ⸜kòm haí² ‿tsöng fú²-⸜mò ‿waí ⸜t‘aí toí² mán² lok꜀:—tsau² shí² pat‿ háu⁾ lok꜀. Tsoí² ‿p‘ang-⸜yau ‿chí ‿ts‘ín, shüt꜀-wá² tsò² sz² ‿m ‿chan shat‿; pín² ‿sau-yuk‿ fú²-⸜mò:—yik‿ haí² pat‿ háu⁾ lok꜀. Yök‿ haí² ⸜néí-téí² tsò² ‿piug-‿ting-ke⁾, ⸜shöng ꞌchan² ch‘ut‿ chín⁾ ‿chí-‿shí, ‿m ⸜hang ⸜fan-‿yung ‿cháng ‿sín; ling² ‿yan síú⁾ ⸜néí ⸜yün-yök‿'; ⸜kòm tsau² haí² ‿tsöng fú²-⸜mò-ke⁾ ‿waí ⸜t‘aí tsok꜀ tsín² lok꜀, yik‿ haí² pat‿ háu⁾ lok꜀. ‿Yü-‿kam shaí⁾ shöng² ng²-yik‿ ke⁾ ⸜tsaí kik‿ ‿to. Fú²-⸜mò wá² ⸜k‘öü yat‿ köü⁾, ⸜k‘öü tsau² ⸜fán mín²; fú²-⸜mò má² ⸜k‘öü yat‿ shengt, ⸜k‘öü tsau² ying⁾-⸜tsöü,—kíú⁾ ⸜k‘öü höü⁾ ‿tung, ⸜k‘öü ‿fán höü⁾ ‿saí. Kang⁾ ⸜yau ‿tí tsz²-⸜kéí ⸜lò-‿p‘ò ⸜tsaí ⸜nöü, ‿tò ⸜páu-⸜páu ⸜nün-‿nün, fú²-⸜mò ⸜fán ⸜taí ‿kéí shau² ‿ngo. Tsz²-⸜kéí ⸜ye ch‘ut‿ wo² ‿laí, ‿lín-löü² fú²-⸜mò shau² héí⁾. Tsz²-⸜kéí fán² ‿híú sz², ‿lín-löü² fú²-⸜mò ⸜shöng ‿kwún yap‿ ⸜fú.

ters, not with utmost-extent-of (your) heart exert (your) strength; serve prince not faithful, just is treat parents not well one same:—that is not filial, 32. Being officials, if (it) is (that you) are not good, lead the-people (i.e. the hundred surnames) to-laugh (and) revile, so is take parents handed-down-to (your) body treat neglectfully, 32:—just is not filial, 32. In friends' presence, speech, do-ing matters not true (and) firm; that-is (a) disgrace-to (your) parents:—also is not filial, 32. If (it) is (that) you are soldiers, going-up-into the-array (or the marshalled ranks) going-out-to battle's time, not will-ing vigourously-valiantly strive to-advance; cause people to-laugh-at you (being) weak; so just is take parents' left-you-to-inherit body make-into ignoble, 32, also is not filial. At-present world in perverse (or stub-born) sons extremely many. Parents say-to them one sentence, (equivalent of 'a word' in such a connection) they then turn against one; (lit. turn face) parents scold them with-one sound [only], they then answer back,—tell them to-go-to-the East, they back go-to-the West. Besides have some themselves, wives, children very well the west. Again, there are some whose wives and children are warmly clothed and fully fed, while on the other hand their parents are empty and suffer hunger. They rush into misery, and embarrass and disgrace their parents. They themselves transgress the law, and their parents are involved, and brought before the magistrate.

It is needless to say that the laws of superior powers will not tolerate this description of persons; but their own children, beholding their example, will follow closely at their heels, imitating them. Only observe those who have themselves been undutiful and disobedient; where did they ever bring up a good child? Do think a little—will you still not be aroused?

After parents, brothers come next in order. I will not say that these brothers are not two persons; but only that the bones and flesh of their bodies are of the same bones and flesh as my own. Therefore they are called 'hands and feet.' If you treat your brother ill, that is just to treat your parents ill. Suppose they be not brothers by the same mother with you, still they have

噉樣嘅人、不獨理難容、就係自己仔女睇樣、亦會跟住嚟做、你見唔孝順嘅人、邊處養得出好仔女嚟呢、你哋想一想、都唔省悟咩。

除曉爷母、就係兄弟呢、哟兄弟唔係兩個人、佢身上嘅骨肉、就係我身上嘅骨肉、所以叫做手足、你若薄待兄弟、便是薄待爷母咯。即使兄弟唔同老母、亦係一個爷親嘅骨血、唔好話唔同老

satisfied with food and quite warm (*lit.* also full full warm warm), parents on-the-other-hand endure famine, suffer hunger. Themselves bring out (*or* bring into existence) misery come implicate parents to receive reproach. Themselves trangress-having in-matters, involve parents to-appear before (*lit.* to-up) officials to-enter-into departmental (offices).

ˋKòm ᶜyöng* keᵓ ₍yan, patᵓ tukᵓ ᶜléi ₍nán ₍yung; tsau² haí² tsz²-ᶜkéi ᶜtsaí-ᶜnöü ᶜt'ai ᶜyöng*, yik₂ ᶜwúi ₍kan chü² ₍lai tsò². ᶜNéi kínᵓ ₍m háuᵓ-shun² keᵓ ₍yan; ₒpín shüᵓ ᶜyöng takᵓ ch'utᵓ ᶜhò ᶜtsaí-ᶜnöü ₍lai ₒni? ᶜNéi-téi² ᶜsöng yatᵓ ᶜsöng,—₍tò ₍m ᶜsing-ng² ₍me?

So fashion men not only common sense (*or* principles) not allow; just is own sons daughters see the-fashion, also can follow in-order-to do (the same). You see not-filial men what place rear-up able out good children come, eh? 53. You think one thought—also not aroused, eh? 39.

₍Ch'ü ₍híú fú²-ᶜmò, tsau² haí² ₍hing-taí². ₍Ni-₍ti ₍hing-taí² ₍m haí² ᶜlöng koᵓ ₍yan; ᶜk'öü ₍shan shöng² keᵓ kwatᵓ yuk₂, tsau² haí² ᶜngo ₍shan shöng² keᵓ kwatᵓ-yuk₂. ᶜSho-ᶜyí kíúᵓ tsò² ᶜshau-tsukᵓ. ᶜNéi yök₂ pokᵓ-toí² ₍hing-taí², pín² shí² pok₂ toí² fú²-ᶜmò lokₒ. Tsik₂ ᶜsz ₍hing-taí² ₍m ₍t'ung ᶜlò-ᶜmò, yik₂ haí² yatᵓ koᵓ fú²-₍ts'an-keᵓ kwatᵓ hütₒ; ₍m ᶜhò wá² ₍m ₍t'ung ᶜlò-

Deducted having father (and) mother, then there-are brothers. These brothers not are two [*C.*] men; their bodies upon bones flesh just is my body upon's bones flesh. Therefore called hand (and) foot. You if slight brothers, that is slighting parents, 32. Even supposing (*or* though) brothers not same mothers, also is one [*C.*] father's bones blood;

the bones and blood of the same father; hence let it not be said that they are not of the same mother—let them not be treated differently. The most intimate of all relations among men in the world, is that of a wife; but suppose that your wife die, you may still marry another.

But if a brother die, where will you go to seek for another? Reflect seriously then, whether you ought, or ought not, to love [your brothers].

But in what manner is this love and kindness to be manifested to them? Younger brothers should greatly respect elder brothers. In every affair, whether in eating or in putting on apparel—in visiting friends or in conversation, in walking, sitting, or standing,—in all these things the precedence must be yielded to the elder brother. Among men of old, belonging to the same village or hamlet, it was thus—another person, ten years older than myself, I honoured him as an elder brother—if he was five years my superior in age, I walked shoulder by shoulder with him, rather a little behind; but dared not presume to go before him.

If it was proper for me to treat a stranger, who was my superior in

母。世如翻一個。就上最親嘅。重可以娶妻，譬如妻死嘵。開分看待呀。人

兄弟若係死嘵，邊處重你愛，攞得翻一個嚟呢。係着親嘅想一想，係着呀。唔着呀。

點樣親愛致得呢。做細唔飯，做大哥，或係食禮路，佬論乜野着衫，或係行行企，都要時村或係講話，或係行十歲，佢或係坐，或係企哥。佢就僭謙讓，做大哥嘅。古一之人，就是一鄉我哥，嘅，佢若大過我哥，我若挨佢先行。

外人年紀大，我尚且嚟樣敬重佢，何況係我

ₑmò,—tsau² ₑfan-ₑhoí ₑhon-toi² a᷄.
ₑYan shaí᷄ shöng² tsöü᷄ ₑts'an ke᷄
haí² ₑts'aí; peí᷄-yü² ₑts'aí ₑsz ₑhíú,
chung² ᷄hò-ₑyí ts'öü᷄ ₑfan yat₎ ko᷄.

don't say not same mother—then
divide treatment, 2. Men world on
most near is wife; supposing wife
dies, still may take back one [C.].

ₑHing-taí² yök₎ haí² ᷄sz ₑhíú, ₒpín shü᷄
chung² ᷄lo tak₎ ₑfan yat₎ ko᷄ ₑlaí
ₒni? ᷄Néi-téí² ᷄söng yat₎ ᷄söng, haí²
chök₎ ₑts'an-oi᷄ ₑm chök₎ a᷄?
᷄Tím ᷄yöng* ₑts'an-oi᷄ chí᷄ tak₎ ₒni?
Tsò² saí᷄-᷄lò-ke᷄, yíú᷄ king᷄-chung²
táí²-ₑko. ₑM lun² mat₎ ᷄ye sz², wák₎
haí² shik₎ fán², wák₎ haí² chök₀-
ₑshám, wák₎ haí² ₑháng ᷄lai, wák₎
haí² ᷄kong-wá², wák₎ haí² ₑháng-lò²,
wák₎ haí² ᷄ts'o*†, wák₎ haí² ᷄k'éí,—
ₑtò yíú᷄ ₑhim-yöng². Tsò² táí² ₑko
ke᷄:—᷄kwú ₑshí ₑchí ₑyan, tsau² shí²
yat₎ ₑhöng yat₎ ₑts'ün ke᷄, ᷄k'öü
yök₎ táí² kwo᷄ ᷄ngo shap₎ᵬsöü᷄, ᷄ngo
tsau² ₑtsün ᷄k'öü tsò᷄ ko-ₑko; ᷄k'öü
yök₎ táí² kwo᷄ ᷄ngo ᷄ng söü᷄, ᷄ngo
tsau² ₑai ₑkín ₑkan-chü² ᷄k'öü; ₑm
᷄kòm ts'ím᷄ ᷄k'öü ₑsïn ₑháng.

Brother if it-is (that he) dies, what place
yet get able back one [C.] to come,
eh? 53. You think a thought, is
right to dearly-love (or) not right? 2.
How fashion dearly-love in order to do,
eh? 53. Being younger-brother, must
respect hightly elder brother. With-
out-reference-to what thing matter,
whether it-is eating rice, whether it-is
dressing, whether it-is visiting (or per-
forming ceremonials), whether it-is
conversation, or it-is walking, whether
it-is sitting-down, or it-is (standing),
—also must-be yielding. With-regard-
to elder brothers:—ancient times's men,
that were one village one village, he if
older than I ten years, I then honoured
him to-be elder brother; he if older
than I (by) five years, I then against
his-shoulder followed him; not dare
arrogantly first to walk.

Ngoi² ₑyan ₑnín-᷄kéi-táí², ᷄ngo
shöng²-᷄ch'e ₑkòm ᷄yöng* king᷄-
chung² ᷄k'öü, ₑhò-fong᷄ haí² ₑ᷄ngo-

Outside men age-big, I however so
fashion reverently-respect them, how

age, in so respectful a manner, how much more so thus to treat my own elder brother! With regard to elder brothers, they ought tenderly to love their younger brothers. We must, without respect to their age treat a younger brother as a child. For example, your own child, if he be worthless, you are displeased with him, scold him, beat him; and then afterward change your countenance [become pleased] and tenderly love him as before. But you do not act thus towards your younger brothers. Yon will not deliberately advise them, and speak to them; but, as soon as you find some trifling error in them, you begin to wrangle with them. But think that you and your younger brother were nourished and brought up by the same parents:—now, if you beat your younger brother, this is the same as beating yourself. These younger brothers know not good from evil; hence, when beaten by their elder brothers, they also learn to lift their hands. We may compare them to a man's hands and feet; a man slips his hand, and strikes his foot; but would it not be strange to say that he should take his foot and kick at his hand again!

做佬、我待好佢、依舊有慢慢佬爭你母佬、一唔佢個打去。至於細大、我看好佢、罵佢、依舊有慢慢細要共你老細己、又打一手腳。呢、至於痛年紀女女、怒佢一陣、於細佬唔肯、再一著、吓你一個打你自己嘅、大哥如一時錯撳手咩。哥嘅雖係我、認真面佢、轉佢、至好處、再教佢。多想、都係你自己做醜、還手、唔隻。親哥佬當如亦佢痛好佢、勸佢、有鬧細生就樣、知佢亦嘅人親踢翻隻脚。

ke' ‿ts'an tái² ‿ko ‿ni ? Chí' ‿yü
tsò² tái² ‿ko ke', yíú' oí' t'ung'
saí'-'lò. Saí'-'lò ‿söü haí² ‿nín-
'kéí-táí², ⸲ngo ‿yiug tong' ⸲k'öü
haí² ⸲tsaí ⸲nöü ‿hon-toí². 'Péí-‿yü,
⸲ngo-ke' 'tsaí ⸲nöü ‿m 'hò, ⸲ngo yik⸲
ying² ‿chan nò² ⸲k'öü, má² ⸲k'öü,
'tá ⸲k'öü; chün' mín² yat, chan², ‿yí
kau² oí'-t'ung' ⸲k'öü. Chí' ‿yü saí'-
'lò ⸲yau ‿m 'hò ch'ü'. Tsoí ‿m 'hang
mán²-⸲mán* hün' ⸲k'öü, káu' ⸲k'öü ;
yat, yü² saí'-'lò ⸲yau ‿ti ‿to ‿m chök⸲,
tsau² yíú' ‿cháng-tau' 'héí ‿laí. 'Söng
⸲há ⸲néí kung² ⸲néí saí'-'lò, ‿tò haí²
yat, ko' ⸲lò-⸲mò ‿sháng ke'. ⸲Néí
yök⸲ 'tá ⸲néí saí'-'lò, tsau² haí² tsz²-
'kéí 'tá tsz²-'kéí yat, yöng² lok⸲.
Tsò² saí'-'lò-ke', yan² ‿m ‿chí 'hò
'ch'au ; kin' táí²-‿ko 'tá ⸲k'öü, ⸲k'öü
yik⸲ ‿wán 'shau. 'Péí-‿yü yat, ko'
‿yan ke' 'shau ; ⸲yau ‿shí ts'o' ⸲shau
'tá ‿ts'au kök⸲ ; ‿m ‿t'ung yíú' ⸲k'áí
kök⸲ höü' t'ek⸲† ‿fán chek⸲ 'shau
‿me ?

much more (if he) is my own elder
brother, eh ? 53. As-to (those who)
are elder brothers, must fondly love
younger brothers. Younger brothers,
although it-is (that their) age great,
I ought to-consider them as sons
daughters treat. For example, my
children not good, I also seriously angry with them, scold them, beat them;
(then) changing countenance immediately according-to-old fondly love
them. As-to younger brother having
bad points, again not willing slowly
advise him, teach him. If (seeing)
younger brother have a-little not
right, then must wrangle rise come.
Think a-bit you with your younger
brother also are one [C.] mother gave-
birth-to. You if beat your younger
brother, just is yourself beating yourself one same, 32. Being (a) younger
brother further not know good bad,
seeing elder brother beat him, he
also return (the) hand. For-instance-
as if a [C.] man's hand, there-were
times by-mistake (lit. wrongly the
hand) struck the-foot ; is-it-necessary
to-take the foot to-go to-kick back
[C.] hand, eh ? 39.

Now, want of harmony among brothers, generally arises from contentions about property, and from listening to what their wives say. What these wives say may not be wholly destitute of reason; but because it has a little reason in it, it enters their husbands ears before they are aware.

如今兄弟不和、多係爲
爭財起見、多係聽妻
子說話、雖然做妻子
嘅說話、亦唔係總有
道理、正因爲佢嘅說
話、亦有啲道理、便不
知不覺、聽從佢咯。

Thus a sister-in-law [the elder brother's wife] will perhaps say to the elder brother :—'How slothful my little uncle is! how insufferably prodigal! You have painfully and labouriously collected money to support him; and still he is prating about long, and chatting about short. Is it not hard to say that you are his son, and that I am his daughter-in-law; and that we must go and discharge filial duty to him?'

就如做大嫂嘅、向大哥
話、小叔點樣懶惰、點
樣散錢、你辛辛苦苦
賺錢嚟養佢、佢重說
長論短、唔通我哋係
佢嘅仔共媳婦、應該
孝順佢嘅咩。

The wife of the younger brother also knows how to chatter to him :—'With respect to your elder brother,' she says, 'he has, it is true, scraped together money; but you also have scraped together money, and acted your part in the family, both in great and small affairs, just as well as he; yea even a hired coolie has not such

嗰個細佬嘅妻、亦會向
丈夫話、就是大哥會
賺錢、你亦賺過錢、你
在家中做呢樣、做個
樣、即使請個長工、亦
有咁勞苦嘅、偏偏佢
嘅仔女就係仔女、買

ᒡYü-ᒡkam ᒡhing-taí² ·pat⟩ ᒡwo, ᒡto haí²
waí² ᒡcháng ᒡts'oí ᶜhéi-kín⟩, ᒡto haí²
ᒡt'eng† ᒡts'aí ᶜtsz shüt₀-wá². ᒡSöü-ᒡyín
tsò² ᒡts'aí-ᶜtsz-ke⟩ shüt₀-wá², yik⟩ ᒡm
haí² ᶜtsung ᶜmò tò²-ᶜléí ; ching⟩ ᒡyan-
waí² ᶜk'öü-ke⟩ shüt₀-wá², yik⟩ ᶜyau
ᒡti tò²-ᶜléí, pin² ·pat⟩ ᒡchí pat⟩ kok₀,
ᒡt'ing†-ᒡts'ung ᶜk'öü lok₀.

Now brethern not harmonious, much is on-account-of dispute (concerning) wealth arising to-appearance, much is listening-to wife (and) children's words. Although being wife (and) children the words, also not is entirely without doctrine ; properly because-of their speech, also have some doctrine, therefore unconsciously (and) unawares, listen-to-and-follow them, 32.

Tsan²-ᒡyü tsò² taí²-ᶜsò ke⟩, höng⟩ taí²-ᒡko wá² :—'Síú shuk⟩ ᶜtím ᶜyöng* ᶜlán-to⟩, ᶜtím-ᶜyöng* sán⟩ ᶜts'ín*. ᶜNéí ᒡsan-ᒡsan-ᶜfú-ᶜfú chán² ᶜts'ín* ᒡlaí ᶜyöng ᶜk'öü ; ᶜk'öü chung² shüt₀ ᒡch'öng lun² ᶜtün. ᒡM-ᒡt'ung ᶜngo-téí² haí² ᶜk'öü-ke⟩ ᶜtsaí kung² sik⟩-ᶜfú ; ᒡying-ᒡkoí háu⟩-shun² ᶜk'öü-ke⟩ ᒡme ? '

For instance being (an) elder-brother's-wife, towards elder brother (i.e. her husband), say :—' Little uncle how fashion lazy, how fashion waste money. You with greatest trouble have-earned in-order-to rear him ; he still speaks much and little (yarns about him, *for the meaning is necessarily a bad one*). Is-it-that we are his son together-with daughter-in-law ; (and) ought to-have-filial-piety-towards him, eh ? 39.

ᶜKo-ko⟩ saí⟩-ᶜlò-ke⟩ ᒡts'aí, yik⟩ ᶜwúí höng⟩ chöng²-ᒡfú wá² :—'Tsau²-shí² taí²-ᒡko ᶜwúí chán² ᶜts'ín* ; ᶜnéí yik⟩ chán²-kwo⟩ ᶜts'ín*, ᶜnéí tsoí² ᒡká ᒡchung tsò² ᒡni yöng², tsò² ᶜko yöng⟩ ; tsik⟩-ᒡsz ᶜts'eng† ko⟩ ᒡch'öng-ᒡkung, yik⟩ ᶜmò kòm⟩ ᒡlò-ᶜfú ke⟩. P'ín-ᒡp'ín ᶜk'öü-ke⟩ ᶜtsaí ᶜnöü tsau² haí² ᶜtsaí ᶜnöü ; ᶜmáí

The [*C.*] younger brother's wife also is-able toward (her) husband to-say :—' Although (*better still* or admitting it as a fact) (your) elder-brother has-been-able to-earn money ; you also have-earned money, you in family midst do this kind (of thing), do that kind (of thing) ; even engage a permanent-work (servant), also not toil and. labour as you have. His own children are treated as children; "buy this for them to eat, and buy that for them to eat;" but is it not hard to say, that our children are to be allowed to starve?' This kind of prattle, to-day a little of it, and to-morrow a little of it, seldom fails to make an impression on the brothers. From this their affections begin to cool towards each other, and day by day they become more alienated, till finally it ends in wrangling and fighting; not considering that as brothers they were originally one person. Suppose an elder brother be rather destitute of ability, and his younger brother support him; this is just what he ought to do. And if a younger brother be possessed of but little talent, and his elder brother support him; this also is nothing more than he ought to do. If at any time, a few impertinent words, or unbecoming sentences be uttered, they should be looked upon as if spoken when over-come by wine, or when dreaming; then the whole matter will be easily settled. But if you will determinately stand out each for his right: then you are fitly compared to a man's two

呢樣食、買個樣食、唔
通我嘅仔女、就該死
嘅咩。照嗽樣說話、今
日有啲、明日有啲、唔
怪得做大哥嘅唔聽
得入耳、從此就將兄
弟嘅心腸都冷淡、一
日一日積埋、便至到
嗌鬧打架咯、誰不知
兄弟原係一個人、即
使大哥有能幹、做細
佬嘅養佢、亦係應該
嘅、細佬有能幹、做大
哥嘅養佢、亦係應該
嘅、若係一時有啲閒
言閒語、只當佢飲醉
酒或當佢講夢話、就
大家撒開咯、你若認
得真、譬如兩隻手、右
手極其能幹、寫字係
佢、打筭盆亦係佢、搩
乜野物件都係佢、個
隻左手、就好笨拙、未
曾聽見人搣右手去
打左手嘅、一個兄弟
親親嘅手足、點好爭

ₔni yöng² shik₂, ꞈmái ko꞉ yöng² shik₂ ; ₔm ₔt'ung ꞈngo-ke꞉ ꞈtsai ꞈnöü, tsau² ₔkoí ꞈsz ke꞉ ₔme ?' Chíú꞉ ꞈkòm ꞈyöng* shüt₀-wá², ₔkam yat₂ ꞈyau ₔti, ₔming yat₂ ꞈyau ₔti, ₔm kwáí꞉ tak₂ tsò² táí²-ₔko ke꞉, ₔm ₔt'eugꝉ-tak₂-yap₂ ꞈyí. ₔTs'ung-ꞈts'z tsau² ₔtsöng ₔhing-taí²-ke꞉ ₔsam ₔch'öng ₔtò ꞈláng-tám², . yat₂ yat₂ yat₂ yat₂ tsik₂-ₔmáí, pín²-chí꞉ tò꞉ áí꞉-nán² ꞈtá-ká꞉ lok₀ ; ₔshuí pat₂ ₔchí ₔhing-taí² ₔyün haí² yat₂ ko꞉ ₔyan. Tsik₂-ꞈsz táí²-ₔko ꞈmò ₔnang-kon꞉, tsò² saí꞉-ꞈlò-ke꞉ ꞈyöng ꞈk'öü ; yik₂ haí² ₔying-ₔkoí ke꞉. Saí꞉-ꞈlò ꞈmò ₔnang-kon꞉, tsò² táí²-ₔko-ke꞉, ꞈyöng ꞈk'öü; yik₂ haí² ₔying-ₔkoí ke꞉. Yök₂ haí² yat₂ ₔshí, ꞈyau ₔti ₔhán ₔyín, ₔhán ꞈyü, chík₀ tong꞉ ꞈk'öü ꞈyam tsöü꞉ ꞈtsan, wák₀ tong꞉ ꞈk'öü ꞈkong mung² wá² ; tsau² táí²-ₔká sát₀-ₔhoí lok₀. ꞈNéí yök₂ ying² tak₂ ₔchan ; p'éí꞉-ₔyü ꞈlöng chek₀ ꞈshan,—yau² ꞈshau kik₂ ₔk'éí ₔnang-kon꞉,—ꞈse tsz² haí² ꞈk'öü, ꞈtá sün꞉-ₔp'ún yik₂ haí² ꞈk'öü*; ₔning mat₂-ꞈye mat₂-ꞈkín*, ₔtò ₔhaí² ꞈk'öü : ko꞉ chek₀ ꞈtso ꞈshau, tsau² ꞈhò pan²-chüt₀. Méí²-ₔts'ang ₔt'eugꝉ kín꞉ ₔyan ꞈk'áí yau²꞉ ꞈshau höü꞉ ꞈtá ꞈtsó ꞈshau ke꞉. Yat₂ ko꞉ ₔhing-taí² ₔts'an-ₔts'an ke꞉ ꞈshau tsuk₂—ꞈtím ꞈhò ₔcháng

so ardent-toil. Only his sons (and) daughters just are sons (and) daughters; buying this kind-of-thing to-eat, buying that kind-of-thing to-eat. Is it that our sons (and) daughters just ought to-die, eh ? 39.' According-to such kind-of words, to-day have some, to-morrow have some, not to-be-wondered-at (that he who) is elder-brother, not hear able-enter-into ear. From this then render brothers' hearts (and) bowels also lukewarm, one day one day accumulated-together, until arrived-at brawling fighting, 32. Who not know brethren originally are one [C.] person. Supposing elder-brother no ability, being younger-brother support him ; also is (what) ought (to-be-done). Younger brother no ability, being elder-brother support him ; also is (what) ought (to-be done). If there-be at-a time, (that) there-are some idle words, idle speech, then regard him (as) from-drinking drunk-with wine, or consider him as-speaking dream words ; then both separate (i.e. separate without any more quarrel). You, if recognised can (the matter), truly (i.e. seriously) ; for-instance two [C.] hands,—the-right hand extremely it (has) ability—writing is it ; manipulating the-abacus

hands,—the right hand boasts extravagantly of its ability—it writes, it strikes the abacus; it lays hold of every thing: as for the left hand, it is artless in the extreme! But was there ever a man seen or heard of, who took his right hand and set to work to beat the left? Brothers are as nearly related as hands and feet—why then strive and debate about trifles? Reflect for a little. Money is [as] the restless waters—it goes and returns again. As for our wives, they are not of the same parents with us; they have not the same feeling. Only observe brothers that do not agree; their parents most undoubtedly are rendered uneasy. You have but just to notice your own children when they fight; are you then displeased or not displeased? Hence those who discharge filial piety, will never disagree with their brothers.

長論短呢，你想一想，錢銀係倘來之物，去曉又嚟嘅，妻子唔係共我一個老母，佢曉得乜野道理呢，但凡兄弟不和，做父母必然生氣，你試睇你仔女打架，你心裏怒唔怒呢，所以做孝子嘅人，總有唔和衾兄弟嘅。

The common proverb says well, 'To attack the tiger, engage the aid of a brother,' and, 'In advancing to battle, it is requisite to have father and son united in the combat' It is also said, 'A stranger, though extremely good, is still a stranger; my own brother, though extremely worthless, is still part of myself.' It

俗語有話，打虎不離親兄弟，土陣還須父子兵，又話，好極係他人，醜極係自已，又話，兄弟不和旁人欺，只顧你哋爭閒氣，就有人嚟挑唆你，搬弄你哋

‿ch'öng, lun² ʿtün ‿ni ? ʿNéi ʿsöng
yat‿ ʿsöng. ‿Ts'ín ʿngan*‿ haí² ʿt'ong
‿loí ‿chi mat‿—höü‿-ʿhiú yau² ʿwúi
‿laí ke‿. ‿Ts'ai-‿tsz ‿m haí² kung²
⸢ngo yat‿ ko‿ ʿlò-ʿmò ; ʿk'öü ʿhiú
tak‿ mat‿ ʿye tò²-ʿléí ‿ni ? Tán²-
‿fán ‿hing-taí² pat‿ ‿wo ; tsò² fú²-ʿmò
pít‿-‿yín ‿sháng-héí‿. ʿNéi shí‿ ʿt'aí
⸍ʿnéí ʿtsai ʿnöü ʿtá-ká‿ ; ʿnéi ‿sam
‿ʿlöü nò²‿ ‿m nò²‿ ‿ui ? ʿSho-ʿyí tsò²
háu‿ ʿtsz ke‿, ‿tsung ʿmò ‿m
‿wó-yap‿ ‿hing-taí² ke‿.

Tsuk‿-ʿyü ʿyan wá² :—'Tá ʿfú‿ pat‿
‿léí ‿ts'an ‿hing-taí².' 'ʿShöng chan²
‿wáp-‿söü fú²-ʿtsz ‿ping.' Yau²
‿wá² :—'Hò kík‿ ‿haí² ‿t'á ‿yan ;
‿ch'au kík‿ haí² tsz²-ʿkéi.' Yau²-
‿wá² :—'‿Hing-taí² pat‿ ‿wo, ‿p'óng
‿yan ‿héi.' ʿChí (or ‿chík‿) kwú ʿnéí-
téí² ‿cháng ‿hán héi ; tsau² ʿyau ‿yan
‿laí ‿t'iú-‿so ʿnéi, ‿pún-lung² ʿnéí-téí²

also is it ; bringing any article (whatever), also is it : that [C.] left hand
just (is) very inactive. Not-yet
heard of anyone taking right hand
to-go to-strike left hand. One [C.]
(pair of) brothers (are like) nearest
hands (and) feet—How good strive
long (and) speak short, eh ? 53. You
think a think. Cash (and) silver are
suddenly come things, gone again can
come. Wife (and) children not are
with me one [C.] mother ; they understand able what thing-of principle,
eh ? 53, (i.e. principle of loving your
brothers). Whenever brothers not
harmonious ; (those who) are parents
must certainly grieve (or be troubled
in their minds). You test (and)
see your children fight ; your heart
within angry not angry eh ? 53.
Therefore (who) are filial sons (those)
persons, entirely not-have not harmonious (with) brothers.

Proverb does say :—'To-attack tiger,
do-not separate-from own brothers.'
'Going-up-to battle must-needs-have
(union of the) father (and) sons (as)
soldiers.' Again it is said. '(Even
though) good to-the-extreme, (a
stranger) is (still) another man ;
(even though) bad to-the-extreme,
(a brother) is (still) one's self.

is further said, 'When brothers do not agree, those who stand by, will contemn them.' Do but observe your own idle quarrels; and you will find persons ready enough to come and work you up to wrath, by carrying tales between you, about your rights and wrongs; till it perhaps comes finally either to fighting or to lawsuits. Then—to a certainly, your family is ruined. If you discharge filial duty, those of you who are of the people will be good people; and those who are soldiers, will become the spirited sons of *Han* [*i.e.* brave soldiers]. Now among you all, whether soldiers or people, what one is there who knows not that filial piety is a good thing; that harmony among brothers is a good thing? Well, seeing that you are ready to confess that these are right, why do you not, with a true heart, go and exert your strength to do them? It is indispensably requisite to have the heart and thoughts fixed on parents and brothers. Do not content yourselves with merely a polite external appearance. Do not overlook lesser matters. Do not covet a mere empty name from spectators. Persevere in goodness. He who does so, is

嘅是非、或是打鬬、或是打官司、總有一個唔敗家嘅、你哋若係孝順親愛呢、做民嘅、致係良民、做兵嘅、致係好漢、但係你哋兵民、邊一個唔知到孝順係好事、兄弟和翕係好事、旣然知得係好、做也又唔實心實力去做呢、必須心心念念記住爻母兄弟、唔好淨做外面嘅儀文、唔好忽略個啲小事、唔好淨貪外人嘅名聲、唔好前時好、後來又唔好、噉致係眞眞嘅孝子、眞眞嘅好兄弟、你若係唔孝、或係兄弟唔和、就要搣刑法處治咯、但你心裏唔明白、處治你亦係無益。

ke' shí²-ͺféi; wák₂ shí² 'tá-tau',
wák₂ shí² 'tá-ͺkwún-ͺsz. 'Tsung 'mò
yat₂ ko' ͺm paí² ͺká ke'. 'Néi-
téi² yök₂ haí² háu'-shun² ͺts'an oi'
ͺni, tsò² ͺman-ke', chì' haí² ͺlöng
ͺman; tsò² ͺping ke', chì' haí² 'hò
hon'. Tán²-haí² 'néi-téi' ͺping ͺman,
ͺpín yat₂ ko' ͺm ͺchí-tò' háu'-shun²
haí² 'hò sz²; ͺhing-taí² ͺwo-yap₂ haí²
'hò sz²? Ke'-ͺyín ͺchí-tak₂ haí² 'hò,
tsò²-mat₂ yau² ͺm shat₂ ͺsam, shat₂
lìk₂ höü' tsò² ͺni? Pit₂-ͺsöü ͺsam-
ͺsam ním²-ním² kéi'-chü² fú²-'mò
ͺhing-taí². ͺM 'hò tsing² tsò² ngoí'-
mín²-ke' ͺyi-ͺman. ͺM 'hò fat₂-lök₂
ko'-ͺti 'síú sz². ͺM 'hò tsing² t'ám
ngoí² ͺyan-ke' ͺming-ͺshing. ͺM 'hò
ͺts'in ͺshí 'hò, hau²-ͺloí yau² ͺm 'hò.
'Kòm chí' haí² ͺchan-ͺchan-ke' hán'
'tsz—ͺchan-ͺchan-ke' 'hò ͺhing-taí².
'Néi, yök₂ haí² ͺm háu', wák₂ haí²
ͺhing-taí² ͺm ͺwo, tsau² yíú' 'k'áí
ͺying-fat₂ 'ch'ü-chí² lok₀, tán² 'néi
ͺsam 'löü ͺm ͺming-pák₂, 'ch'ü-chí²
'néi yik₂ ͺmò yik₂.

Further, (it is) said, 'Brothers not agree, (standing-by-the) side people deceive (or oppress) (them).' If-only you (or if you do nothing but pay attention-to) regard your disputes-about trifling tempers; then have men come egg-you-on, (and) stir-up your gossip, or it-is (that they-stir you up) to-fighting, or it-is (that they stir you up) to-law-suits. Entirely there-is-not one [C.] (that) does-not ruin (his) family (property). You, if are filial (and) (feel) affection (and) love (for your relatives), being-of the-people, then you-are good people; being soldiers, then you-are brave-men. But you soldiers (and) people, which one [C.] not know filial piety is (a) good thing; brothers harmonious is good thing? If-already know (it) is good, why further not firm mind, firm strength go do, eh? 53. Must-with heart, continually remember parents (and) brothers. Do-not only do outside ceremonies (or outward forms). Do-not make-light-of (or despise) those little things. Do-not only covet outside persons' (giving you a) re-putation. Do-not (in) former times (be) good, afterwards again not good. So only is truly filial son—

truly a dutiful son—truly a good brother. If you be not obedient to your parents, or do not live in harmony with your brothers, the penal law will lay hold of, and correct you; but even that, if you are without understanding, will fail to reform you.—'*The Sacred Edict.*'

LESSON, XXX.

The daughter-in-law was called Coral Cheng. She was a very beautiful girl, had a low, soft-toned voice, and was very polite and kind. She waited upon her mother-in-law, making a point of going to her, early each morning, to ask how she was, at the same time bringing cakes and tea to her. She could not but tidy herself up, before presenting herself to her mother-in-law; and, with her features properly composed, she came and attended respectfully upon her. Nevertheless Old Cross Sticks, who had been of a giddy disposition, seeing Coral so charming, felt ashamed of her own looks and thereupon loudly scolded her, saying:—'It is an everyday occurrence for a daughter-in-law to wait upon a

新婦姓鄭、名珊瑚、生得十分美貌、極有禮義、柔聲下氣、奉事家婆、每朝晨早、定必到家婆處問安、捧茶獻餅、少不免修飾顏容、威儀致敬、誰不知橫紋柴一向性情佻儺、見珊瑚美麗、自覺懷慙、遂大聲罵曰、做新婦敬家婆是平常事、你估好時典麼。何用支支整整、聲聲色色、搣得個樣嬌嬈、想來我處賣俏嗎。我當初做新婦時、重好色水過

truly good brother. You, if are not filial, or-if (it) is (that you) are (a) brother, not harmonious, then must take instruments-of-torture, (and) law to-deal-with (you), 32; but-if your heart within not understand, dealing-with you also is-not profitable.

LESSON, XXX.

꜀San-꜅fú sing꜆ Cheng², ꜀meng* ꜀Shán-꜄wú. ꜀Sháng tak꜄ shap꜆ ꜀fan ꜅méi-máu², kik꜆ ꜅yau ꜅laí-yí², ꜄yau ꜀shengt há² héí꜆, fung²-sz² ꜀ká-꜄p'o. ꜅Múi ꜀chíú-꜄shan ꜅tsò ting² ꜀pít tó꜆ ꜄ká-꜄p'o shü꜆ man² ꜄on, ꜅f'ung (i.e. ꜅p'ung) ꜄ch'á hín꜆ ꜅pengt. ꜅Shíú pat꜄ ꜅mín ꜄sau-shik꜄ ꜄ngán-꜄yung; ꜄waí-꜄yí chí꜆ king꜆. ꜄Shöü-pat꜄-꜄chí ꜄Wáng-꜄man-꜄shái yat꜄ höng꜆ sing꜆-꜄ts'ing ꜄t'íú-t'át꜄₀, kín꜆ ꜀Shán-꜄wú ꜅méi-laí², tsz² kok꜀₀ ꜄waí-꜄ts'ám, söü꜆ táí² ꜄shengt má² yüt꜄ :— ꜆Tsò² ꜄san-꜅fú king꜆ ꜄ká-꜄p'o shí² ꜄p'íng-꜄shöng sz². ꜅Néí ꜅kwú ꜅hò ꜄shí-hing ꜄mo? ꜄Ho yung² ꜄chí-꜄chí-꜅ching-꜅ching, ꜄shing-꜄shing shik꜄-shik꜄, pán² tak꜆ ko꜆ ꜅yöng* ꜄kíú-꜄yíú? ꜅Söng ꜄loí ꜅ngo shü꜆ máí²-ts'íú꜆ má꜆? ꜅Ngo. ꜄tong-꜄ch'o tsò² ꜄san-꜅fú ꜄shí, chúng² ꜅hò shik꜄-꜅shöü kwo꜆

The daughter-in-law, surnamed Cheng, named Coral, grew (so as to be) able (to be) ten parts beautiful, extremely had politeness (and) kindness, soft sound, low breath. Respectfully-waited-upon the-family mother, each morning, early-morning, fixed heart arrived-at family mother's place, asked welfare, offered tea, presented cakes. Must necessarily *(This is a mandarin phrase, but is understood and used by educated people)* improve appearance : correct department in-order-to-be respectful. Nevertheless Cross-grained-firewood, before-time (or all-along-up-to-the-present-time) temperament giddy, seeing Coral (so) nice looking, she felt ashamed (of her own appearance), thereupon (with) loud voice scolded, saying :—

mother-in-law. Do you think it is a new thing to do? What is the use of your mincing walk, affected tones, ogling eyes, and expressive face? Do you, dressed up in that fascinating style, wish to come and *woo* me? When I was first a bride, I was ten times prettier than you are. I never thought that old age would now make me ugly and diminish my good looks.' When Coral heard this, she hung down her head, and received the rebuke submissively without presuming to say a word.

你十倍、唔估今日老
得個樣醜態、減去三
分。

Coral again, early the next morning, presented cakes and tea, and asked for her mother-in-law. She was dressed plainly though nicely, and looked neat and clean; she had on a washable, blue jacket; and had neither powdered nor rouged herself. As soon as Old Cross Sticks had set eyes on her, her ire again rose; and she greeted her with :—'I only said a word to you yesterday, and you come this morning then, without putting a flower in your hair, or powder on your face, or your best clothes on. You want to come and make me angry. Do you think I don't know? Do you think I

珊瑚聽罷、低頭順受、不
敢出聲、明早又奉茶
餅問安、粧得雅淡、潔
淨、着件洗水藍衫、頭
面不施脂粉、橫紋柴
一見又發怒曰、昨朝
話一句、今朝嗽就花
唔戴、粉唔搽、新衫唔
着、想來激惱我、你估
我唔知、你估我唔知。
珊瑚又低頭無語、自
怨不曉奉承。

ᶜnéi shap₂-ᶜp'öü. ₌M ᶜkwú ₌kam-
yat₂ ᶜlò tak₎ ko⁾ ᶜyöng* ᶜch'au-
t'ái⁵, ᶜkám höü⁾ ₌sám ₌fan. ₌Shán-
₌wú ₌t'engʈ pá², ₌tai ₌t'au shun²
shöü², pat₎ ᶜkòm ch'ut₎ ₌shengʈ.

'Being (a) daughter-in-law reverenc-
ing mother-in-law is ordinary matter.
You think very fashion able, eh?
What (is the) use (of) mincing
walk, affected tones, ogling-eyes-and-
expressive-face? Dressed (in) that
fashion fascinating, wish to-come
my place to-show-off-your-beauty (to-
me), eh? 35. I, when at-first was
a-bride time, still better colour
than you tenfold. Did-not think
to-day, oldened that appearance, ugly
reduced gone three tenths.' Coral
hearing finished, bowed-down head,
compliantly received, not dare utter
sound.

₌Ming-ᶜtsò yau² fung² ₌ch'á ᶜpengʈ
man² ₌on; ₌chong-tak₎ ᶜngá-tám²
kit₀-tsing², chök₀ kíu² ᶜsai-ᶜshöü ₌lám-
₌shám: ₌t'au mín² pat₎ ₌shí ₌chí-
ᶜfan. ₌Wáng-man-₌shái yat₎ kín⁾,
yau² fát₀ nò², yüt⁾:—'Tsok₎ ₌chíú wá²
yat₎ köü⁾, ₌kam ₌chíú ᶜkòm tsau²
₌fá ₌m tái⁾, ᶜfan· ₌m ₌ch'á, ₌san
₌shám ₌m chök₍. ᶜSöng ₌loí kik₎ ᶜnò
ᶜngo. ᶜNéi ᶜkwú ᶜngo ₌m ₌chí?
ᶜNéi ᶜkwú ᶜngo ₌m ₌chí?' ₌Shán-
₌wú yau² ₌tai ₌t'au ₌mo ᶜyü, tsz²
yün⁾ pat₎ ᶜhíú fung²-₌shing.

Next morning again presented tea,
cakes, asked (after) welfare. Adorned
plainly, cleanly-neatly; wearing article
washable, blue jacket; head, face
not put red (or) white cosmetics.
Cross-grained-fire-wood one see again,
got angry, said:—'Yesterday morning, said one sentence, this morning,
so-then flowers not wear, powder not
applied, new clothes not wear. Wish
to-come make angry me. You think
I not know? You think I not know?'
Coral again stooped head, no words,
herself blamed, (because she did) not
understand to-wait-upon (and) please
(her grandmother).

don't know?' Coral again hung down her head and said nothing, but blamed herself for not knowing how to present herself properly before her mother-in-law.

After this, if the mother-in-law kicked against a stool, Coral was scolded ; if the fowls would not eat, Coral was scolded. Coral went to pay the visit [made by a young bride] to her own family, and, when she came home after three days, she was scolded for ten days. Tai-Shing, seeing that his mother was displeased, gave Coral a severe beating to please his mother. * * * * *.

The mother-in-law stood at the door, one night, and scolded loudly, only because some trifle did not suit her. Coral brought out a bamboo chair, and asked Granny to rest herself on it. Old Cross Sticks sat down, and leaned back, while, with her hand upraised and stamping her foot, she scolded without stopping. Coral boiled a cup of tea, and, brought it, asking Granny to slake her thirst. Old Cross Stick's throat was moistened after drinking it ; and then, with a shriller voice and more penetrating sound, she scolded till the third watch of the night, when

自後踢着樓仔,將珊瑚罵,鷄唔食米,將珊瑚罵,珊瑚去探外家三日歸來,被罵了十日。大成見老母不悅,遂將珊瑚拷打,以順母心。 * * * * *

一晚不過因些小事,不合意,便企在門口,大罵一塲,珊瑚捧張竹椅出來,請婆婆安坐,橫紋柴坐下,腰骨挨斜,手指天,腳拍地,罵不絕聲,珊瑚煲茶一碗,捧來,請婆婆解渴,橫紋柴飲了,喉嚨既潤,氣更高,聲更响,罵到三更,聲漸低,力漸微,氣漸喘。

Tsz²-hau², t‘ek † chök₂ tang²-‘tsaí, ₍tsöng ₍Shán-₍wú má²; ₍kaí ₍m shik₂ ‘maí, ₍tsöng ₍Shán-₍wú má². ₍Shán-₍wú höü² t‘ám³ ngoi² ₍ká ₍sám yat₂, ₍kwaí ₍loí, péí² má² ‘líú shap₂ ₍yat₂. Táí²-₍shing kin² ‘lò-‘mò pat₂ ₍yüt₂. söü² ₍tsöng ₍Shán-₍wú ₍háu ‘tá, ‘yí shun² ‘mò ₍sam. * * * * *

Afterwards, kicked against stool. took Coral to-scold; fowls not eat rice, took Coral to-scold. Coral went to-visit her-own-family, (*lit.* the outside family) three days home came, was scolded ten days. Tai-shing seeing (his) mother not pleased, then took Coral tortured, to comply (with his) mother's heart. * * * * *.

Yat₂ ‘mán, ₍pat₂ kwo² ₍yan ₍se-‘síú sz² pat₂ ₍hóp₂ yí², pín² ‘k‘éí ₍mún ‘hau táí² má² yat₂ ₍ch‘öng. ₍Shán-₍wú ‘fung (*i.e.* ‘p‘ung) ₍chöng chuk₂ ‘yí ch‘ut₂ ₍loí, ‘ts‘engt ₍P‘o-₍p‘o ₍on ‘ts‘o*t. ₍Wáng-₍man-₍shaí ‘ts‘o*t há², ₍yiú-kwat₂ ₍áí ₍ts‘e. ‘shau ‘chí ₍t‘in, kök₀ p‘ák₀ téí², má² ₍pat₂ tsüt₂ ₍shing. ₍Shán-₍wú ₍pò ₍ch‘á, yat₂ ‘wún, ‘fung (*i.e.* ‘p‘ung) ₍loí, ‘ts‘engt ₍P‘o-₍p‘o ‘káí hot₀. ₍Wáng-₍man-₍shaí ‘yam ‘líú, ₍hau-₍lung ke² yun²; héí² kang² ₍kò, ₍shengt kang² ‘höng, má² tò² ₍sám ₍káng, ₍shengt tsím² ₍taí, lik₂ tsím² ₍méí, héí² tsím² ‘ch‘ün.

One night, not more than on-account-of (some) trifling thing not agreeable (to her) wish, forthwith stood in (the) doorway. great scolded one [C.]. Coral brought [C.] bamboo chair out come, invited, 'Granny peacefully sit.' Cross-Grained-Fire-wood sat down, backbone leaned-back awry, hand pointed-to heaven, foot stamping the-earth, scolded without stopping sound. Coral boiled tea one bowl, brought-in-two-hands. came invited Granny slake thirst. Cross-grained-fire-wood drank finished, throat being moistened, breath still-more high sound, still-more resonant, gradually her voice got fainter, her strength diminished, and her breath was gradually reduced to a whisper.

Coral knelt before her and said:—'Granny I have heard everything you have said. I know now, and I will be good. I beg you, Granny, to go to bed and rest quietly: so as not to get the cold wind on you here, and be calling out the whole night with colic.'

Old Cross Sticks said:—'I will scold; I will scold;' and she *would* not lie down, but scolded till dawn, Coral weeping and wailing at her side. The neighbours then came in a body, and advised the old woman to stop her scolding. Coral, having lighted a lamp, came and led and supported her mother-in-law to her room for her to rest quietly. She put right the bed-clothes and the mosquito-net, and put straight her pillow, telling her:—'Granny, go to sleep quietly;' and then she went away. * * * * *.

Tai-Shing knew from the first that Coral was an admirable wife; but there was no help for it—she did not suit his mother; so he wrote out a Bill of Divorcement, and directed Coral, as follows:—'I have heard that a wife is married to wait upon

珊瑚跪下禀曰，婆婆所教，媳婦盡得聽聞，今知，改過咯，請婆婆同牀安睡，免至在此受了生風，通夜叫肚痛。

橫紋柴曰，我要罵，我要罵，拼之唔睡，罵到天光，珊瑚從旁啼哭鄰里共來勸止，珊瑚點燈來引，扶住，歸房安歇，整好被鋪，蚊帳，移正枕頭，囑咐婆婆安睡而去。* * * * *

大成本來知得珊瑚賢孝，無奈，老母不合意，遂寫分書一紙，吩咐珊瑚曰，我聞娶妻所以事母，今致老母時時激惱，要妻何用，我

‚Shán-wú kwaí² há², ‚pan yüt₂ :—‘ ‚P'o-
‚p'o ‚sho kánʾ, sik₎-‚fú tsun² tak₎
‚t'eng† ‚man. ‚Kam ‚chí, ‘koi kwoʾ
lok₀. ‘Ts'eng† ‚P'o-‚p'o ‚wúi ‚ch'ong
‚on shöü² : ‚mín-chí tsoí² 't'sz shan²
‚líú ‚sháng-‚fung, ‚t'ung ye² kíúʾ
‚t'ó t'ungʾ.’

‚Wáng-‚man-‚shái yüt₂ :—‘ ‚Ngo yíúʾ
má² ; ‚ngo yíúʾ má².’ ‘Ping ‚chí ‚m
shöü², má² tóʾ ‚t'ín ‚kwong, ‚Shán-
‚wú ‚ts'ung ‚p'ong ‚t'ai huk₎. ‚Lun-
‚léí kung² ‚loí hünʾ ‘chi. ‚Shán-
‚wú ‘tím ‚tang, ‚loí ‚yan, ‚fú-chü²
‚kwai ‘fong* ‚on hít₀. ‘Ching ‘hó
‚p'éí-‚p'ó, ‚man-chöngʾ, ‚yí chingʾ
‘cham-‚t'au, chuk₎-fúʾ ‚P'o-‚p'o ‚on
shöü², ‚yí höüʾ. * * * * *.

‚Táí²-‚shing ‘pún-‚loí ‚chí tak₎ ‚Shán-
‚wú ‚yín-háuʾ ; ‚mò noí²—‚lò-‚mò
pat₎ hòp₂ yíʾ ; söü² ‚sé ‚fan ‚shü, yat₎
‘chí, ‚fan-fúʾ ‚Shán-‚wú, yüt₂:—‘ ‚Ngo
‚man ‚ts'öü ‚ts'aí ‚sho-‚yí sz² ‚mò.
‚Kam chíʾ ‚lò-‚mó ‚shí-‚shí kik₎
‚nò. Yíúʾ ‚ts'aí ‚ho yung²? ‚Ngo

scolded until third watch, voice gradually lowered, strength gradually small, breath gradually gasping.

Coral knelt down, petitioned, saying :—‘Granny whatever taught, daughter-in-law entirely obtained the-hearing. Now knowing, change (from) error, 32. Invite Granny return-to bed, peacefully sleep, to-avoid, at this (place), receive draft, throughout the-night call-out stomach ache.’

Cross-Grained-Firewood said:—‘I want-to scold ; I want-to scold.’ And would-not sleep, scolded till (the) sky (was) light. Coral from (her) side wept (and) cried. The (people of the) neighbouring lane together came, advised (her) to-stop. Coral lighted a-lamp, (and) came, (and) led, (and) supported (her) home to (her) room to-quietly rest, made right bedding, mosquito-net, changed straight pillow, enjoined Granny peacefully sleep, and-then went-away. * * * * *.

Tai-Shing originally knew Coral was-virtuous (and) filial ; (but) there-was-no help-for-it—(his) mother (did) not (find her to) suit her-mind ; then wrote divorce deed, one paper, directed Coral, saying :—‘ I have-heard in-taking a-wife (it is) for-the-purpose-

one's mother. Now you cause my mother to be continually angry. What is the use of having a wife? I give you a Deed of Divorce. You can go elsewhere, look for a good place, and marry someone else. It is not fit for you to live in my house.'

After he had said this, he twirled his sleeves in anger, and went away.

將分書與你，你可別尋好處，另嫁他人，不宜在我屋住也。

話完翻袖出門而去。

ₜtsöng ₜfan-ₜshü ᶜyü ᶜnéí. ᶜNéí ᶜho
pít₂ ₜtsʻam ᶜhò shüʾ, ling² kaʾ ₜtʻá
ₜyan. Pat,-ₜyí tsoí² ᶜngo-ukₗ chü²
₍yá.ʾ

of serving the-mother. Now it-has-
come-to mother always exasperated
(*or* provoked). Want wife what use?
I take divorce deed give-to you. You
can elsewhere look-for good place,
besides marry another man. Not be-
seeming (*or* it is unbecoming) in my
house live (final).ʾ

Waʾ²-ₜyün ₜfán tsau², chʻut, ₜmún ₜyí
höüʾ.

Speak finished, turned sleeves, went-
out-of door, and then went-away.

HONGKONG.

Printed by KELLY & WALSH, Limited.

1894.